REASON™ 3
IGNITE!

By Eric D. Grebler
and Chris Hawkins

THOMSON
★
COURSE TECHNOLOGY™
Professional ■ Technical ■ Reference

A Thomson Course Technology Professional, Technical, Reference Publication

R E A S O N ™ 3
I G N I T E !

Publisher and General Manager, Thomson Course Technology PTR: Stacy L. Hiquet

Associate Director of Marketing: Sarah O'Donnell

Manager of Editorial Services: Heather Talbot

Marketing Manager: Kristin Eisenzopf

Senior Acquisitions Editor: Todd Jensen

Senior Editor: Mark Garvey

Marketing Coordinator: Jordan Casey

Project Editor and Copy Editor: Dan Foster, Scribe Tribe

Technical Reviewer: Steve Pacey

Thomson Course Technology PTR Editorial Services Coordinator: Elizabeth Furbish

Interior Layout Tech: Danielle Foster, Scribe Tribe

Cover Designer: Michael Tanamachi

Indexer: Kelly Talbot

Proofreader: Kate Welsh

Reason™ is a trademark of Propellerhead Software AB, Stockholm, Sweden.

All other trademarks are the property of their respective owners.

Important: Thomson Course Technology PTR cannot provide software support. Please contact the appropriate software manufacturer's technical support line or Web site for assistance.

Thomson Course Technology PTR and the authors have attempted throughout this book to distinguish proprietary trademarks from descriptive terms by following the capitalization style used by the manufacturer.

Educational facilities, companies, and organizations interested in multiple copies or licensing of this book should contact the publisher for quantity discount information. Training manuals, CD-ROMs, and portions of this book are also available individually or can be tailored for specific needs.

ISBN: 1-59200-666-3

Library of Congress Catalog Card Number: 2004115274

Printed in Canada

05 06 07 08 09 WC 10 9 8 7 6 5 4 3 2 1

THOMSON

COURSE TECHNOLOGY ™

Professional ■ Technical ■ Reference

Course Technology PTR,
a division of
Thomson Course Technology
25 Thomson Place
Boston, MA 02210
www.courseptr.com

About the Authors

Eric D. Grebler is an IT professional, author, and certified trainer who has demystified the world of computers for thousands of people. Originally from Ottawa, he currently resides in Toronto, Canada. Grebler has developed curriculum and resource material on a wide range of technical topics, including desktop publishing, graphics, XML, and operating systems. He is also the author of *Lindows Fast & Easy* (Premier Press, 1-59200-060-6) and *Windows XP Media Center Edition Fast & Easy* (Premier Press, 1-59200-083-5).

Chris Hawkins has been working with computer music production both professionally and personally for 13 years. Hawkins is a graduate of Columbia Academy's Recording Arts program in Vancouver, Canada, and currently resides in Nagoya, Japan. He is the founder/publisher of Streamworks Audio—The Online Magazine for Recording Professionals and Hobbyists (www. streamworksaudio.com). Hawkins was also a member of the Steinberg support team on their online Cubase community forums, helping with end-user support issues. In addition to Streamworks Audio, he is the managing director of SWA Video (www.swavideo.com)—an online video tutorial site for audio/MIDI applications. Hawkins is also the author of *Reason 2.5 Ignite!* from Thomson Course Technology PTR. He runs a small recording studio that he uses to produce his own material.

Contents

CONTENTS }

❅ ❅ ❅

} Introduction

Reason 3 Ignite! is here to help you explore the vast creative possibilities and updated tools within Reason 3. Both beginners and experienced users can benefit from this book, which will teach you, through straightforward examples, Reason's main features and functions and will show you how to use them to create musical masterpieces of your own. This book will help you take control of the synths, samplers, effects, and other devices that make up Reason; connect them; and expand them so that you can turn your computer into a music making machine!

Who Should Read This Book?

Reason 3 Ignite! was written with the beginner in mind. Programming synthesizers and drum patterns, and mixing them well, can sometimes require a steep learning curve. The goal of *Reason 3 Ignite!* is to seriously shorten that learning curve by giving you clear step-by-step instructions for creating music with the diverse set of tools that Reason offers. Each chapter has been organized to provide a simplified workflow, and the instructions in the chapters are accompanied by clear illustrations, so you'll easily be able to see and understand what you are learning.

Helpful Advice

In addition to the tasks you'll learn as you read through this book, you will find useful information in sidebars that expand on a particular topic related to the task—providing helpful tips, additional details, or warnings.

In addition to the chapters, helpful information is available in the appendixes at the back of the book. The appendixes cover how to ReWire Reason to a ReWire master application, general tips on publishing your song and preparing it for CD, as well as overviews of the Combinator and MClass effects.

The creative possibilities within Reason are almost limitless. It will take you as far as your imagination cares to go. Begin the journey now!

1 } Setting Up Your Computer to Run Reason 3.0

Reason 3.0 is a hybrid, or dual-platform, application, which means that it runs equally well on Windows PCs and Macintosh computers. The Reason CD contains complete versions for each platform. Reason 3.0 comes with three CDs. Disc One contains the actual program for Windows and Mac OS X (as well as OS 9). The remaining two discs contain the sounds and samples to be used in Reason. In this chapter, you'll learn how to

※ Install Reason 3.0 on your Windows XP or Mac OS X computer.

※ Set your preferences for Reason's configuration.

Installing and Starting Reason 3.0

When you install Reason, of course the program is installed on your computer, but in addition there are two CDs full of sounds and samples for use in Reason. During the setup you have the option of installing these files. They are large files, and may require gigabytes of hard-disk space; however, most reasonably current computers will have adequate storage space for them.

For Windows XP

After placing Disc One into your CD drive, AutoPlay will take over and the setup will begin automatically. Follow the setup, which is very straightforward. If your computer has the AutoPlay feature disabled, you will need to run the installer manually.

1 Click on the Start button at the left side of the Windows Taskbar.

2 Click on My Computer.

3 Right-click on the CD-ROM drive containing the Reason Install CD and Select AutoPlay from the CD-ROM shortcut menu. The installation will begin; follow the instructions on the screen.

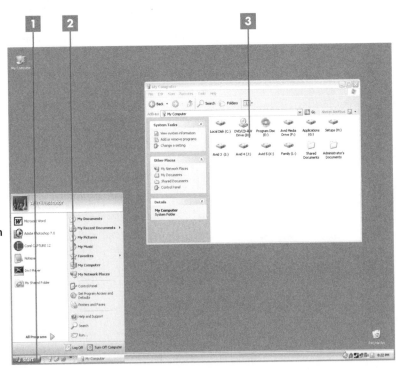

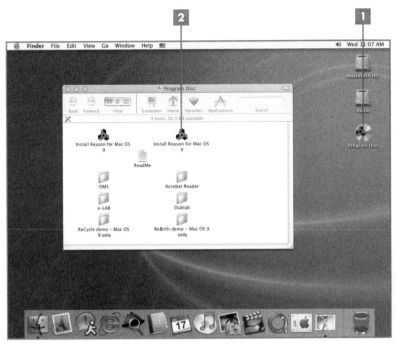

For Mac OS X

After placing the CD into your CD drive:

1 Double-click on the Program Disc icon to open the disc's contents.

2 Double-click on Install Reason for Mac OS. The installer will launch.

❋ REASON AND THE MAC OS

Reason is compatible with both Mac OS 9 and Mac OS X. When installing, be careful to choose the appropriate install icon for your operating system.

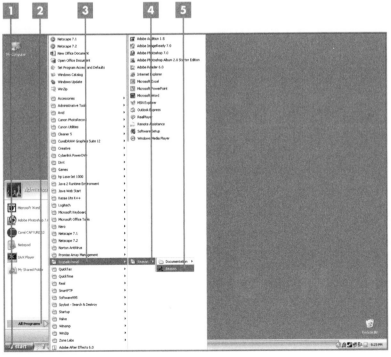

Starting Reason

Before you can set up Reason to work best with your computer, you need to launch the program.

Starting Reason in Windows

1 Click on the Start button at the left side of the Windows Taskbar.

2 Click on All Programs. The programs list will appear.

3 Click on the Propellerhead group.

4 Click on the Reason group.

5 Click on the Reason program icon. The program will launch.

3

❋ ❋ ❋

Starting Reason in Mac OS X

1 Click on the Go menu.

2 Click on Applications. The Applications window will appear. Double-click on the Reason folder.

3 Double-click on the Reason program icon. The program will launch.

❋ **REASON IN THE DOCK**

If you're a Mac OS X user, you may want to drag the Reason icon from the Reason folder to the Dock, where you can quickly launch the program in the future without having to navigate through the Finder each time.

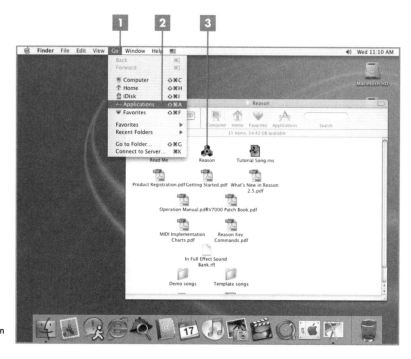

Setting Your Preferences

Before you can start working with all the devices in Reason and create any music, you need to tell the application which audio card and MIDI devices you will be using.

To set your preferences in Reason, you will first need to open the Preferences panel.

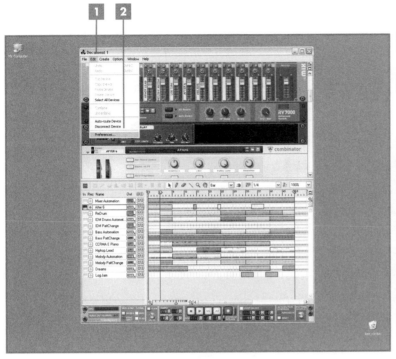

1 Click on Edit. The Edit menu will appear.

2 Click on Preferences. The Preferences panel will appear.

❈ PREFERENCES ON THE MAC

Mac users will find the Preferences panel under the Reason menu in the main Reason screen.

After authorizing the program during initial launch, the Preferences panel will open automatically. However, if you accidentally closed it, or if there are ghosts in your machine and the panel did not open, merely follow the steps above to access the Preferences panel.

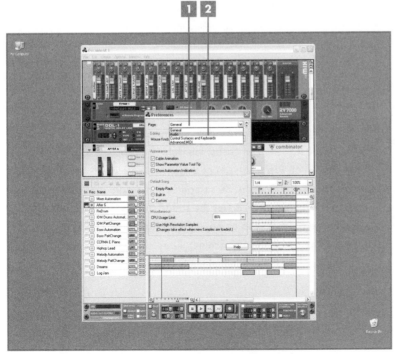

Configuring Your Audio Card

With the Preferences panel open, you can set up your audio hardware preferences.

1 Click on the Page menu drop-down arrow. The Page menu will appear.

2 Click on Audio. The Audio preference panel will appear.

Next, you can set the sound card that Reason will use. From the Audio panel, you can adjust how Reason will interact with your audio hardware.

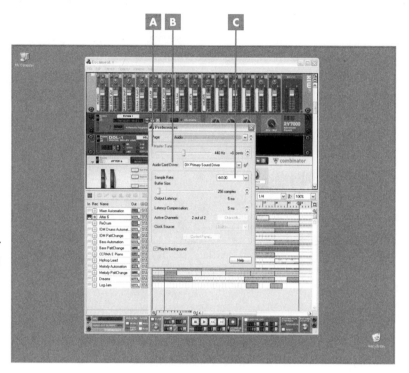

A Master Tune. This control allows you to change Reason's overall tuning, in increments called *cents*. This will not change the tune of just one device or sound, but of all devices and sounds.

B Audio Card Driver. This is where you choose an audio card to use with Reason. The sound-card drivers that appear will be those currently installed in your computer, so your specific list of drivers will be different than the ones shown in the figure.

❊ AUDIO DRIVERS AND REASON

Windows users: If you have an audio card that comes with an ASIO driver, then selecting this driver will result in better performance than using the standard Windows driver. Mac OS X users will achieve similar performance by using Core Audio drivers with Mac OS X's Audio system. It is also a good idea to check your audio card manufacturer's Web site to ensure that you have the latest drivers.

C Sample Rate. From this drop-down menu, select the desired sample rate for Reason. In most cases, the default of **44100** is sufficient; however, if you use a sample of a different rate it will be re-sampled automatically by Reason. Re-sampling can create extra work for your computer and can lower the sound quality, but if you really want to use a drum loop or any other sample that's at a rate different than your current project, Reason will have no problems playing it.

❋ LOCKED SAMPLE RATES

Some audio cards may have their sample rates locked by their drivers, and this option will be grayed out. If this is the case, then consult your audio card's manual for instructions on how to adjust the sample rate.

D

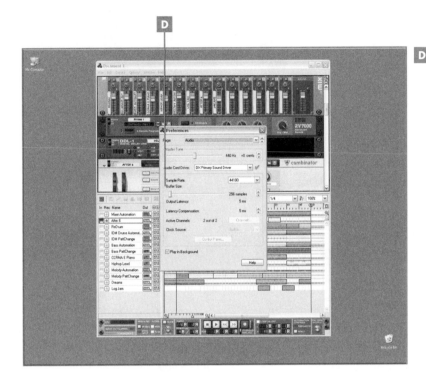

D Buffer Size. **Buffer size affects** *latency*—**the time it takes Reason to respond to MIDI commands, such as notes from a keyboard or other device. For example, if you use a MIDI keyboard to play Reason's synthesizers in real time, there will be a slight delay from the moment you hit a controller's key to the moment when you hear Reason's synthesizer actually play that note. This delay is latency. The Buffer Size slider will either increase or decrease that delay. A smaller buffer rate means lower latency, but it also means a higher load on your CPU, which can create unwanted artifacts, such as cracking and clicks in the audio. With modern systems, low latencies are becoming easier to achieve. With most modern systems, a setting of around 512 samples is adequate for achieving a stable and usable latency.**

❋❋❋

E Output Latency. **Reason will report the latency of your system, in milliseconds (ms). This measurement will rise or fall depending on how you set the Buffer Size slider.**

F Latency Compensation. **Due to latency created by your system, when synchronizing to an external MIDI device, Reason will be delayed to the external device and will not achieve solid synchronization. Use the Latency Compensation control to compensate for the latency (see Chapter 9, "External Control of Reason," for more on external synchronization).**

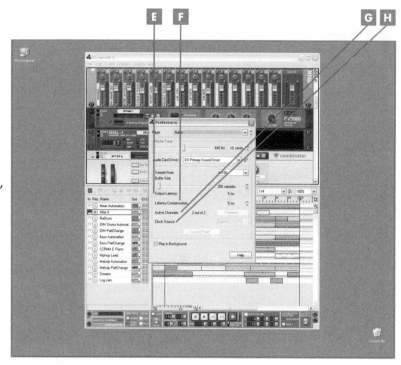

G Active Channels. If you are using an ASIO driver on the Windows platform or a Core Audio driver for the Mac OS X platform with an audio interface that is equipped with multiple inputs and outputs, you will be able to choose which outputs are used in Reason. If you are using a standard Windows MME driver, this option will not be changeable. The benefits of having more than one output are many. For example, you could run a Reason device's virtual output to a dedicated output on your audio card. From there you could run it to an effects processor or EQ (equalizer). See Chapter 3, "Analog Emulated Synthesizers," for more information on audio routing.

H Clock Source. If you use more than one audio card, one of them will need to be a "master" for the other cards to follow. In most cases, only one audio card is being used and should be set to the internal clock of your audio card.

❋ CHANGING THE CLOCK SOURCE

Some audio cards may not allow you to change the clock source. Refer to your audio card's documentation for more information on changing the clock source.

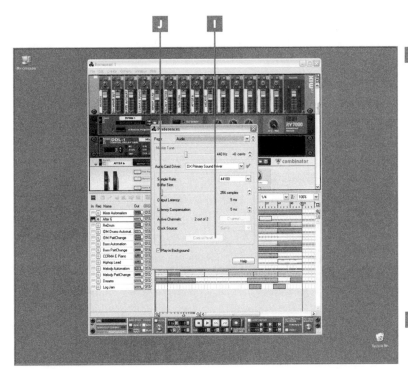

I Control Panel. **Click this button to access the control panel of your ASIO device (available only to those using an audio card with ASIO drivers). For information regarding the control panel, please consult the documentation that accompanied your audio card. The control panel of your audio card will allow you to make adjustments pertaining to the settings and performance of the card.**

J Play in Background. **When this option is checked, the audio from Reason will continue to play, even if you place Reason in the background. When this option is unchecked, Reason will stop playback of any audio if the user places Reason as a background task.**

Configuring Advanced MIDI

Next you will configure your MIDI devices.

1 Click on the Page drop-down menu. The Page menu will appear.

2 Click on Advanced MIDI. The MIDI panel will appear.

Advanced MIDI settings on this page allow you to use Reason as a stand-alone synthesizer that receives MIDI from an external source. This could be a sequencer program such as Cubase SX or Sonar, or an input device such as a MIDI keyboard.

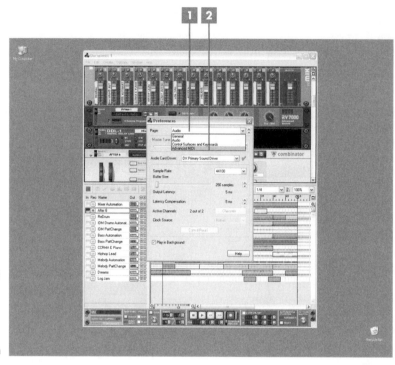

A External Control. From here you can select up to four separate MIDI interfaces to play back Reason devices loaded in your song. These are divided into four MIDI busses: A, B, C, and D. After assigning an interface to a bus, you will be able to access it though the MIDI In device. (You will learn more about the hardware interface in Chapter 4, "Digital Samplers and the Rex File Loop Player.")

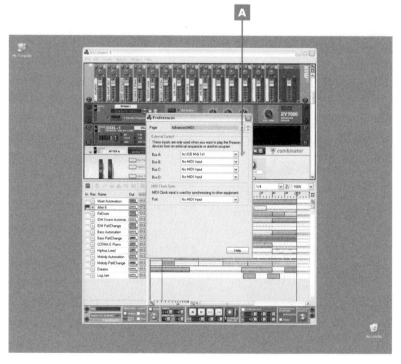

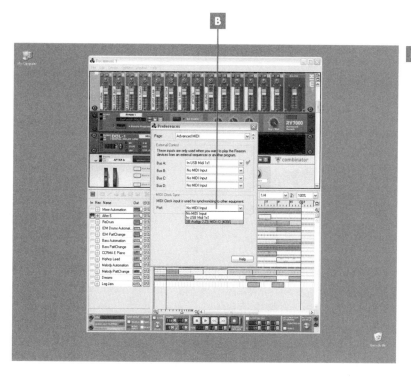

B MIDI Clock Sync. **Here you can slave Reason to external MIDI hardware or software applications that are either on or connected to your computer. Select the MIDI interface you wish to use to synchronize Reason to an external device. (You'll find more on the remote control and synchronization in Chapter 9).**

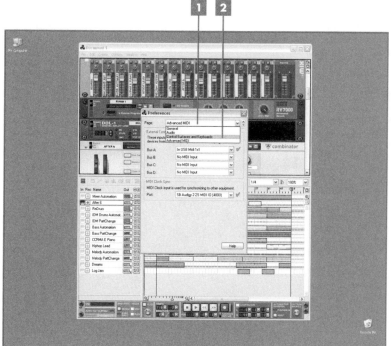

Control Surfaces and Keyboards

Having configured Advanced MIDI settings, you'll now be able to configure the Control Surfaces and Keyboards settings to be able to connect a keyboard to Reason.

1 Click on the Page drop-down menu. The Page menu will appear.

2 Click on Control Surfaces and Keyboards. The Control Surfaces and Keyboards panel will appear.

1 Auto-Detect Surfaces. **Here is the quick and easy method for connecting a keyboard to Reason. Click on this button, and Reason will search for any attached keyboards. When it finds one, it will appear in the Attached Surfaces window.**

2 If you didn't auto-detect a keyboard, click on the Add button. The Control Surface window will appear.

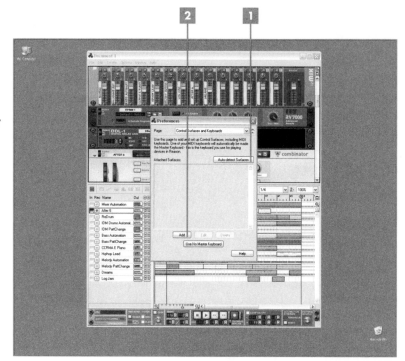

3 Click on the Manufacturer drop-down menu and select your keyboard manufacturer's name from the list. If it's not listed, click <Other>.

4 Click on the Model drop-down menu and select the appropriate model. If you selected <Other> from Manufacturer, choose Basic MIDI Keyboard or Basic MIDI Keyboard with Controls, depending on the keyboard you are connecting. The name and manufacturer of your keyboard will be shown under Name.

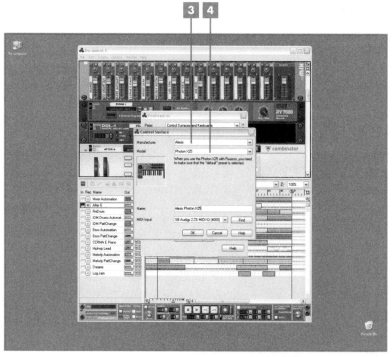

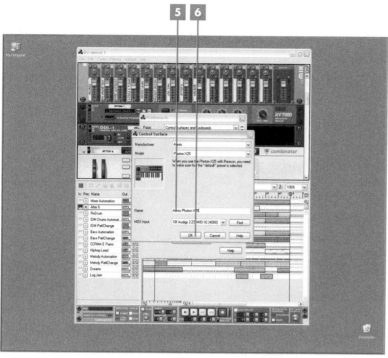

5 Click on the MIDI Input drop-down menu and choose the MIDI connection you are using to connect your keyboard to Reason. You can also click on the Find button, which will ask you to press a key on your keyboard to auto-detect the MIDI input you are using.

6 Click OK to accept your settings. You are now returned to the Preferences window.

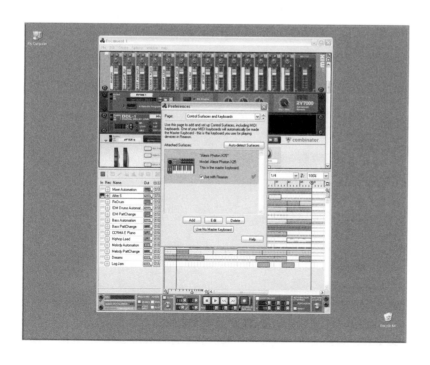

General Program Preferences

In the final preference panel, you will set general preferences for the program.

1. Click on the Page drop-down menu. The Page menu will appear.

2. Click on General. The General preferences panel will appear.

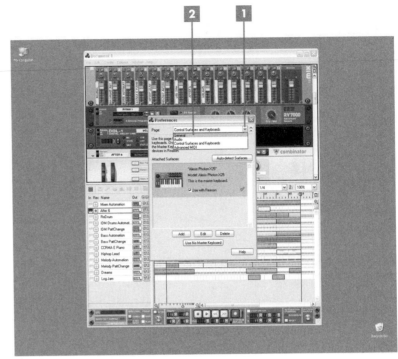

A. Editing: Mouse Knob Range. When using the mouse to change a parameter on a device, the cursor will move the parameter in predetermined increments. When the Mouse Knob Range is set to Normal, the cursor will move the knob or other control in larger increments. If you choose Precise, the increments become smaller, and even smaller if you select Very Precise.

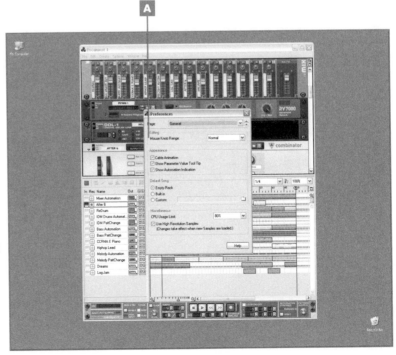

B Appearance: Cable Animation. **When you turn around Reason's rack to view the rear panel, the cables will move in order to look realistic. This is also true when you are patching devices—the cables move realistically. Although this is a very cool-looking feature, it puts more of a workload on your CPU, so perhaps it is better to leave this option unchecked. If you have a fairly powerful CPU, you may want to leave this option checked.**

C Appearance: Show Parameter Value Tool Tip. **When you move your cursor over one of Reason's devices or parameters (or change the value of a parameter), a small Tool Tip will display that parameter's value. If you uncheck this box, the Tool Tip will be disabled.**

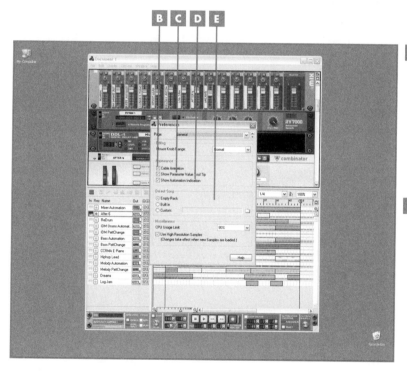

D Appearance: Show Automation Indicator. **If a device has automation changes in the song, this will be indicated by a green box around the automated parameter. Uncheck this box if you wish to disable this feature.**

E Default Song. **Whenever you start a new song, Reason will load with the option you choose here. If you choose Empty Rack, an empty rack will open each time you start a new song. If you choose Built in, Reason will open with its own built-in song. If you choose Custom, you can specify any song you wish as your default startup song. This would be handy if you wish to use a particular template for starting each new project.**

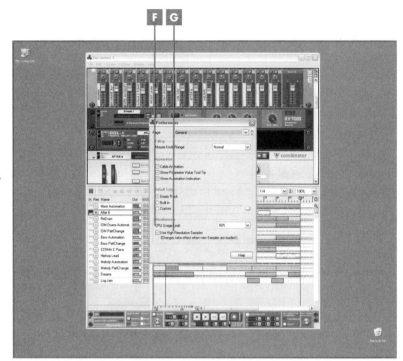

F Miscellaneous: CPU Usage Limit. This setting is meant to ensure that Reason will not overload your system to the point at which everything crashes. Set this to a limit that seems safe to you. I find that the default value of 80 percent is more than adequate.

G Use High Resolution Samples. This setting determines whether Reason will play back samples with a 24-bit resolution or 16-bit resolution. With this option checked, a 16-bit file will play back at 16-bit resolution and a 24-bit sample will play back at 24-bit resolution. If this option is unchecked, then all files will play back at a 16-bit resolution, even if they're 24-bit files.

2 } Fast Start

Now that you have made it through the installation and you have set up your machine to run Reason, it's time to take a look at what Reason can do. In this chapter, you will dive a little deeper into the program, have a look at some of the components that comprise this application, and begin learning how to work with them. In this chapter, you'll learn how to

※ Play back a song in Reason.

※ Work with the rack window and the transport bar.

※ Perform basic audio routing.

※ Identify the functions of the various devices available in Reason.

Playing the Demo Song

Now play back a song to ensure that all your configurations went as planned in Chapter 1, "Setting Up Your Computer to Run Reason 3.0," and to get some sense of just what can be accomplished in Reason. The following steps show you how to load a demo song that was copied onto your computer when you installed Reason.

1 Click on the File menu. The File menu will appear.

2 Click Open. The Song Browser window will appear.

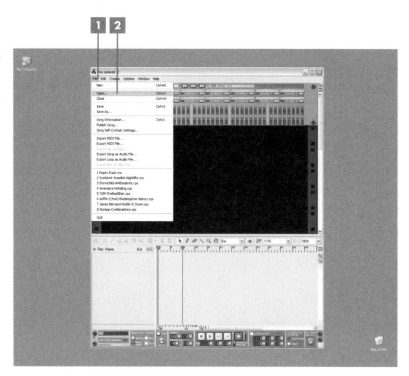

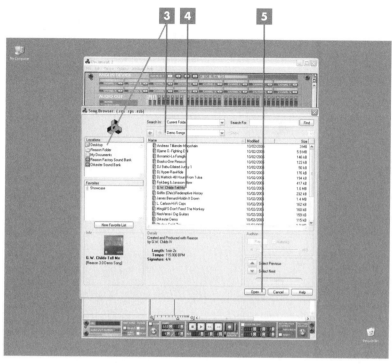

3 Select the Demo Songs folder, C:\Program Files\ Propellerhead\Reason Folder\ Demo Songs, by navigating in the Song Browser window.

4 Click on the file G.W. Childs-Tell Me. The file will become highlighted.

5 Click Open. The song will be loaded into Reason.

Navigating with the Song Browser

Reason 3.0 has updated the Song Browser, which makes navigating to find songs, samples, and patches much easier. In addition, you can see details about the selection and even audition it.

A Click in the Locations window to find the main location of the song or file you are looking for.

B Click on the folders in the main Song Browser window to browse to the file you're searching for, just like you would within the operating system.

C Click the down arrow to identify the folder you are looking to search through next to Search In.

D Enter the file name (or type of file) in the Search For entry field to specify what you're looking for.

E Click the Find button to begin your search.

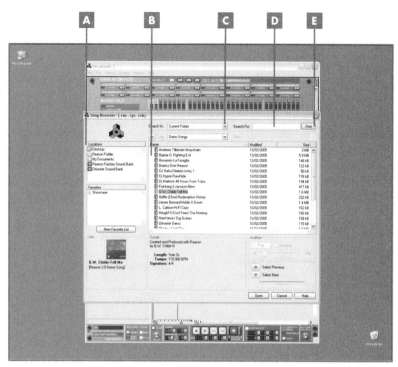

F Click the left/right arrows to go forward or backward in the folder tree you are navigating.

G Click the New Favorite List to create a folder where you can store your commonly used files.

H Info shows the picture related to the item selected, it's name, and the version of Reason associated with it.

I Details lists more information about the creators of the file, the length, tempo, and time signature.

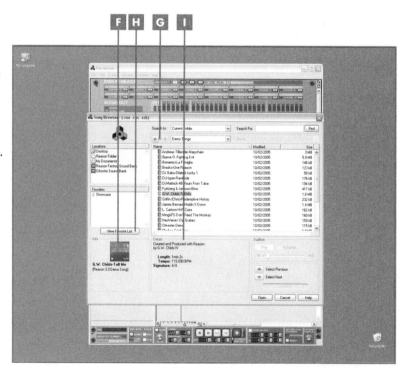

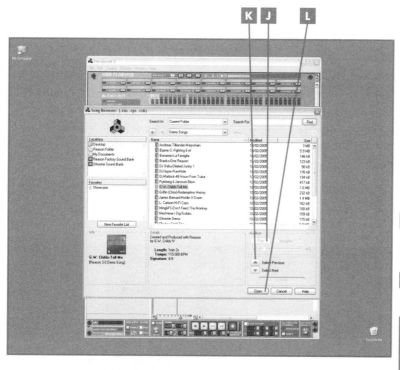

J Click Play in the Audition section to hear the item selected. You can also control the volume here using the volume slider. Keep the Autoplay box checked to automatically start playing whichever file you choose in the main window.

K Click the up/down arrows to move through the files in the main windows.

L Click Open to load the file.

✳ WHERE TO FIND THE SONG ON THE MAC

Mac OS X users can find this song in the Applications\Reason\Demo Songs folder.

When the song loads you will be presented with a splash screen about the artist.

1 Click OK to continue.

2 Click the Play button on the transport bar to begin playback. If all went well with the configuration, you should be listening to a pretty cool tune right about now.

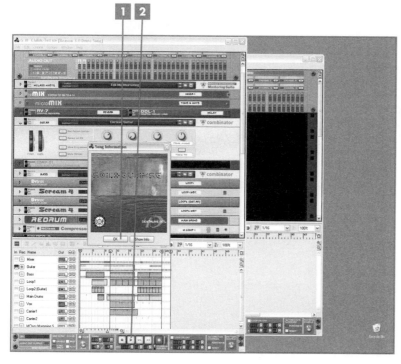

After listening to the song, click the Stop button and close the demo song.

Working with the Rack

To begin making your own cool tune, you need to create a palette in which to place your "colors"; in Reason we call that the *rack*. The rack is modeled after a rack full of outboard gear that can be found in many professional recording studios. The rack is the core of Reason and is where you will manage all the devices you load.

Starting with an Empty Rack

First, begin with an empty rack.

1 Click on the File menu. The File menu will appear.

2 Click on Open. The Song Browser will appear.

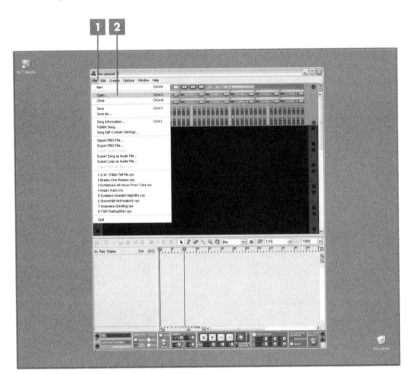

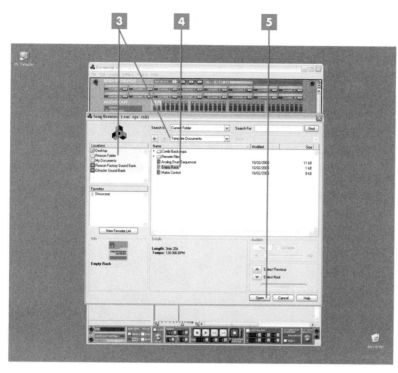

3 Navigate to **the folder C:\Program Files\ Propellerhead\Reason Folder\ Template Documents.**

4 Click **on the file** Empty Rack. **The file will become highlighted.**

5 Click Open. **A new song with an empty rack will appear.**

❄ LOADING AN EMPTY RACK USING A MAC

Mac OS X users can load this song from the folder Applications\Reason\Template Songs\Empty Rack.rns.

❄ CREATING A DEFAULT EMPTY RACK

Remember that you can set the Empty Rack as the default when creating a new song. Set this preference in the Sound Locations Preference (as described in Chapter 1).

An empty rack contains only the hardware interface, the sequencer, and the transport bar.

The Rack, Front and Back

❋ The rack has two views: the front panel and the rear panel. The front panel gives you access to control various parameters of your devices.

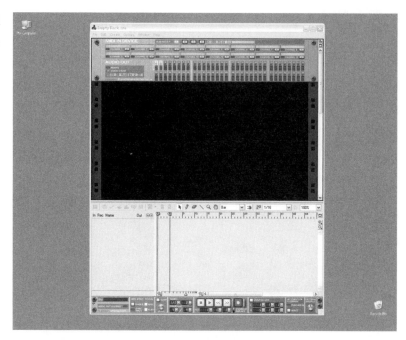

1. Click on the Options menu. The Options menu will appear.
2. Click on Toggle Rack Front/Rear. The rack will turn to show the rear view.

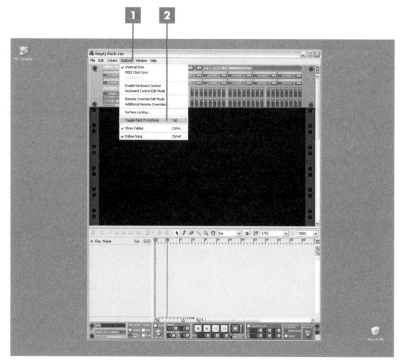

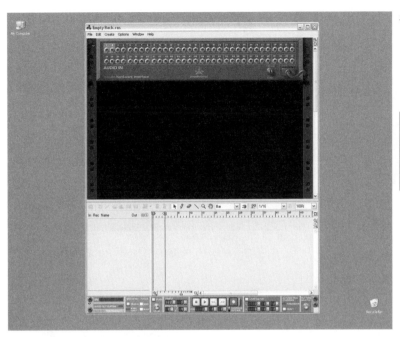

❋ The rear panel allows you to use virtual cables to route audio and other information between devices in the virtual rack.

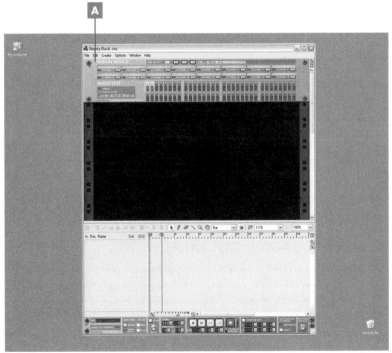

Hardware Interface

You will use the hardware interface to route the signal from any device in the rack to the outputs on your audio card.

A MIDI In Bus Select. This is where you will map incoming MIDI data from an external MIDI sequencer and/or MIDI controller keyboard to devices loaded in the rack. As described in the preferences section of Chapter 1, Reason has four MIDI input busses. Use the Bus Select button to choose an interface you want to assign to a Reason device.

B Channels. All MIDI interfaces are equipped with 16 input and 16 output channels. To assign a channel to a device, click on the down arrow beside the channel number and select your device from the list. As we do not have any devices loaded into the rack as of yet, the list of course will be empty.

C Audio Out channels. This is your virtual patch bay. With the Audio Out device you can connect the outputs of your devices to the outputs of your audio card. The channels correspond to the number of channels you have set in the Audio Preferences panel (Refer to "Configuring your Audio Card" in Chapter 1). Output 1 of the hardware interface routes to Output 1 of your audio card.

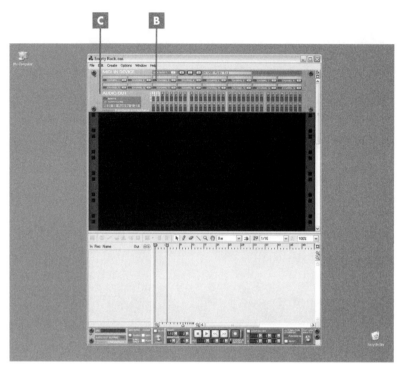

WHAT MIDI IN SHOWS YOU

The MIDI In Channel assign button will display only devices that are loaded in your song. If you have no devices in your song, this menu will have an empty list.

WHAT THE AUDIO OUT PANEL SHOWS

When viewing the front panel of the Audio Out device, no options are configurable. The front panel will display each output's volume level and whether it's in stand-alone mode, in which you are running the program on its own, or in ReWire mode (see Appendix A, "ReWire,") in which the program can be run from another application, such as Cubase SX. The rear panel view becomes the Audio In device where you connect Reason's devices.

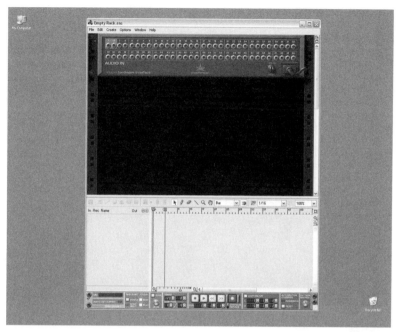

❋ Press Tab to spin the rack around, and you will see that the Audio Out device has 64 virtual outputs. Most users will not have 64 physical outputs on their audio interfaces; however, if you run Reason in ReWire slave mode, you can route 64 channels via ReWire to your master/host application—for example, Cubase.

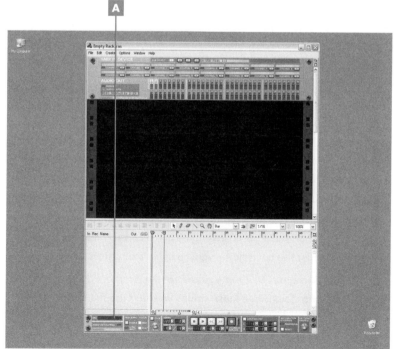

The Transport Panel

The transport panel is where you will typically start and stop playback of your songs, but there's a lot more to the transport panel.

Ⓐ CPU Meter. This meter allows you to watch over your system performance. If the meter gets too high, you may find your system to be less responsive and the audio performance will tend to suffer with crackling sounds and breakups.

✳ KEEP YOUR EYES ON THE CPU METER

For optimal performance, keep the CPU meter from getting too high. As a general rule, I try to keep the meter under 80%. This way there is room for the other portions of my system to remain responsive and keep the audio performance from suffering.

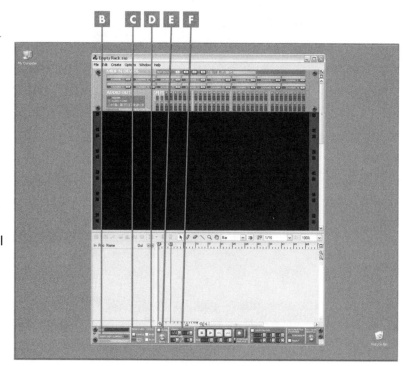

B Audio Out Clipping. **This indicator lets you know if your audio output is** *clipping.* **Clipping happens when the audio is too loud for your audio card to handle, and the signal produces a clicking or crackling noise.**

C MIDI Sync. **This button toggles between Reason's internal sync and sync from an external source. (See Chapter 9, "External Control of Reason," for more info on MIDI sync.) In Most situations you will want to leave this switch in the off position unless you are synchronizing Reason to another machine.**

D Focus. **If you have multiple songs loaded, this function will allow you to choose which song is played back when Reason receives MIDI sync.**

E Click. **Selecting this option will start a simple metronome that follows the tempo Reason is set to. A metronome is helpful when you are recording to ensure your audio parts are played in the correct time. The level knob directly under this controls the volume of the metronome.**

F Tempo and Signature. **Here you can set the tempo and time signature of your song. To change these values you must use the arrows to the right of the number; you cannot enter a number via your keyboard.**

✳ ✳ ✳

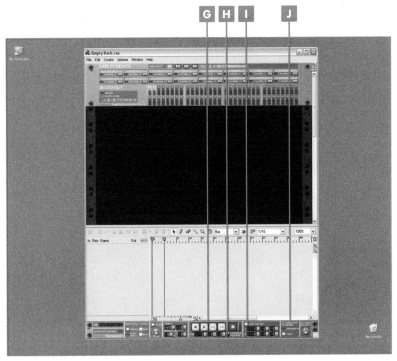

G Transport Controls. **These
four buttons control Reason's
transport: Stop, Play, Rewind,
and Fast-Forward. Fast-
Forward and Rewind will move
the playback cursor through
the song in increments of
one bar. The red button is for
recording your performance
from your master MIDI
controller (if you have one).
The Play button starts the
playback of Reason.**

H Overdub/Replace. **This switch
sets the record mode. If you
record while in Replace mode,
the new recording will erase
the previous performance.
In Overdub mode, the new
performance will be added to
the existing recording.**

I Loop. **You can set the points at which you want Reason to loop while
playing or recording. This button enables or disables looping. The
displays and controls below the Loop On/Off button allow you to
set the beginning and end points of the loop.**

J Automation Override. **The red indicator labeled Punched In will light
up if a track has automation recorded on it and new automation
data is being recorded over the top of the exiting automation,
or if you change the value of a parameter on a device that has
automation recorded to it; the newly created automation will be
temporary until the Reset button is clicked (more on automation in
Chapter 7, "The Sequencer").**

K Pattern Shuffle. **Reason contains a few pattern-based devices, such as Redrum and Matrix Pattern Sequencer. When using these devices, you can apply a shuffle to all loaded pattern devices. Shuffle will slightly alter the timing of the pattern devices randomly to make them sound more natural. Turning this knob to the right will increase the shuffle amount, but be careful—too much can produce unwanted timing effects.**

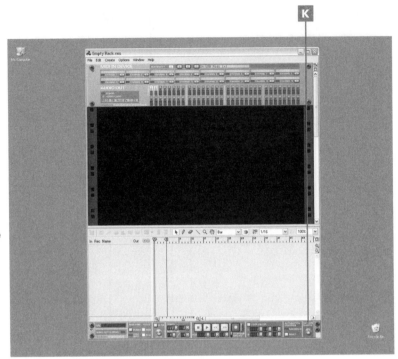

Adding and Removing Devices

Before you can begin to use Reason, you must load a device into the virtual rack. You can begin by adding a simple synthesizer.

1 Click on the Create menu. **The device menu list will appear.**

2 Click on SubTractor Analog Synthesizer. **The SubTractor synth will appear in the rack.**

> ❄ **STAY TUNED FOR MORE ON REASON'S DEVICES**
>
> The parameters for each of Reason's devices will be covered in detail, beginning in Chapter 3, "Analog Emulated Synthesizers."

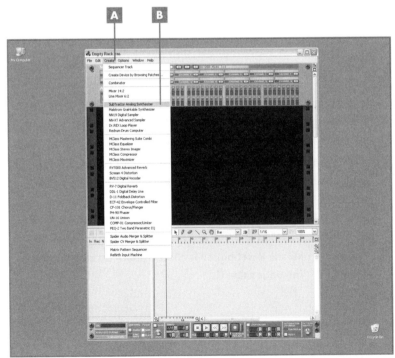

❄ ❄ ❄

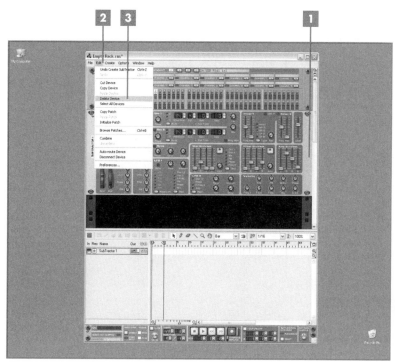

If you wish to remove this or any other device that has been added to the rack:

1 Click on the device you wish to remove. The device will be highlighted.

2 Click on the Edit menu. The Edit menu will appear.

3 Click on Delete Device. The device will be removed from the rack.

Organizing Devices and the Rack

As mentioned, Reason can load as many devices as your computer's CPU can handle, so you might imagine that the rack, both front and back, can get fairly confusing. But the rack can be organized just about any way you like. You can move devices around the rack without have to worry about re-routing the cables (something I wish I could do with real hardware in a real rack).

Moving a Device

You can move the devices around the rack to place them to your liking.

❅ ❅ ❅

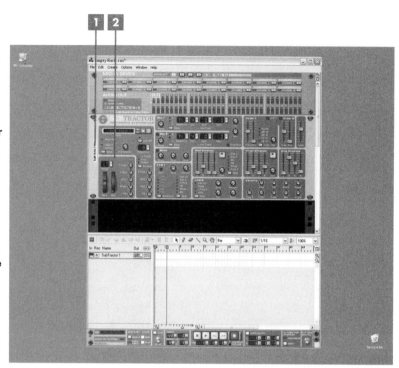

1 Click on the side of the device you wish to move (left side or right side). The device will become highlighted.

2 Drag and drop the device up or down to move it.

❄ THIS IS JUST A (MOVING) TEST

At this point you will have only one device loaded in the rack, so clicking and dragging on the device will give you the idea of how to move a device, but you will not be able to actually move it.

❄ ORGANIZING DEVICES

Moving devices is a good way to keep similar components together—for example, you can categorize them by type of device or by the nature of the parts they are playing, such as percussion, bass, or pads.

Folding Devices

To conserve rack space, each Reason device can be folded, or collapsed, into a smaller version of itself.

1 Click on the down arrow on the left side of the device. The device will fold up.

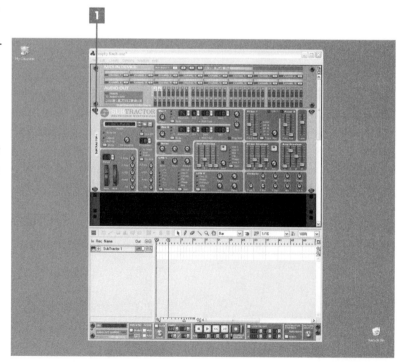

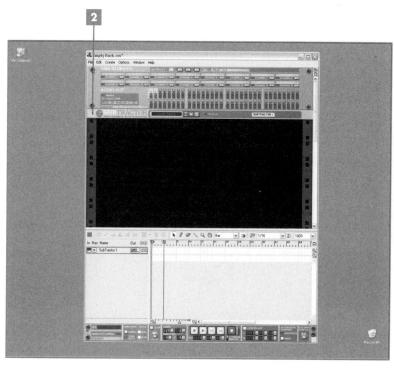

2 Click on the right arrow on the left side of the device. The device will unfold.

✳ FOLDING THE LOOPING DEVICES

Folding is great for looping devices such as the Dr:rex Loop Player. More often than not, loops are tweaked then left to play. Once they're tweaked the way you like them, you can simply fold them out of your way.

Labeling Your Devices

You can label each of the Reason devices you have loaded. This can be particularly helpful if you have loaded more than one instance of the same device. The label is made to look like a piece of masking tape, which many real-world audio engineers use for labeling consoles and outboard gear.

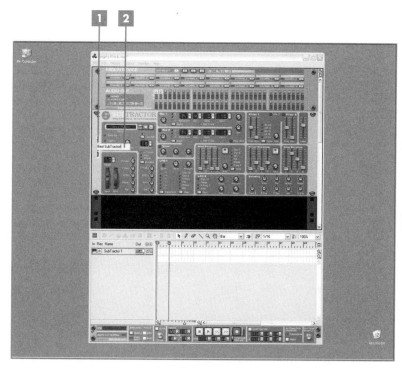

1 Click on the tape strip on the left side of the device. The current name will become highlighted.

2 Type the desired name for the device and press Return. The device name will reflect the changes.

Basic Audio Routing

After adding the SubTractor synth to the empty rack, flip the rack around to the rear view and see how Reason has automatically routed the SubTractor's output to Input 1 on the Audio In device. This is the most basic form of audio routing.

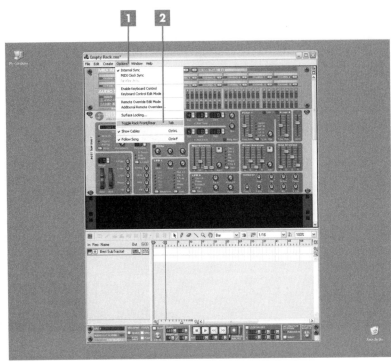

1 Click on the Options menu. The Options menu will appear.

2 Click on Toggle Rack Front/Rear.

❋ **TOGGLE VIEW SHORTCUT REMINDER**

A little reminder: Pressing the Tab key will also toggle the rack between front and rear views.

A The cable connects the output of the SubTractor to Input 1 of the audio interface.

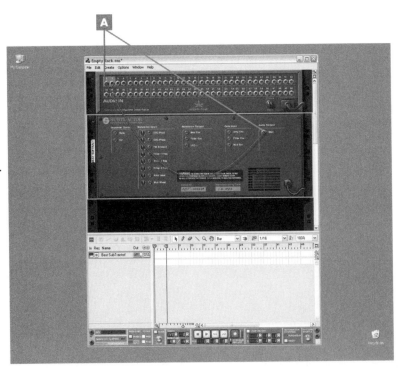

Keep in mind that the Audio In device represents your audio card outputs, and if you have only one stereo output, then you have only two channels. If SubTractor is taking one of them, how will you route audio from other devices you load into the rack? You need a mixer, and, luckily, Reason includes one called Mixer 14:2.

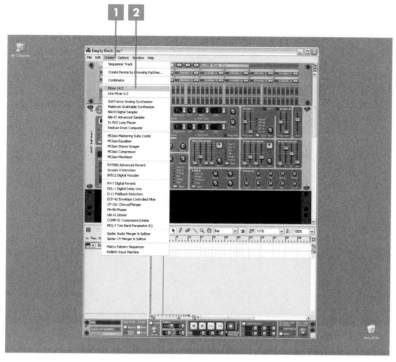

Next you'll learn to load the mixer into the rack and take a look at how to route devices with it.

1 Click on the Create menu. The Create menu will appear.

2 Click on Mixer 14:2. The mixer will be added to the rack.

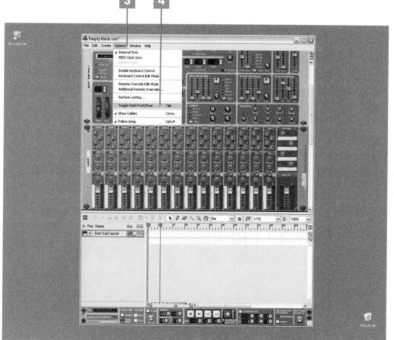

3 Click on the Options menu. The Options menu will appear.

4 Click on Toggle Rack Front/ Rear. The rack will turn to the rear view.

As you can see, the mixer is not connected to any device. First you need to connect the SubTractor to the mixer.

1. Click on Input 1 of the Audio In device. The Connections menu will appear.

2. Click on Disconnect. The cable connected to Channel 1 will be removed.

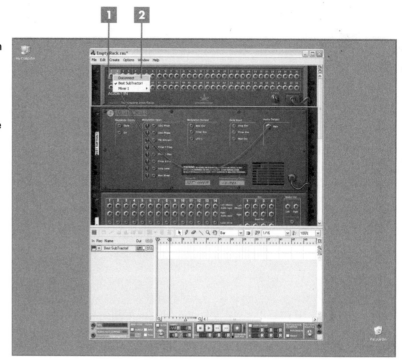

3. Click on SubTractor's Audio Output. The Connections menu will appear.

4. Click on Mixer 1. The mixer's inputs will appear.

5. Click on Channel 1 Left. A cable connecting the SubTractor and the mixer will appear.

Now you can connect the mixer to the Audio In device.

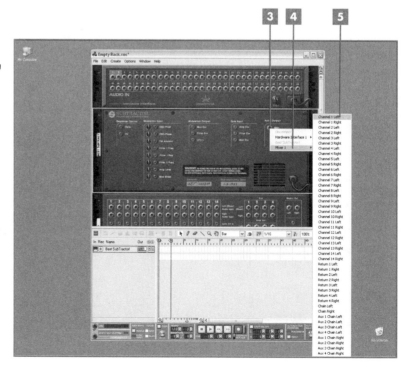

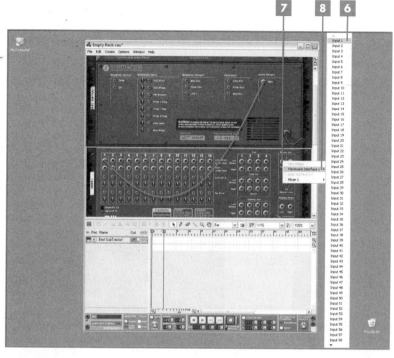

6 Click **on the** Mixer Left Master Output. **The Connections menu will appear.**

7 Click **on** Hardware Interface. **The hardware interface input menu will appear.**

8 Click **on** Input 1. **The output of the mixer will be connected to input Channels 1 and 2 of the hardware interface.**

✤ INSTANT CABLES

Two cables will automatically appear. This is because Channels 1 and 2 of the Audio In device are a ganged stereo pair and any device with a stereo output that is connected to either Channel 1 or 2 will be automatically routed in a stereo pair.

✤ ANOTHER WAY TO ROUTE CABLES

You can also route by clicking and dragging cables. This is done by clicking and holding the end of a cable, dragging it to the location where you want to make the connection, and "plugging" the cable in by releasing the mouse button.

In most cases when working in Reason you will want to have a mixer loaded in the rack before loading any other devices. That way, when you do load devices, they will route to the mixer automatically. You could simply try to remember to load a mixer first, or to make it simpler, you could create a template song that has only a mixer loaded into an empty rack.

1. Open the Empty Rack template (as described earlier in the section, "Starting with an Empty Rack").

2. Click on the Create menu. The Create menu will appear.

3. Click on Mixer 14:2. The mixer will be added to the rack.

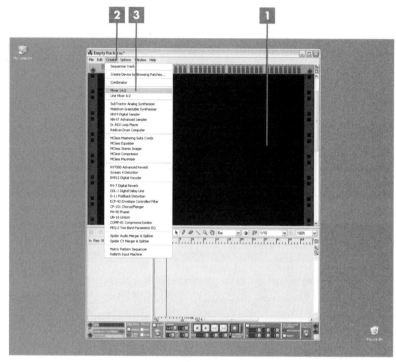

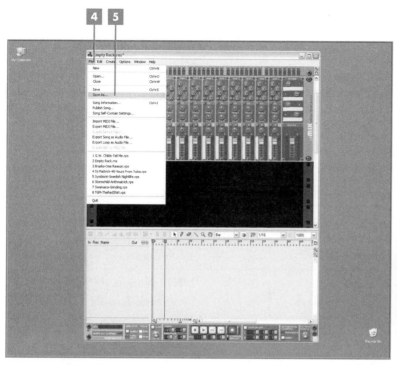

4 Click on the File menu. The File menu will appear.

5 Choose Save As from the File menu. The Save As window will appear.

6 Navigate to the location where you wish to save the template and click Save.

❄ **SETTING UP TEMPLATES AS DEFAULTS**

Remember that you can then set the template to be your default sound when you start a new song (see "General Program Preferences" in Chapter 1).

Now you can route more devices to your audio card's outputs by using the mixer. In fact, you can load as many mixers into the rack as your CPU will allow (this goes for all devices in Reason). You'll learn about more advanced routing in Chapter 8, "Advanced Audio Routing with Effects."

Introducing Reason's Devices

At this point you have configured your computer to run Reason, and you've seen what Reason can do with the playback of a demo song. Furthermore, I briefly covered adding devices and how to arrange and route audio. In the next chapter, you'll get a closer look at the devices included in Reason 3.0. Reason includes a list of over 20 devices—a very impressive list at that (see Table 2.1).

To acquire an equivalent amount of hardware gear, you would spend a fortune. And what is even more impressive is that you can load multiple instances of each device. Would you like to have three samplers in your rack? With Reason, it's as easy as simply adding another one to your rack! With Reason, your creativity is limited only by the power of your computer and the depth of your imagination.

Because the list of devices is extensive, I want to make navigating through the device section of this book as easy as possible. With that in mind, I have divided the devices into five separate chapters. Table 2.1 demonstrates how the devices are categorized by chapter:

Table 2.1   Where to Find Reason Devices in This Book

Chapter	Devices
Chapter 3 Analog emulated synthesizers	SubTractor synthesizer; Malström Graintable synthesizer
Chapter 4 Digital samplers	NN19 Sample; NN-XT Advanced Sampler; Dr:rex Loop Player
Chapter 5 Effect processors and dynamics	RV7000 Advanced Reverb; Scream 4 Distortion; BV512 Digital Vocoder; RV-7 Digital Reverb; DDL-1 Digital Delay Line; D-11 Foldback Distortion; CF-101 Chorus/Flanger; PH-90 Phaser; UN-16 Unison; COMP-01 Compressor/Limiter; PEQ-2 Two Band Parametric EQ
Chapter 6 Pattern sequencers	Redrum Drum Computer; Matrix Pattern Sequencer; ReBirth Input Machine
Chapter 8 Audio routing devices	Mixer 14:2; Spider Audio Merger and Splitter; Spider CV Merger and Splitter
Appendixes D and E	The Combinator, MClass Mastering Suite Combi; MClass Equilizer; MClass Stereo Imager; MClass Compressor; MClass Maximizer; Line Mixer 6:2

3 } Analog Emulated Synthesizers

Reason contains several devices, referred to as *Sound Modules*, that are responsible for creating the sounds you hear. Some of them are based on the emulation of analog-style synthesizers that use FM (frequency modulated) synthesis to create their sounds with various oscillators and filters, while others generate sounds through the use of digital audio recordings, or samples. First I'll discuss the FM synthesizers. In this chapter, you'll learn how to

❋ Load and save patches.

❋ Initialize devices.

❋ Reset device parameters.

❋ Work with the SubTractor synthesizer.

❋ Work with the Malström Graintable synthesizer.

Loading and Saving Patches

All of Reason's Sound Modules allow you to select patches, or sounds, to play. You can either load a preset patch from Reason's factory CDs or from other sources, such as third-party ReFills, or you can create, save, and reload your own patches. Loading and saving works the same in each of Reason's devices.

Loading the SubTractor to the Rack

Later in this chapter you'll get a close look at the SubTractor Analog synthesizer, but first you should load it into the rack so that you understand how to load and save patches and also how to initialize devices.

To load the SubTractor:

1 Click on the Create menu. The Create menu will appear.

2 Click on SubTractor Analog Synthesizer. The SubTractor device will be added to the rack.

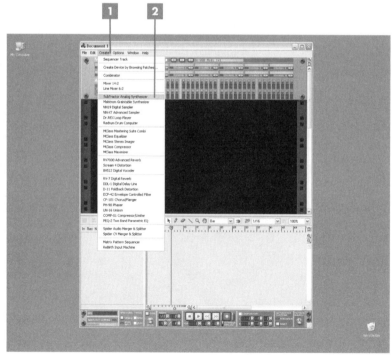

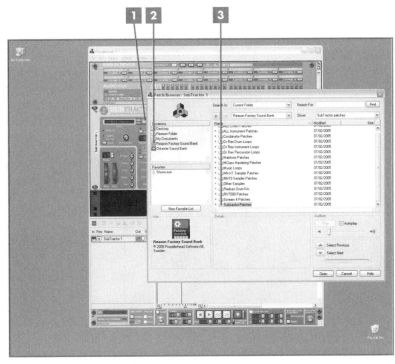

Loading a Patch

To load a patch:

1 Click on the folder icon. The Patch Browser will appear.

2 In the Locations window, click on the Reason Factory Sound Bank.

3 Double-click on the Subtractor Patches folder.

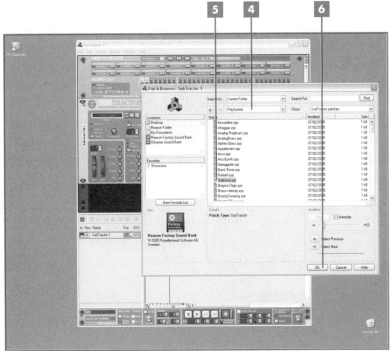

4 Navigate to the PolySynths folder.

5 Select the Balinese.zyp patch.

6 Click the OK button. The patch will be loaded into the device.

Saving a Patch

Here's how to save a patch:

1. Click on the disk icon. The Save Synth Patch window will appear.

2. Navigate to the folder where you wish to save the patch.

3. Type a file name.

4. Click Save.

❄ **THE PATCH FILE TYPE**

The File Type menu in the Save Synth Patch window will automatically add the file extension that is relevant to the device you used to create the patch. These patch files can be opened only in the same device.

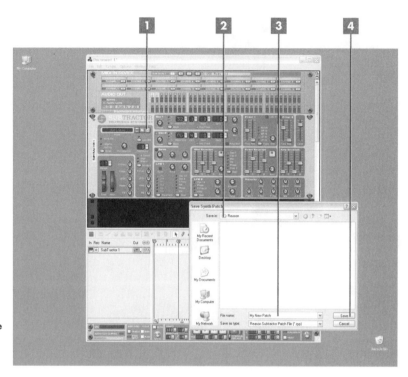

Initializing a Device

While working on the different exercises with the devices throughout this book, there is a good chance that the sounds you create may become unpleasant due to all the changes you're able to make—sometimes once you start tweaking parameters, it's hard to stop! So, to begin each exercise with a clean palette, you will initialize the devices often. Initializing brings the instrument back to its default state, giving you a fresh starting point. To initialize a device:

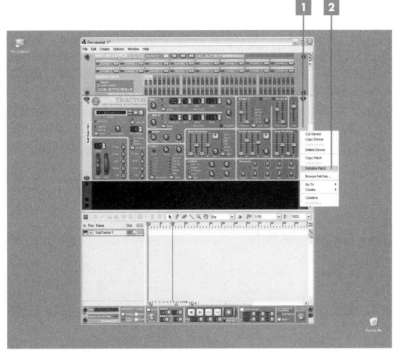

1 Right-click **on the** front panel **of the device. The Devices menu will appear.**

2 Select Initialize Patch. **The device will initialize with its default settings.**

❄ START WITH AN EMPTY RACK

As you follow the exercises in this chapter and the chapters to follow, it's a good idea to start with an empty rack each time you begin working with a new device. That way, you won't need to worry about re-routing the audio each time you add a device to the rack. I will cover audio routing in detail later. To make this even easier for you, I recommend choosing Empty Rack as the default when creating a new song. Refer to Chapter 1, "Setting Up Your Computer to Run Reason 3.0," for more details on how to do this.

❄ COMMON FEATURES SHARED BY REASON DEVICES

As you learn about Reason's devices, you'll soon notice that many of them share common features. I will cover the parameters for each device but will move quickly through the explanation of any parameters and controls that have already been discussed.

Resetting Device Parameters

There may be a few times in this book when you want to reset some parameters of a device without having to initialize the entire device. To do this:

1 Press the Ctrl key on your keyboard.

2 Click on the parameter you wish to reset.

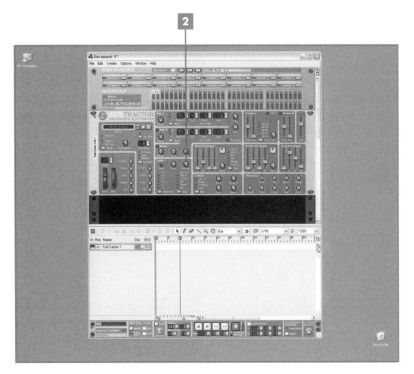

The SubTractor Analog Synthesizer

The SubTractor analog synthesizer is modeled after the classic analog synthesizers that made their boom in the late 70s and early to mid 80s. Earlier in this chapter, you loaded the SubTractor into the rack. Now you will start your tour of the devices with this classic-sounding synthesizer.

If all went well during the setup, you should now be able to hear the SubTractor synthesizer by playing your master MIDI keyboard. If not, check your connections and settings by reviewing "Configuring Advanced MIDI" in Chapter 1.

To get better acquainted with the SubTractor, you can load a simple bass guitar patch and see how adjusting some of the parameters affects the sound.

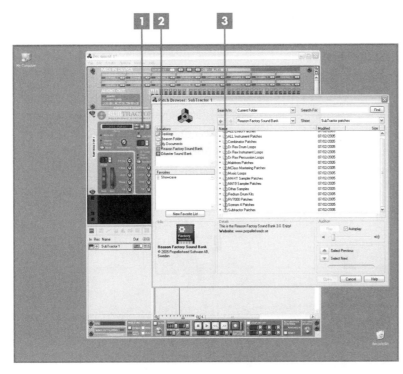

Loading the Sample Patch

First you will need to load the patch into the SubTractor.

1 Click on the Browse Patch button. The Patch Browser will appear.

2 Click on Reason Factory Sound Bank in the Locations window.

3 Navigate to the folder SubTractor Patches.

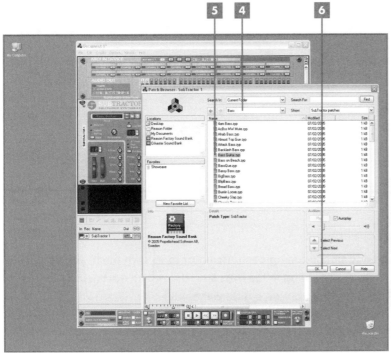

4 Navigate to the subfolder Bass.

5 Click on the file Bass Guitar. zyp. The patch will become highlighted.

6 Click on OK. The patch will be loaded into the SubTractor.

❋ QUICK ACCESS TO PATCHES

After the first time you load a patch for any device from the original installation CDs, you can access a pop-up menu displaying all available patches in the last folder loaded by clicking on the Patch Name window.

After the patch is loaded, play a few notes from your MIDI controller to familiarize yourself with the sound of the patch before you start experimenting with the parameters.

The Oscillators

All sounds created in SubTractor are generated from the oscillator section. Think of an oscillator as an engine that is used to produce waveforms. These waveforms produce the actual sounds that you hear. SubTractor comes with two individual oscillators: OSC 1 and OSC 2. By adjusting the frequencies of these oscillators, you can change the pitch of the sounds they create.

Tuning the Patch

1. Double-click the up arrow for Oscillator 1's octave tuning. The value of the octave tuning will be 5.

2. Double-click the up arrow for Oscillator 2's octave tuning. The value will be set to 5.

Now when you play a note from your MIDI controller, the pitch of the bass guitar will be two octaves higher than before.

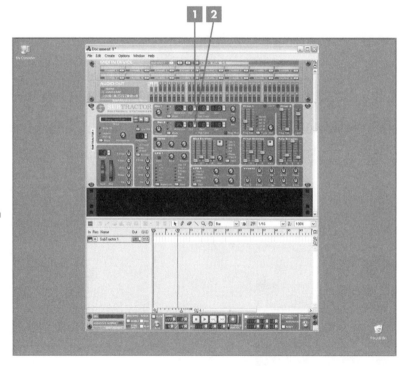

Doubling

In addition to tuning each oscillator to its own pitch, you can also create a doubling in the bass sound in which each oscillator plays the same note but on a different octave.

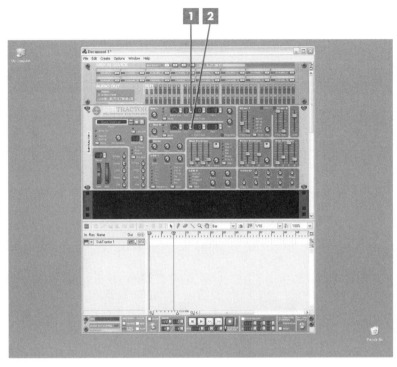

1 Double-click the down arrow for Oscillator 1's octave tuning. The value will now be 3.

2 Click the down arrow four times for Oscillator 2's octave tuning. The value will now be 1.

Now play a key on your MIDI controller. The SubTractor will produce two bass tones, two octaves apart. Doubling is a great technique for fattening the sound of the SubTractor.

❄ FINE-TUNING THE OSCILLATORS

Each oscillator on the SubTractor can also be tuned in semi steps as well as cents. The Semi tuning parameter will tune either up or down in semi tones (one note). Cents are generally used for very fine amounts of tuning.

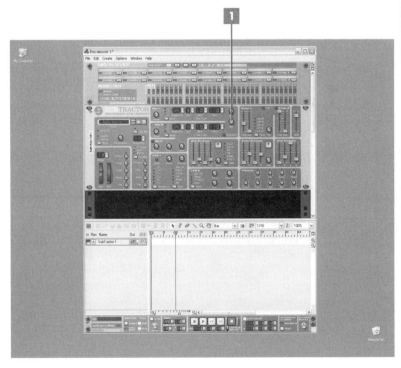

Mixing the Two Octave Tones

Now that you have created two separate tones by tuning each oscillator to a different octave, you can control the balance of the two.

1 Turn the Mix knob all the way to the right. You will hear only the sound from Oscillator 2, which is the lower octave tone.

2 Turn the Mix knob all the way to the left. Now you will hear only the higher octave tone produced by Oscillator 1.

3 Turn the Mix knob to the center position to create a 50/50 blend of the two tones.

Playing the Same Pitch from Any Key—Keyboard Tracking

The SubTractor will automatically readjust the tuning to match the note you're playing from your MIDI controller—that is, if you play a C note, the SubTractor will retune the oscillators to produce a C; this is referred to as Keyboard Tracking. However, if you wish to play the same note regardless of the key you play, you need to disable Keyboard Tracking.

1 Click on the Kbd. Track button on Oscillator 1. Keyboard Tracking will be disabled on Oscillator 1.

2 Click on the Kbd. Track button on Oscillator 2. Keyboard Tracking will be disabled on Oscillator 2.

Now play several different notes from your MIDI controller. No matter which note you play, the same tone will be produced by the oscillators.

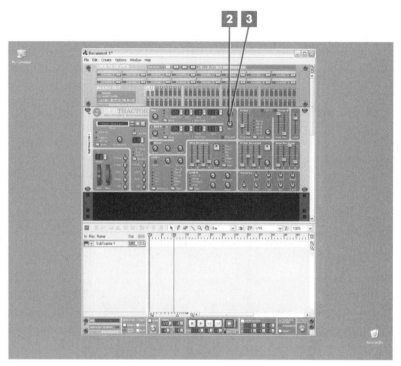

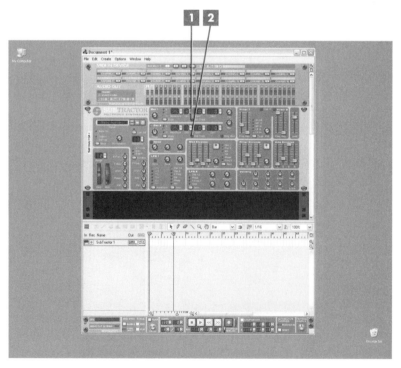

✳ EXPERIMENTING WITH KEYBOARD TRACKING

In most cases you will want to leave Keyboard Tracking turned on; however, a good experiment to try is to have Keyboard Tracking enabled on only one of the oscillators, which will create a thicker detuning sound. It's also helpful to adjust the mix to create a good blend between the two tones.

Playing Parameters

The SubTractor has several parameters that control the playing style of the instrument. Here is a look at some of these.

Single Notes or Chords—Polyphony

The bass patch that you loaded into the SubTractor will allow you to play only a single note at one time. (The number of notes playable at one time is known as the instrument's *polyphony*). Typically, bass players play one note at a time, so single-note polyphony (known as *monophony*) is usually not a problem with a bass patch; however, perhaps you would like to play some chords with your bass.

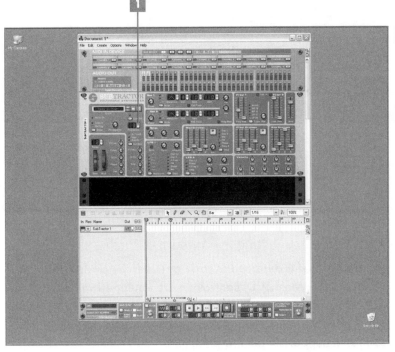

1 Double-click on the Polyphony up arrow. The value will now be 3, meaning that three notes can be played at one time.

2 Play a three-note chord from your MIDI controller. You will be able to reproduce all three notes. If you try to add a fourth, the first note played will cease playing.

✳ POLYPHONY AND THE BASS PATCH

Since you are using a bass patch as an example, low polyphony settings will be sufficient. However, if you are using the SubTractor to play a pad or string sound, you may want to set the polyphony value to a higher number in order to be able to play more notes simultaneously.

Portamento

Portamento applies a small pitch glide when you move from one note to another on your MIDI keyboard. The direction of the pitch glide depends on whether you move up or down to the next note.

1. Turn the Portamento knob to the full position.

2. Play a single C3 note from your keyboard. A simple tone will be produced.

3. Play a single G3 note from your keyboard. A G3 note will be produced, but with a rising glide at the start of the note.

4. Play the original C3 note again. This time, a C3 will be produced with a falling glide.

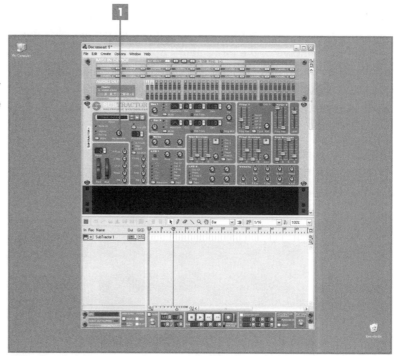

Pitch Wheel—Adjusting the Amount of Pitch

The pitch wheel is designed to raise or lower the pitch of the note being played. Most MIDI controllers are equipped with a pitch wheel that allows you to control SubTractor's pitch wheel (please check your MIDI controller's documentation to verify that your controller supports a pitch wheel).

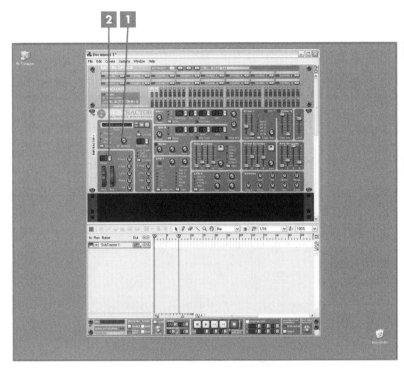

1. Turn the Portamento knob all the way to the left to disable the feature (so there will be no confusion caused by the pitch glide effect from the Portamento).

2. Click on the Range up arrow three times. The pitch bend value will be 5. Play a note and turn the pitch wheel up to its full position; the pitch will bend five semi tones.

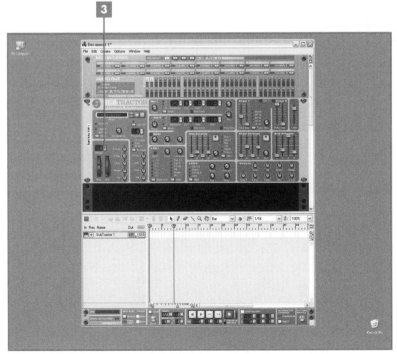

3. Click on the Range down arrow two times. Now when you apply a pitch bend the bend will be only 2 semi steps.

Noise

Noise is just that—noise. If you have ever fallen asleep late at night with the TV on and awakened a few hours later to find only white snow on the screen along with some kind of awful noise, then you know the noise I am referring to. This is called "white noise," and it can create quite an interesting effect when added to your sounds in SubTractor.

Adding the Noise

1 Click on the Noise section's power button. The Noise section will be enabled.

2 Turn the Level knob all the way to the right. This will set the noise to its highest level.

3 Turn the Decay knob to the maximum setting. The Decay knob controls how fast the noise level decreases.

4 Turn the Color knob to the right position as you play your MIDI controller. The Color knob controls the tone of the noise.

Play a note on your MIDI controller and you will hear noise mixed with your bass guitar.

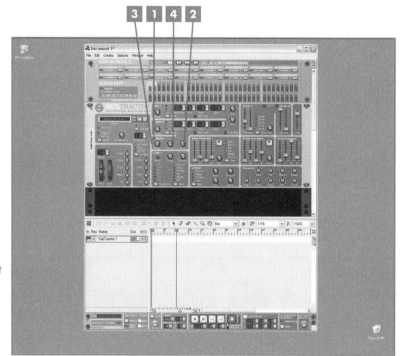

Noise: Tone, Decay, and Volume

Using these knobs, you can control the level and tone of the noise as well as how long it lasts after you initially strike the key.

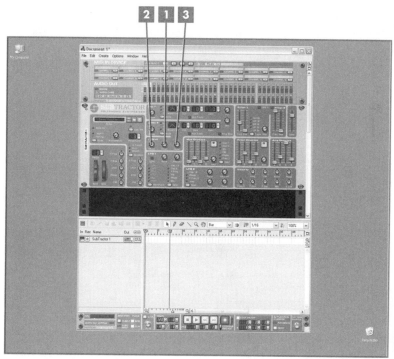

1 Turn the Color knob to the left. As you play your MIDI controller and turn the knob, the tone of the noise will become darker.

2 While playing your MIDI controller, turn the Decay knob to the left. The length of the noise will become shorter.

3 Turn the Level knob to the left. The volume of the noise will decrease.

❄ **DECAY TIME AND TONE**

Short decay time can be effective when using noise to add punch to the attack of the SubTractor's tone.

Modulation—LFO

LFO stands for Low Frequency Oscillator, which is yet another engine that creates waveforms; however, unlike OSC 1 and OSC 2, these waveforms are of a lower frequency and are used to modulate (change the character of) Oscillators 1 and 2, by merging the low-frequency waveform with the waveforms they create.

Adding a Vibrato

LFOs are often used to add vibrato to the sound.

1. Turn the Rate knob to the center position. This will set the speed of the vibrato by increasing the frequency of the LFO.

2. Turn the Amount knob to the right as you play your MIDI control. You will begin to hear the vibrato being mixed into the bass patch.

3. As you continue to play, turn the Rate knob to the right to increase the speed of the vibrato.

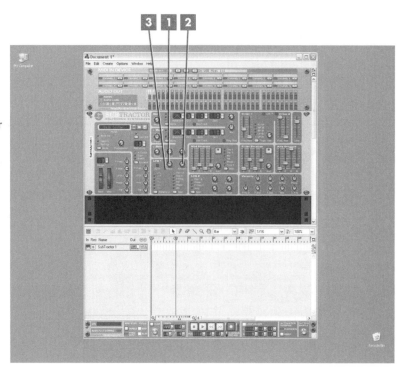

You can add vibrato to the tones from both of the oscillators or the tone from just Oscillator 2.

1. Click on OSC 2 to add the vibrato to the tone of Oscillator 2.

2. Click on OSC 1, 2 to add vibrato to the tones of both oscillators.

❋ WAVEFORM CHOICES

Clicking on the Waveform button will scroll through the different waveform shapes for the vibrato. For more information on the effects of the different waveforms, consult Reason's documentation.

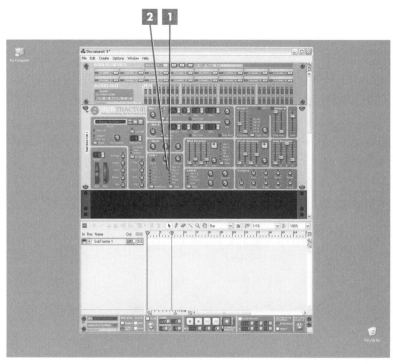

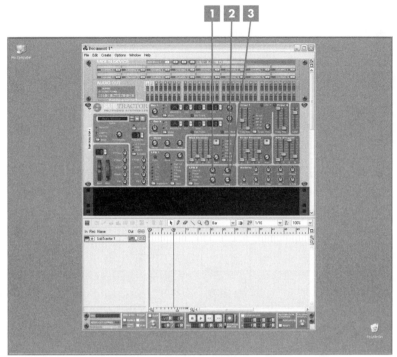

Adding a Second Vibrato

By using the LFO 2 section you can add a second vibrato to create something really interesting.

1 Turn LFO 2's Rate knob to the center position.

2 Turn the Amount knob to the right as you play your MIDI controller. You will begin to hear a second vibrato being added to the bass patch.

3 Turn the Delay knob to the right. This will increase the time before the second vibrato is added after striking a key on your MIDI controller.

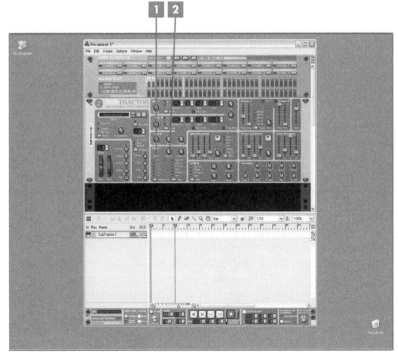

Sync'ing the Vibrato to the Song's Tempo

Using the Rate knob you can control the speed of the vibratos; however, you can have more control by sync'ing the speed to the tempo of the song.

1 Click the Sync button in the LFO 1 section. The rate will be sync'ed to the song's tempo.

2 Turn the Rate knob. Instead of values of 1-127, the Rate knob can now be adjusted to time measurements of the song—i.e., quarter notes, etc.

※ **LFO ROUTING DESTINATION**

The outputs of the LFO section can be routed to other areas of the SubTractor, such as the filters. Use the Dest. button to indicate where in SubTractor you want the LFO's output to go.

Filtering

The SubTractor is equipped with two filters that provide basic tonal control over the instrument. The filters allow you to cut or boost certain frequencies in the sound. Before you continue, I recommend resetting the LFO parameters (see "Resetting Device Parameters" earlier in this chapter).

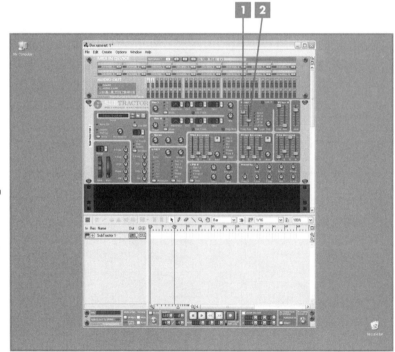

1 Move the Frequency fader up, then down, as you play your MIDI keyboard. When you move it up, the sound will have more of a treble tone. When you move it down, the bass's decay will begin to cut shorter and shorter as you pull the fader down; this is because you are now filtering out the low tones and, since this is a bass patch, most of the tone is in the lower range.

2 Move the Resonance fader up. This will raise the level of resonance (see note); you will notice that the bass guitar will take on more of a synthesizer bass character.

CREATING A THINNER SOUND

The Resonance control enhances the frequencies around the "cut off" point of the filter, creating a thinner sound.

LINKING FILTERS

The SubTractor has two filters, allowing you to filter or enhance more than one frequency. The two filters can be linked by clicking on the Link button. When the filters are linked, any changes made to Filter 1's frequency setting will also affect Filter 2's frequency setting in relation to Filter 1. (Even though the filters can be linked, moving one fader will not physically move the fader of the other filter.)

Working with Envelopes

Envelopes allow you to alter the volume of a patch over time, create a fade in, or even change the length of the note. In addition to controlling volume levels, Envelopes can be used to control various parameters such as the SubTractor's tuning. (Before moving on to the Envelope exercises, the filters should be reset.)

Envelopes Fader Labels—What Do They Mean?

Here's what the Envelope faders' labels mean:

❄ A: Attack controls how fast the Envelope opens. A larger value produces slower opening times.

❄ D: Decay controls how fast the attack's peak amplitude level falls to the sustain level.

❄ S: Sustain controls amplitude level of the note that will play while holding the key. If this value is lower than the decay value, then the decay value will determine the note's length.

❄ R: Release controls how long you can hear the note after the keys are released.

Fade In and Note Length—Amp Envelope

This Envelope is used to control the overall volume of the Sub-Tractor device.

1 Move the A fader up as you play your keyboard. The time it takes the note to reach its full volume will become longer.

2 Decrease the S fader setting. The amplitude level of the note while holding the key will become shorter.

3 Increase the R fader. This will increase the length of time the note plays after you release the key.

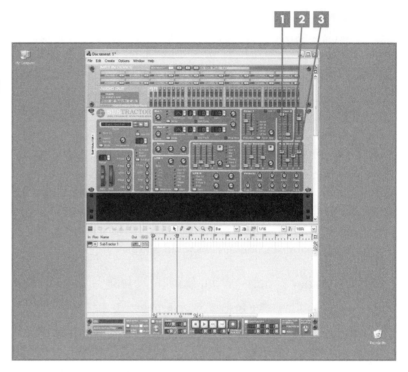

Rising and Falling Pitch—Mod Envelope

With the Modulation Envelope you can change the tuning of the device over time. To demonstrate this, you are going to make the pitch of the bass slowly rise and fall. (Reset the Amp Envelope settings before continuing.)

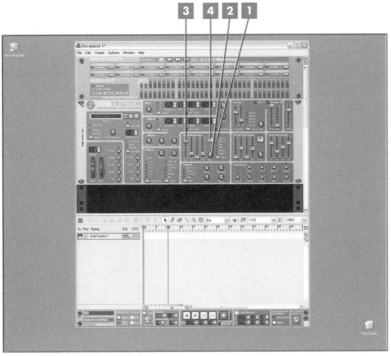

1. Click on Osc 1. This will make the Envelope control the tuning of Oscillator 1.

2. Turn the Amt knob to its full position. The Envelope will now have full control of Oscillator 1's tuning.

3. Move the A fader up to the top. As you play, the note will start at the key you play and slowly rise in pitch.

4. Click on the Invert button. When you play your MIDI controller, the notes will now fall in pitch after you play the key.

❋ MODULATION EXPERIMENTATION

In the previous exercise you used the Modulation section to change the pitch of the SubTractor. The modulator can also be used to create other interesting effects; experimentation is always encouraged.

Sweeping Synthesizer Bass—Filter Envelope

The Filter Envelope allows you to control the filter's setting over time. As an example, you will turn the bass guitar into a sweeping synthesizer bass.

First you need to set the filter's settings so that the bass sounds more like a synthesizer bass. (Before continuing, please reset the Modulation Envelope Amt. knob.)

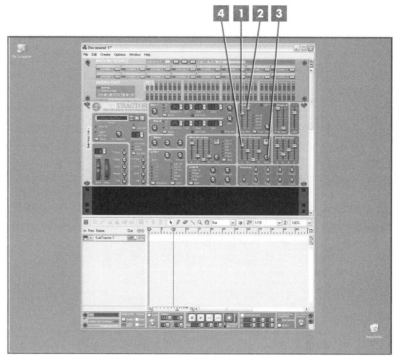

1 Move the Frequency fader to about 3/4. This will allow more midrange frequencies to pass through the filter.

2 Move the Resonance fader to the top. This will enhance the frequencies around the filter's frequency setting, and produce a very synthetic bass sound.

Now you will use the filter Envelope to create a sweeping sound.

3 Turn the Amt knob to the full position. This will give the Envelope control of the filter.

4 Move the A fader to about 3/4. Now when you play a note on your MIDI controller, you will notice the synthesizer's resonance value slowly increase after playing the note, creating the sweeping effect.

❋ OVERDOING THE VOLUME LEVEL

When increasing the Filter Envelope's amount, you are increasing the level of the filter and could easily overdo the volume of the SubTractor. Please be careful when increasing the filter amount.

❋ ❋ ❋

Malström Graintable Synthesizer

In many ways, the Malström Graintable synthesizer works like the SubTractor does: It has two oscillators to create the sounds, as well as several parameters that allow you to further shape the characteristics of the sound. However, instead of using traditional oscillators, the Malström's oscillators use actual audio recordings to generate the sounds. This form of synthesis is not the same as wavetable synthesis, which is a method in which an actual sample or recording is played back when a note is struck. Graintable chops these samples into smaller segments, which are referred to as *grains*. This method allows users to alter each segment or grain with the various parameter controls.

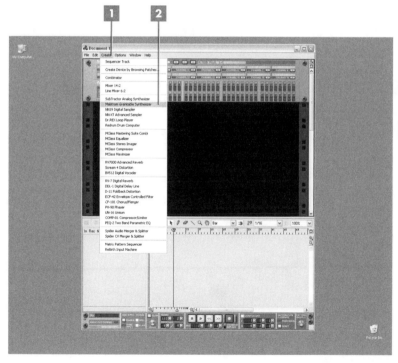

Loading the Device to the Rack

1 Click on the Create menu. The Create menu will appear.

2 Click on Malström Graintable Synthesizer. The device will be loaded in the rack.

Loading the Test Patch

Before exploring Malström's parameters, you will load up a test patch. You will load a simple patch of a bell sound.

1 Click on the Browse Patch icon. The Patch Browser window will appear.

2 Click on the Reason Factory Sound Bank in the Locations window.

3 In the main Patch Browser window, double-click Malström Patches, then double-click the PolySynths subfolder to open it.

4 Click on the Bells.xwv patch.

5 Click on OK. The bells patch will be loaded into Malström.

After loading the patch, play some notes from your keyboard to get familiar with the patch's sound.

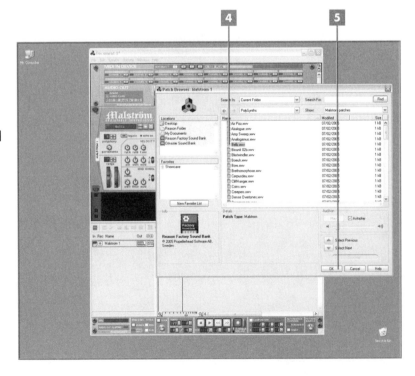

Changing the Sound's Characteristics—Oscillators

Since the Malström is a graintable synthesizer, the most notice-
able changes to the sound characteristics will be in the oscillator
section. As mentioned earlier, unlike the SubTractor, which uses
waveform generation to produce its sound, the Malström uses
small audio recordings to generate sound. There are two oscillators in Malström.

Changing the Sample

You'll start by diving straight into the most important part of the
oscillator section— the sample. Changing the sample will change
the foundation of the synthesizer.

The bell patch uses the sample "Chime" as its base, loaded into
both oscillators. You are going to change this sample.

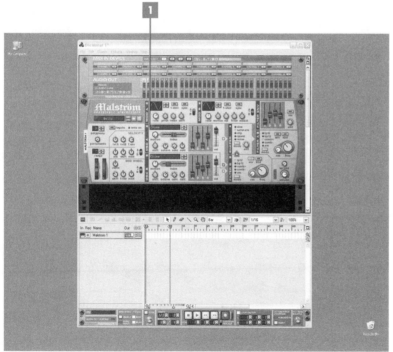

1 Click on the sample window
in the oscillator section.
The Malström sample menu
will appear.

2 Click on Synth: FM1. The sample window will change to display the newly loaded sample.

Now change the sample of Oscillator B.

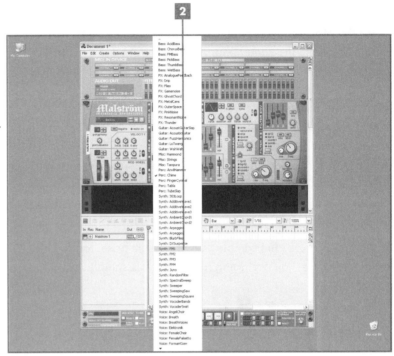

3 Click on the sample window of Oscillator B. The Malström sample menu will appear.

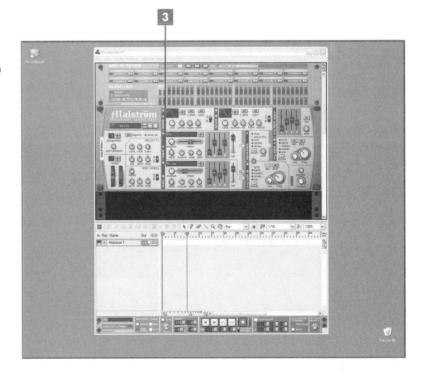

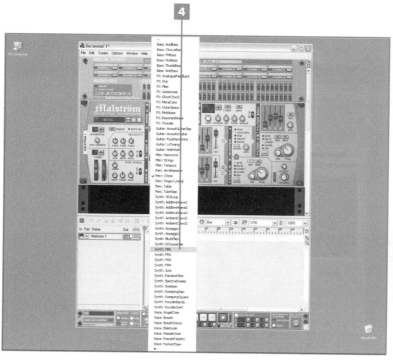

4 Click on Synth: FM1. The sample window will reflect the change to the FM1 sample.

Now when you play your keyboard you should hear an analog-sounding synthesizer instead of the bells you heard before.

❄ **SCROLLING THROUGH THE SAMPLE LIST**

If you wish to scroll through the sample list one sample at a time, use the up and down arrows next to the sample LCD window.

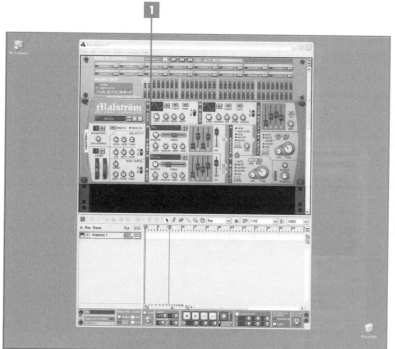

Two Synthesizers in One

Since there are two oscillators that you can load graintable samples into, the Malström becomes a very flexible synthesizer. Next you'll see how you can use the two oscillator sections to layer the sounds of two different graintable samples.

1 Click the sample window of Oscillator A. The sample menu will appear.

2 Click on the sample Bass: Pick Bass. The sample will be loaded into Oscillator A.

Play a key on your keyboard. You will now have the FM synthesizer sound and a picked bass guitar sound playing together.

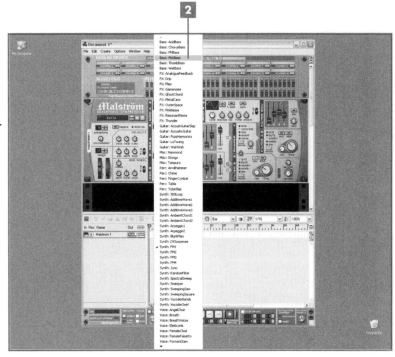

Adding Some Movement—Motion

The speed of the samples loaded into the oscillators (how fast the sample plays from start to end) can be altered. In Malström this is referred to as *motion*.

1 Play your MIDI keyboard and listen carefully to the FM 1 sample. The sample should have a slight downward pitch glide that starts shortly after you hit the key. This is part of the sample itself.

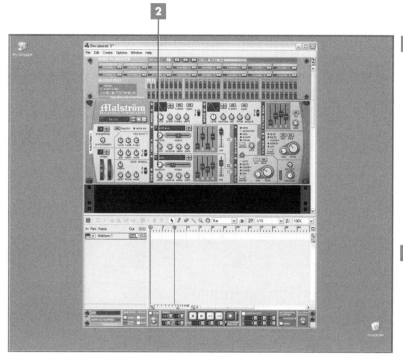

2 Turn the Motion knob of OSC B to the left as you play your MIDI keyboard. The length of time after you strike the key to the pitch glide will increase. This is because the sample speed is being slowed down. If you turn the knob too far, the sample will become slow enough that you will no longer be able to hear the pitch glide.

3 Continue to play your MIDI keyboard while you turn the Motion knob to the right. The length of time to the pitch glide will become faster the farther to the right you turn. Turning it too far will make the pitch glide become extremely fast and produce a fluttering effect.

4 Turn the Motion knob back to the half-way point to restore the original speed.

❊ **MOTION AT TWELVE O'CLOCK**

When the Motion knob is at the half-way point, no speed changes are applied to the sample.

Tone Changes—Shift

Using the Shift knob you can change the tonal characteristics of the sample.

1 Turn the Shift knob to the left while playing your MIDI controller. The sound will have a lower tone.

2 Turn the Shift knob to the right. The sound will become brighter and have a higher tone.

❄ **SHIFT AT TWELVE O'CLOCK**

When the Shift knob is in the center position no tone changes are applied.

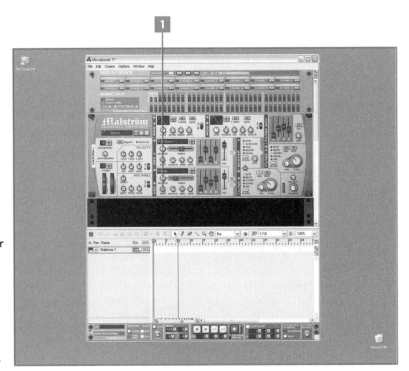

Sample Start Position—Index

With the Index parameter you can control which point in the sample should be marked as the start point that's triggered when you strike a key on your MIDI keyboard.

1 Move the Index slider on Oscillator A all the way to the left. When you play your MIDI keyboard, the bass guitar will have a bigger synthesizer sound when you first strike the key.

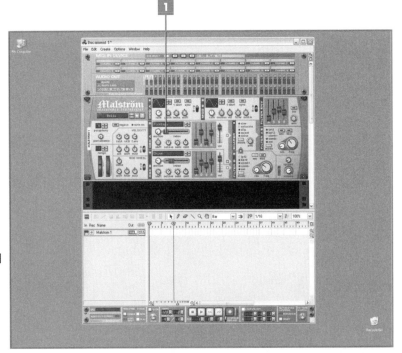

2 As you play, move the slider to the right. This will change the start point to farther into the sample and will remove the synthetic sound at the beginning of the bass.

Oscillator Volume

With the SubTractor, you mixed the volumes of the two oscillators using a mix knob, but with the Malström the oscillators can be mixed by using their own individual volume controls.

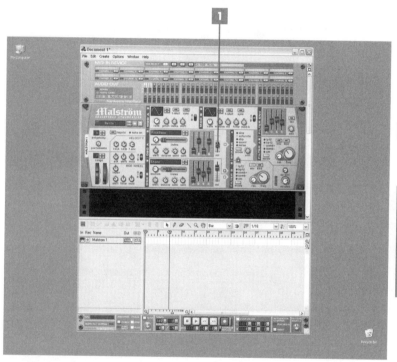

1 Move Oscillator A's volume fader down to decrease the volume of the sample in Oscillator A.

2 Move the fader up. The volume will increase.

❋ **OSCILLATOR VOLUME FADERS**

Each oscillator has its own volume fader that affects the volume of that oscillator. Each oscillator also has its own Envelope, to control the amplitude of the oscillator over time.

Modulation

The Malström's Mod section works similarly to the LFO section of the SubTractor. It generates waveforms that are mixed into the sample recordings (oscillators) to alter the sounds' characteristics, such as the vibrato you created with the SubTractor.

Pitch Modulation

To modulate the pitch of a sample:

1 Turn the Pitch knob to the full position.

2 Play a note on your MIDI controller, and the bass guitar sample will play with a looping pitch bend that will eventually fade out.

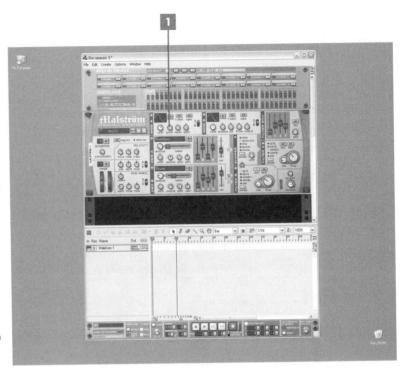

❄ THE PITCH KNOB: LEFT AND RIGHT

Turning the Pitch knob to the right will force the pitch loop to start at a high note and glide downwards. If you turn the Pitch knob to the left, the pitch bend loop will start from a lower note and move upwards.

Now try increasing the speed of the pitch bend.

1 Turn the Rate knob to the right. The speed of the pitch bend will increase.

2 Turn the Rate knob to the left. The speed of the pitch bend will decrease.

3 Turn the Rate knob to the lowest position. No pitch bend will be applied.

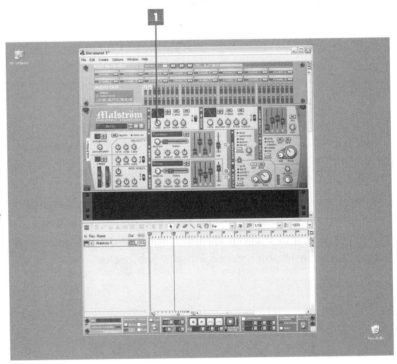

❋ SYNC'ING WITH TEMPO

As with SubTractor's LFO section, you can set the rate to sync with the tempo of the song by clicking on the Sync button located at the top of the Mod section. After enabling the sync option, the Rate knob can be used to select time measures such as quarter note, eighth note, etc., for the speed of the modulation.

Modulating the Start Position—Index

You can also use the Mod section to control a sample's start point (index). (Once again, please reset the previous modulation changes before continuing.)

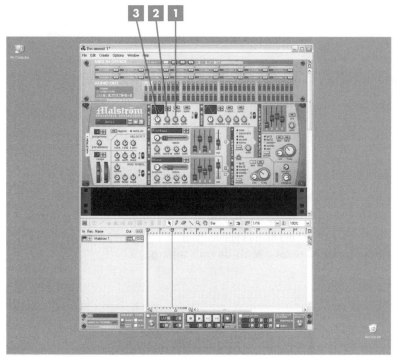

1. Turn the Index knob to the full position.
2. Turn the Pitch knob to center position.
3. Turn the Rate knob to the center position
4. Play a key on your MIDI controller. An additional bass sample will be added and delayed. Also, the new bass sample will start from the beginning of the sample.

5 Turn the Index knob to the left while playing your MIDI controller. The start point of the second bass sample will move further into the sample, reducing the synthetic sound at the beginning. Once the Index knob gets to the center position, you will no longer be able to hear the additional sample.

❄ LOOPING MODULATION

Since the modulation is a continuous loop, the second bass sample will remain looped as long as you hold the key on your MIDI controller.

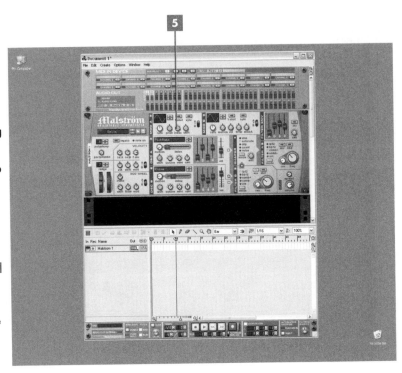

Modulating the Tone

Use the Mod section to adjust the tonal characteristics of the sample. Before moving on, please reset the modulation controls. Hold down the Ctrl key (Command key on Macs) and click on the knob/fader to reset it to its default setting.

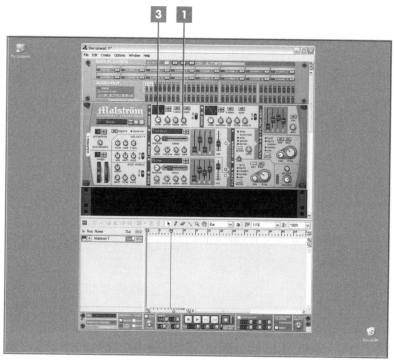

1. Turn the Shift knob to the full right position.

2. Play a note on your keyboard. There will be a sweeping tonal change to the bass sample's character that will start with a low tone and move toward a higher tone.

3. Turn the Rate knob to the right as you play your MIDI controller. The speed of the tone change will increase.

4. Turn the Rate knob to the left. The speed of the tonal change will decrease.

❄ SHIFT KNOB TONE CHANGES

When the Shift knob is turned to a positive value, the tonal changes will start with a low tone and move toward a high tone. If you turn the Shift knob to a negative value, the tone change will begin from a high tone and move toward a lower tone.

Motion Modulation

It is also possible to use the speed of sample as a method of modulation. (Reset the modulation controls before continuing.)

1. Turn the Motion knob to the right as you play your MIDI controller. You will begin to hear modulated versions of the samples being mixed with the original sample. The speed of the modulated samples will be faster than the originals (which is actually what creates the modulated sound).

2. Turn the Rate knob to the left. The modulation speed of the new samples will begin to decrease.

3. Turn the Motion knob back to center position, and the additional samples will be removed.

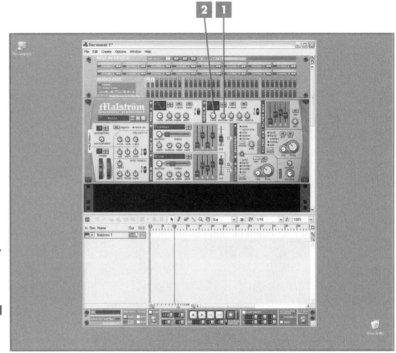

Controlling the Volume— Tremolo

The Mod section can also control the volume of the samples, and one good example of this is to create a tremolo effect. (Again, please reset the modulation parameters first.)

1. Turn the Volume knob to its full positive position.

2. Play a note on your keyboard. The note will slowly rise to full volume, then fall to zero, then rise again.

3. Turn the Rate knob to the right to increase the speed of this effect. Turn the knob to the left to decrease the speed.

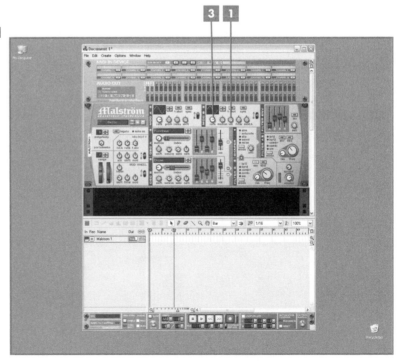

❋ 1-SHOT BUTTON

The waveform created by the Mod section is continuous, meaning that if you use modulation to create a pitch shift, that pitch shift will continue to bend up and down as long as you hold the key. There is an option to have the waveform produced only once, after you first strike the key. Click on the 1-Shot button at the top of the Mod section to enable this feature.

Selecting the Oscillator to Modulate

There are two modulation sections in Malström; each can be assigned to modulate one or both of the oscillators.

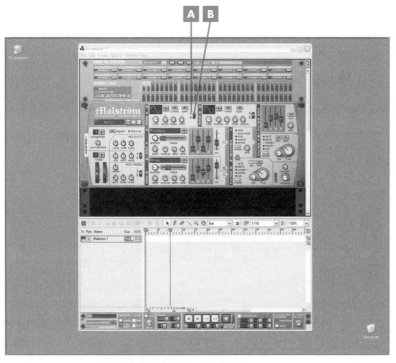

A Move **the** oscillator selector switch **to** A **to apply the** modulation to Oscillator A only.

B Move **the** oscillator selector switch **to** B **to apply the** modulation to Oscillator B only.

C Move **the** oscillator selector switch **to the** middle **position to** apply the modulation to both oscillators.

Adding Some Color—Shaper

The Shaper section works much as the Noise section does on the SubTractor; it adds noise to the oscillator to enhance the shape of the sound. (Please reset the modulation controls.)

1 Click on the Shaper power button. The Shaper section will become enabled.

2 Turn the Amt (amount) knob to the right to increase the Shaper's volume.

3 Play your MIDI controller. You will hear the noise that has been added to the oscillators.

✸ **OVERLOADING MALSTRÖM**

Be careful when adjusting the Shaper's Amt control; it is easy to overload the output of the Malström if too much noise is added. If you still desire more noise, bring down the volume level.

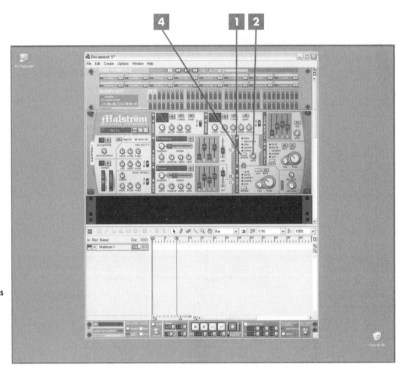

4 Click on the Mode button to toggle between the different noise characteristics.

Increasing the Stereo Width

The Malström is able to spread its two oscillators left and right to increase the perceived stereo image of the device.

1 Turn the Spread knob to the right to increase the stereo width.

2 Play your MIDI controller. The bass sample from Oscillator A will be on the left, and the FM synthesizer sound from Oscillator B will be on the right.

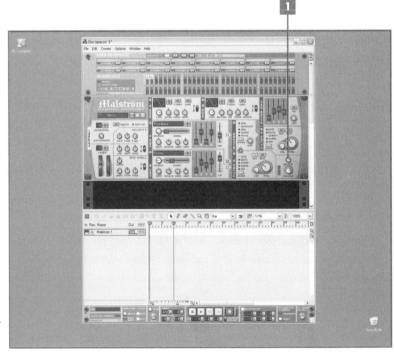

✸✸✸

4 { Digital Samplers and the Rex File Loop Player

Samplers first arrived on the music scene several years ago, and in many ways revolutionized the way many songwriters, engineers, and producers work. A sampler works by recording a small piece of an instrument's sound, or any other sound for that matter, and then allowing you to play back that recording from a keyboard. These devices used to be big, bulky, and very expensive; however, samplers have since evolved into many different shapes and forms. Samplers are becoming software based, allowing your computer to become the equivalent of a hardware-based sampler. Reason comes equipped with two such software samplers. In addition to these samplers, you also have a loop player. A loop player will play back recordings of drum beats that play in a continuous loop, and loop players are helpful when building the rhythm foundation of your songs. In this chapter, you'll learn how to

* Work with the NN19 Digital Sampler.

* Work with the NN-XT Advanced Digital Sampler.

* Work with the Dr:rex Loop Player.

NN19 Digital Sampler

The first of two digital samplers in Reason is the NN19. The NN19 has the features you would expect to find in a much more expensive hardware equivalent. And Reason allows you to add as many of these samplers to your rack as your computer can handle, removing any limitations to the number of patches or samples you can load (depending on the power of your computer).

Loading the NN19

Begin by adding the NN19 to an empty rack.

1 Click on the Create menu. The Create menu will appear.

2 Click on NN19 Digital Sampler to load the NN19 into the rack.

❈ ANOTHER WAY TO ADD A DEVICE TO THE RACK

Remember that you can also add any device to the rack by right-clicking on an empty space in the rack and selecting the device from the pop-up menu.

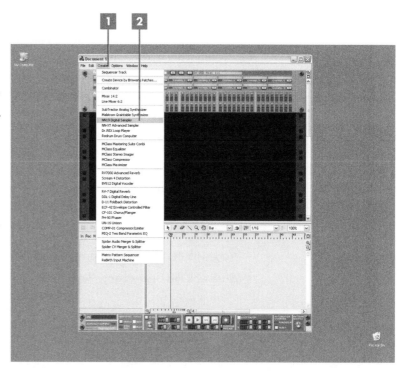

Loading a Sample Patch

Begin by loading a Grand Piano patch into the NN19 in an Empty rack.

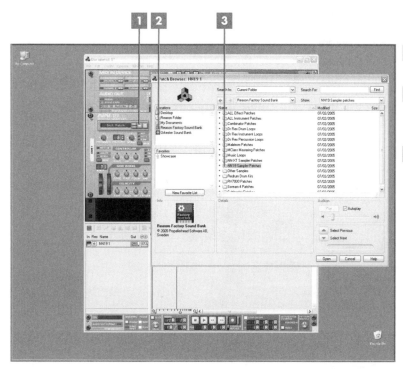

1. Click the Folder icon. The Patch Browser window will appear.

2. Click on the Reason Factory Soundbank in the Locations window.

3. Double-click on the NN19 Sample Patches folder.

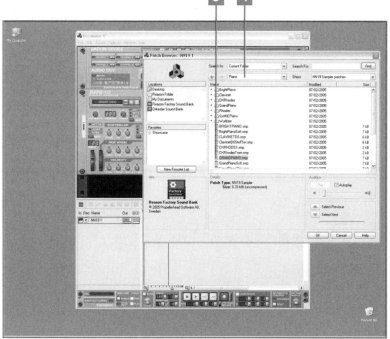

4. Navigate to the folder NN19 Sampler Patches: Piano.

5. Double-click on GRANDPIANO.smp. The Grand Piano patch will be loaded into the NN19.

Play a few notes from your MIDI controller to get familiar with the sound of this Grand Piano patch.

Modulation—LFO

Just as with the SubTractor and Malström in Chapter 3, "Analog Emulated Synthesizers," the NN19 is also equipped with an LFO section that is used to further shape the sound of its patches.

Now use the LFO to create a stereo tremolo effect with the Grand Piano.

1. Click on Pan. This will assign the LFO to modulate the panning of the instrument.
2. Turn the Amount knob all the way to the right.
3. Turn the Rate knob to the half-way point.
4. Play your MIDI controller and listen to how the notes will now bounce between the left and right speakers.

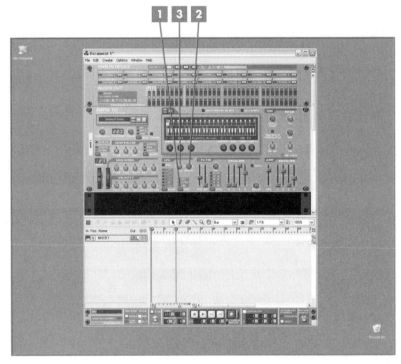

Filters

NN19 has filtering capability, similar to that in the SubTractor and Malström synthesizers.

A Softer Touch

Use the filters to give the Grand Piano a warmer sound.

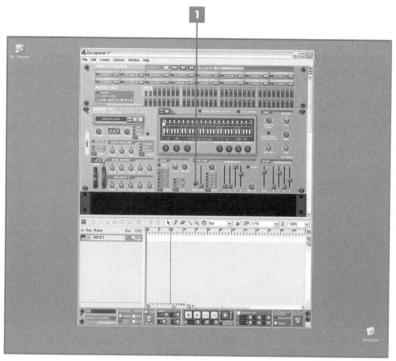

1 Move the Freq fader down to just about the bottom.

2 Play your MIDI controller. The piano will have a slightly muffled tone.

The filter here removed some of the higher frequencies and left the lower frequencies more dominant, so the result is a warmer sound.

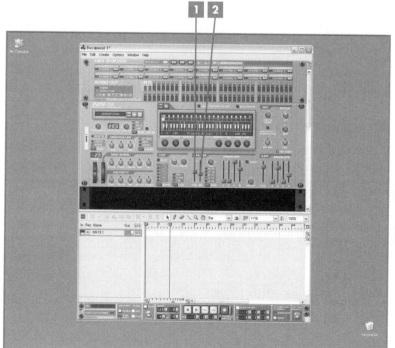

A Bright Piano

Next, tweak the filters to give the piano a brighter tone.

1 Move the Freq fader to the half-way point. This will allow some of the higher tones to pass through the filter.

2 Move the Resonance fader to just below the half-way point.

3 Play your MIDI controller. The piano will have a brighter, sharper tone.

Amp Envelope

With the Amp Envelope section, you can control the characteristic of the instrument's volume. Before continuing, you will need to reset the filter settings by holding down the Ctrl key (Command key on Macs) and clicking on the filter parameters.

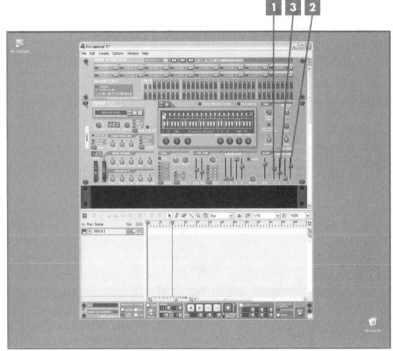

1 Raise the Attack fader. Listen to how the piano becomes softer as you touch the keys. Continuing to move the fader will eventually make the piano inaudible.

2 Move the Release fader up as you play your MIDI controller. Listen to how the piano's notes last longer after you release the keys.

3 Bring the Decay fader down lower than the Attack. The piano will start to resemble a synthetic computer beeping sound.

Sample Playback Controls

In the OSC section of the NN19 you can control how the samples used in the Grand Piano patch will play as you play your MIDI controller. (Before you begin, please reset the Amp Envelope section.)

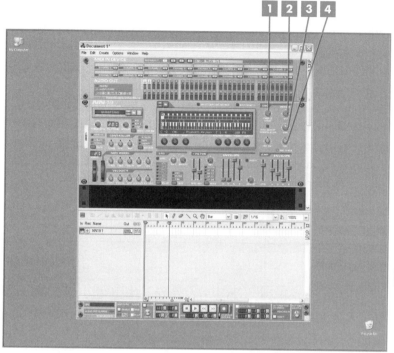

1. Turn the Sample Start button to the right as you play your MIDI controller. The sound will become softer. The Sample Start button alters the point at which the sample starts its playback.

2. Turn up the OCT knob. The pitch of the NN19 will increase in octave steps.

3. Turn up the SEMI knob. The pitch of the NN19 will increase in semi note steps.

4. Turn the FINE knob to the right. The pitch will increase slightly.

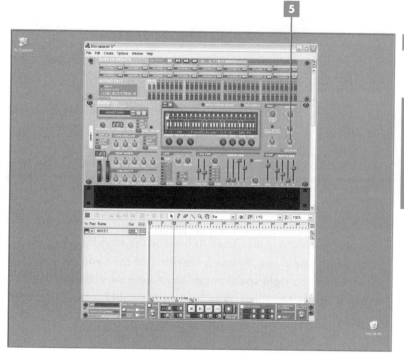

5. Turn the FINE knob to the left. The pitch will decrease slightly.

❅ PITCH CONTROLS AT TWELVE O'CLOCK

When the SEMI control is set to zero, no pitch change will be applied. With the OCT and FINE controls, the knob must be in the center position for no pitch changes to be applied.

Stereo Width

With the NN19 you can set how the notes will be placed in the stereo image.

Widening the Piano

If you have ever played a real piano you may have noticed that the instrument has a natural panning law. What I mean by this is that the low sounds are generally on your left, and higher-pitched sounds are on your right. This is due to the physical design of the piano. To recreate this:

1. Turn the Spread knob to the full position.
2. Play some low notes from your MIDI controller. The notes will be played from the left side.
3. Play notes from the higher octaves. The notes will be played from the right side.

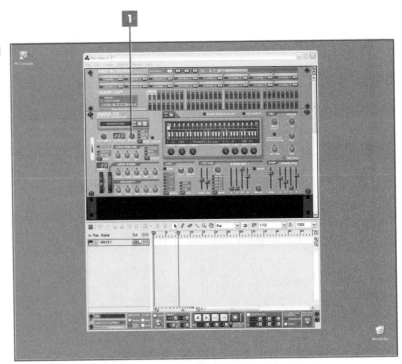

Bouncing Pan

The Spread feature is also used to bounce the keys between the left and right speakers, meaning that the first note you play will be placed on the right speaker and the next note you play will bounce to the left speaker, then back to the right for the next note, and so on.

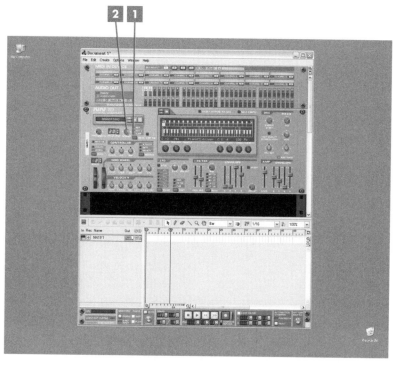

1. Click on Jump. This enables the bouncing pan effect.

2. Turn the Spread knob to the right.

3. Play your MIDI controller. Every second note you play will bounce between the left and right speakers.

Key Zone Editor—Building Your Own Patch

Every sample loaded into a sampler must be mapped to a key or group of keys on your MIDI controller; these groups are called "key zones." In the Grand Piano you loaded earlier, all the samples were already mapped to their respective keys for you. However, the beauty of the sampler is that you can import samples and create your own patches. Next you will import a few simple drum samples to build a small three-piece drum kit.

Before you begin you will need to initialize the NN19 to clear all the samples and key zones created by the Grand Piano patch.

❄ DRUM SAMPLES WEB SITE

For this exercise, download the drum samples from this book's companion Web site: http://www.courseptr.com/downloads. In the search field enter "Reason 3.0 Ignite!" The search return will offer you the file nn19drums.zip. Download it and extract the files to a folder on your hard drive.

Building the Key Zones

After initializing the NN19 there will be only one key zone, so the first thing you will need to do is build more key zones into which the samples will be imported. Since this is going to be a three-piece drum kit, you will need three zones—one for each piece of the kit. You will also create the zones so that each piece of the kit will be played on its individual key from your MIDI controller.

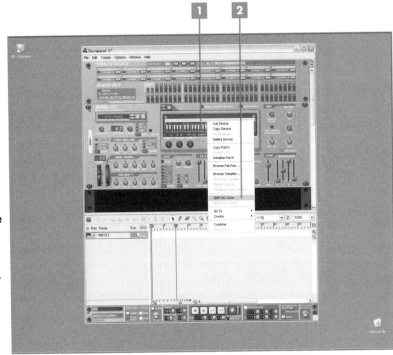

1. Right-click on the key zone window. The NN19's pop-up menu will appear.

2. Click on Split Key Zone. Two key zones will appear in the window.

3. Click and drag the key zone marker to C3. The Lo Key value will show you what note the marker is set to. Use this to guide you to C3.

4. Right-click on the highlighted key zone window again. Click on Split Key Zone.

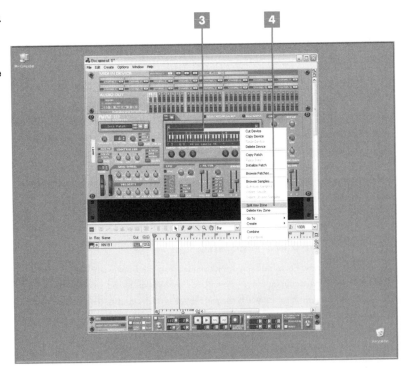

❋ SPLITTING THE RIGHT KEY ZONE

When splitting key zones it is important that you right-click on the zone you wish to split. If you accidentally right-click on any other zone, Reason will automatically change the selected key zone and the split will be performed on the incorrect zones.

❋ FINDING THE KEY ZONE MARKER

Sometimes after performing a key zone split you may need to scroll through the key zones to locate the newly created key zone marker.

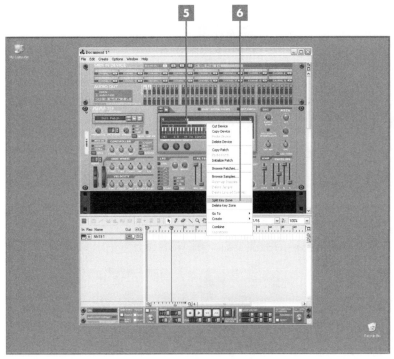

5 Click and drag **the newly created** key zone marker to C#3. **(Remember to use the Lo Key value to guide you.)**

6 Right-click **on the highlighted** key zone window **again, and** click **on** Split Key Zone **from the pop-up menu. The key zone will be split again.**

7 Click and drag **the** third **key zone** marker to D3.

8 Right-click **on the** key zone window **a final time, and** click **on** Split Key Zone **from the pop-up menu. The key zone will be split yet again.**

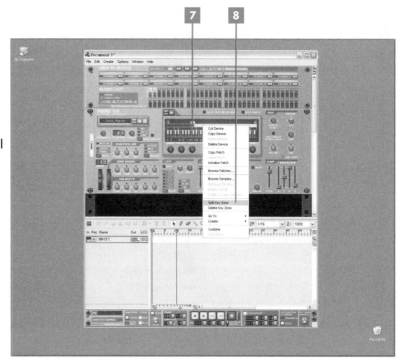

9 Click and drag **the** last **key zone** marker to D#3.

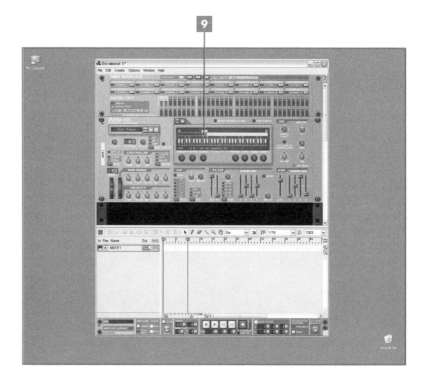

Importing the Samples

Now that you have created the three required zones, you can import the drum samples to them. First, import the kick sample.

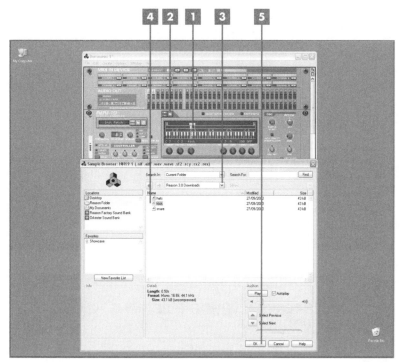

1 Click on the key zone that starts at C3. The key zone will become selected.

2 Click on the Sample Browser icon. The Sample Browser window will appear.

3 Navigate to the folder where you extracted the drum sample that you downloaded.

4 Select the file kick.wav. The file will become highlighted.

5 Click OK. The sample will be loaded into the key zone.

Import the hi-hats sample.

1 Click on the key zone that starts at C#3. The zone will become highlighted.

2 Click on the Sample Browser icon. The Sample Browser window will appear.

3 Click on file hats.wav. The file will become highlighted.

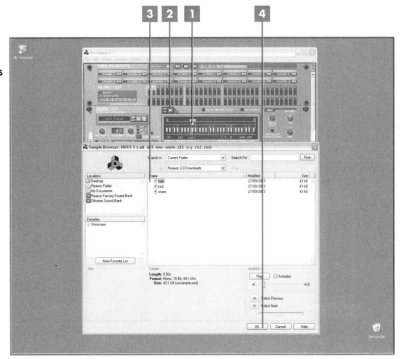

SAMPLE BROWSER WINDOW RETURNS TO LAST IMPORT LOCATION

Because we just finished importing the kick drum, when we click the Sample Browser icon the window will automatically return to the folder where you imported the kick from, as this was the last folder used by the Sample Browser window.

4 Click OK. The hi-hat sample will be loaded into the key zone.

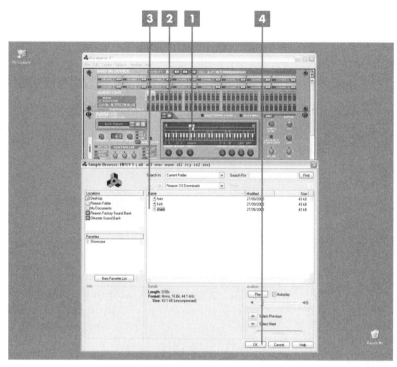

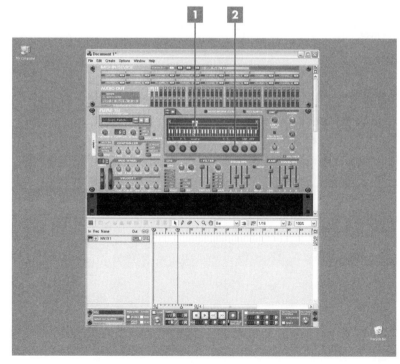

Import the snare drum.

1 Click on the key zone that starts at D3. The zone will become highlighted.

2 Click on the Sample Browser icon. The Sample Browser window will appear.

3 Click on the file snare.wav. The file will become highlighted.

4 Click OK. The snare drum sample will be loaded in the key zone.

Now play the note C3 from your MIDI controller; you will hear a kick drum from this key. Play a C#3 and you will hear a hi-hat; play a D3 and you will hear a snare drum. Congratulations— you have just built a simple kit. Now you can use the Save Patch feature to save this drum kit for later use.

Tuning the Samples

Sometimes you may need to fine-tune a sample that is loaded into a key zone. Here's how:

1 Click on a key zone with one of the drum samples to select it.

2 Turn the Tune knob to the left to lower the pitch. Turning it to the right will raise the pitch. The tuning difference will be very slight, since this is intended for fine-tuning (in cents) adjustments.

Setting a Key Zone Volume

You can also set the volume level of each key zone independently from the others.

1 Select the key zone whose volume you wish to adjust.

2 Turn the Level knob to the left to decrease the key zone's volume and to the right to increase it.

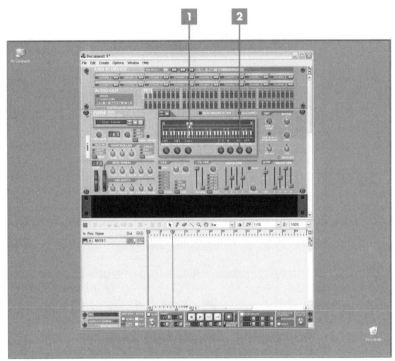

Sample Looping

One of the attractive features of working with samplers is that they can loop (repeat) a sample as long as you are holding the key. Typically, you wouldn't loop individual drum instrument samples, since the nature of the drum is to produce the sound every time you strike the key. However, to get an idea of what looping will do, you will apply it to the snare sample.

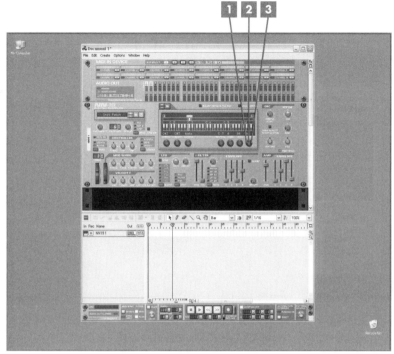

To have a sample automatically loop itself:

1 Turn the Loop knob until the value reads FW. Play and hold the snare drum sample from your MIDI controller. When the snare reaches the end of the sample, it will automatically play again. This will continue as long as you hold the key.

To have the loop of the sample play reversed:

2 Turn the Loop knob to FW BW. Play and hold the snare sample key again. This time when the snare reaches the end of the sample it will also automatically play again; however, when it does, the sample will play in reverse. The repeating reversed sample will repeat as long as you hold the key.

To turn looping off:

3 Turn the Loop knob to OFF. No looping will take place.

Assigning a Sample to a Key Zone

Sometimes you may wish to move a sample from one zone to another. For example, let's say you want to move the sample kick from C3 to D3, and the snare from D3 to C3 (so that the kick and snare swap places).

1 Select the kick drum's key zone. The zone will become highlighted.

2 Turn the Sample knob to the right until the sample value above the knob reads snare.wav. The snare will now be mapped to this zone.

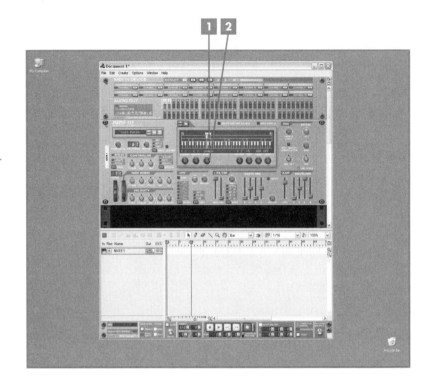

3 Click on the snare's key zone (starting at D3). The zone will become highlighted.

4 Turn the Sample knob to the left until the sample value reads kick.wav. Now the kick will be mapped to this zone.

❋ LOADED SAMPLES AND THE SAMPLE KNOB

The Sample knob will only allow you to select a sample that has been loaded into the NN19, whether or not it is being used by a key zone.

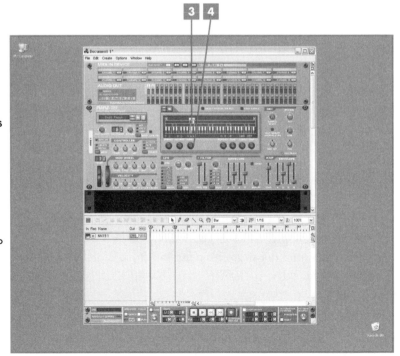

Selecting a Zone from Your MIDI Controller

With this drum kit, you're only using three zones; therefore it is fairly easy to remember which sample is on which zone. However, there may be some situations in which you are working with many more zones; at times it can be hard to be certain that you have selected the correct zone. One way to be sure you have selected the correct zone is to select it from your MIDI controller.

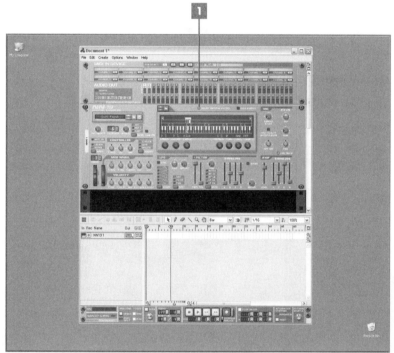

1 Click on Select Key Zone Via MIDI. The feature will be activated.

2 Play the snare drum sample from your MIDI controller. The snare drum key zone will become selected.

3 Play the kick drum sample from your MIDI controller. The kick drum key zone will become selected.

❊ ORGANZING SAMPLES AND PATCHES

Many users dedicate a portion of their hard drive for holding all samples and patches. In fact, some users (such as myself) even have a separate drive for them. This is a good idea, not only to help with file management but also to help with system performance.

NN-XT Advanced Digital Sampler

In many ways, the NN-XT is similar to the NN19, but, as the name implies, it is a far more advanced sampler. One of the biggest advantages of the NN-XT over the NN19 is that all the parameters such as filters and envelopes are individual for each key zone, allowing you to have more control over the samples you use. Most important is the fact that with the NN-XT you can edit individual samples—something you can't do with the NN19.

Loading the NN-XT

Load the NN-XT to your rack.

1 Click the Create menu. The Create menu will appear.

2 Click on the NN-XT Advanced Sampler. The NN-XT will be loaded into the rack.

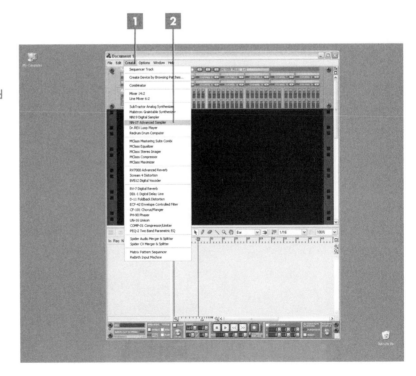

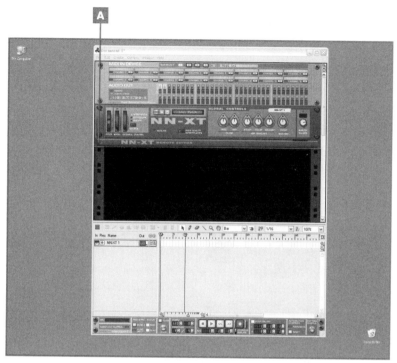

The Sampler and the Remote

As with most hardware samplers today, the NN-XT consists of the body, which is the brains of the device, and a remote unit, the device that allows you to tweak the parameters. By default, the NN-XT's remote is folded out of the way.

A Click on the arrow to open the Remote Editor.

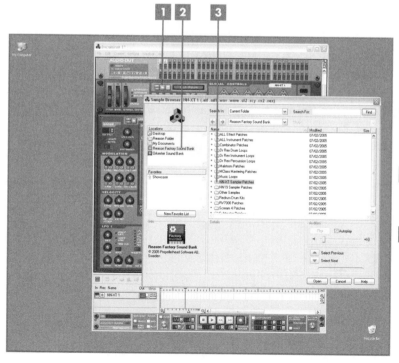

Loading Patches

Now load a Grand Piano patch into the NN-XT.

1 Click on the Browse Patch icon. The Patch Browser window will appear.

2 Click on the Reason Factory Sound Bank in the Locations window.

3 Double-click on the NN-XT Sampler Patches folder.

4 Navigate to **the** Piano **folder.**

5 Select GrandPiano.sxt.

6 Click OK. **The Grand Piano patch will load into the NN-XT.**

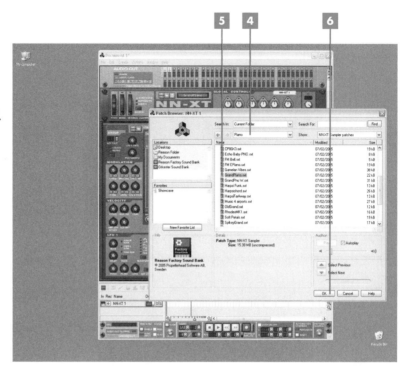

The Key Zone Editor

As with the NN19, all samples loaded into the NN-XT must be mapped to a key zone. The NN-XT's key zone editor is simpler than the NN19's although it may appear to be more complicated. With the Grand Piano patch that you loaded, you can see how the samples are already mapped to several key zones across the keyboard. Because most of the advancements of the NN-XT over the NN19 are in how the key zones are edited, you can now concentrate mostly on the key zone editor.

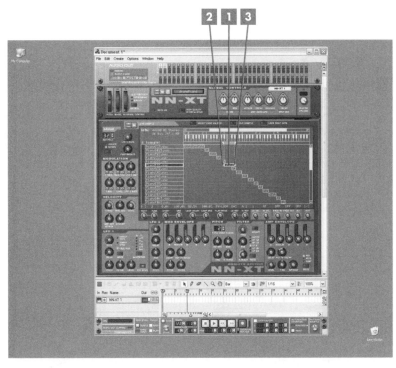

Changing the Key Zones

With the NN19, you used the Lo Key and Hi Key settings to change the start and stop points of a key zone. To change these on the NN-XT:

1 Click on the key zone you wish to change.

2 Click and drag the small box on the left of the key zone. The start point of the key zone will be set.

3 Click and drag the box on the right side of the key zone. The stop point of the key zone will be set.

❊ EDITING KEY ZONE START AND STOP POINTS

The key zone start and stop points can also be set by clicking and dragging on the key zone markers below the keyboard in the key zone editor.

❊ SELECTING A KEY ZONE

You can select a key zone by clicking on the key zone directly or by clicking the sample it is assigned to in the left-side sample list.

Setting the Key Zone's Root Key

When you import a sample into the NN-XT (or the NN19) you need to be careful to map it to a key that will match the pitch of the sample. For example, if you import a bass sample that is pitched to an A note then you would want to make sure that the sample is mapped to an A note; when a sample is mapped to a key of equal pitch to the sample, that key is referred to as the *root key*.

To set the root key of sample:

✺ ROOT KEY DEMO

For a demonstration of a root key in use take a look at the Grand Piano patch. On the left side of the key editor window is a sample list of all the samples used that make up the Grand Piano. Click on the sample, PianoC33.wav, and the key zone will also become highlighted. If you notice that one of the notes is grayed out in the key zone, this indicates the zone's root key. You may also notice that this root key is set to a C2 note. Now look at the sample's file name, and you'll notice there is a C in the file name. This is because this sample's pitch is a C2 note; therefore the root key has been set to C2.

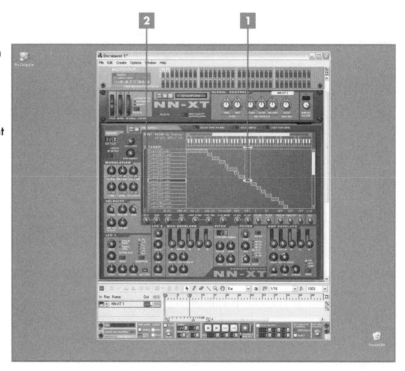

1 Click on the key zone for which you wish to change the root key. The key zone will become highlighted.

2 Turn the ROOT knob to the right to raise root key value. Turn it to the left to lower the value.

✺ ROOT KEY DISPLAY

The root key is displayed on the key zone by highlighting the note; as you change the root key value the highlighted note will change to reflect the changes.

Automatically Assigning the Root Key

The purpose of the root key is to ensure that when you play a note from your MIDI controller the sample is played with the correct pitch; this means that the pitch of the sample you use should also be the pitch of the root key. For example, if you use a sample of a C4 note from a piano, then the root key should also be set to C4. Sometimes, however, you may come across a sample for which you do not know the pitch. If this ever happens, you can have the NN-XT automatically detect the pitch of the sample, and assign the root note accordingly.

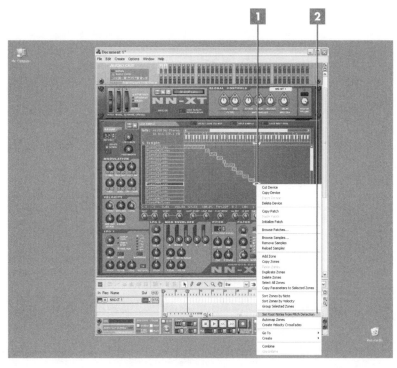

1 Right-click on the key zone for which you wish to set the root key. The NN-XT's pop-up menu will appear.

2 Click on Set Root Notes from Pitch Detection. The root key value will be automatically set to match the pitch of the sample.

Sample Tuning

From time to time, a sample may need some fine-tuning in order to match the root key. To fine-tune the sample:

1 Select the key zone whose pitch you wish to tune.

2 Turn the TUNE knob to the right to raise the pitch of the sample. Turn to the left to lower the pitch.

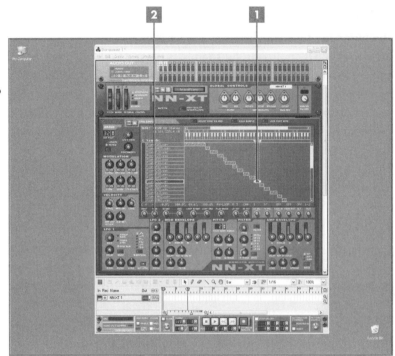

Setting the Volume of a Key Zone

When working with various samples from different sources, sometimes you may find that their volume levels are not consistent. One way to fix this is to control the level of the individual key zones.

1 Select the key zone whose volume you wish to edit.

2 Turn the LEVEL knob to adjust the key zone's volume.

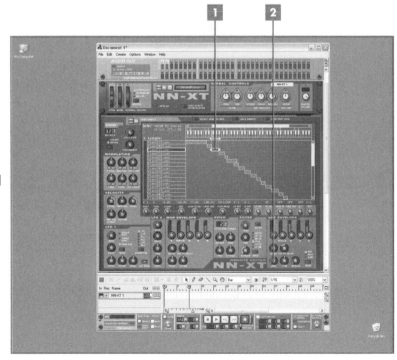

Key Zone Layers

With the NN19 you could set only one sample to a key zone, but with the NN-XT, you can map several samples to a single key zone; this is known as *layering*.

To demonstrate how layering works, you will to add a bass guitar sample that will be played along with the piano sample.

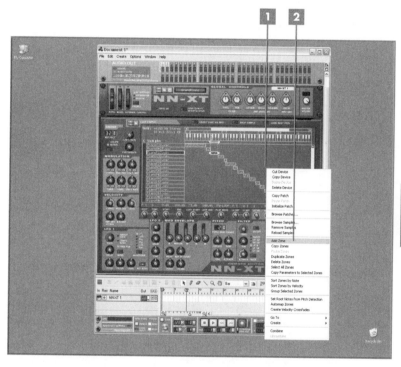

1 Right-click on the key zone window. The NN-XT pop-up menu will appear.

2 Click on Add Zone. A new zone will be created in the key zone window.

❋ **FINDING THE NEW ZONE**

Most likely, you will have to scroll to the bottom of the zone list to see the newly created key zone.

3 Click on the new key zone to select it.

4 Click on the Load Sample icon. The Sample Browser window will appear.

❄ ANOTHER WAY TO LOAD A SAMPLE

Double-clicking on the Sample Name Field will also open the Sample Browser window to load a sample into the key zone.

5 Click on the Reason Sound Factory Bank.

6 Double-click on the NN-XT Sampler Patches folder.

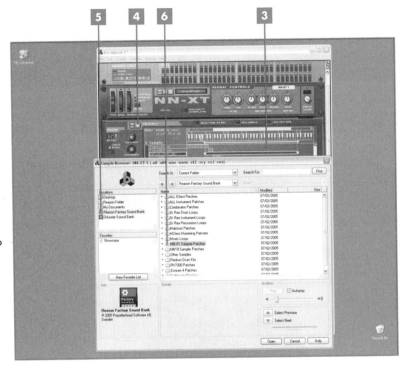

7 Navigate to Bass: Finger Bass Samples.

8 Click on the sample C6FulA_ 1M-M.wav. The file will become highlighted.

9 Click OK. The sample will be loaded into the key zone.

Next you will set the key zone of the bass to play between the notes A1 and E2.

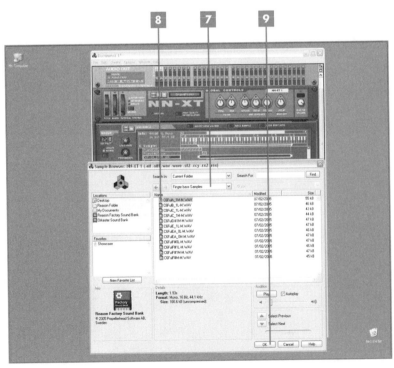

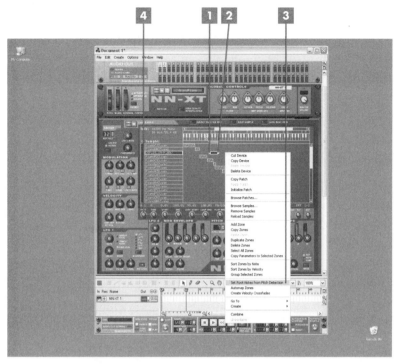

1 Click and drag **the bass key zone's** low setting to C2. **The start point of the zone will be set to C2.**

2 Click and drag **the bass key zone** high setting to E2. **The stop point of the zone will be set to E2.**

Next you will need to set the root key of the sample. Although you can guess the pitch of the sample by the file name (C) you can also use pitch detection.

3 Right-click **on the** bass key zone. **The NN-XT's pop-up menu will appear.** Click on Set Root Notes from Pitch Detection.

4 Play **a few** notes between A1 and E2 **on your MIDI controller. You will now hear a bass sample playing along with the piano. The bass guitar sample's root key will be set to A1.**

❋ **THE IMPORTANCE OF SETTING THE ROOT KEY**

If you forget to set the root key of the bass sample, when you play your MIDI controller between the notes A1 and E2, the bass sample will be pitch-shifted to match the key you are playing. The result is a very high-pitched bass sample!

Auto Mapping

If you are loading several patches into the NN-XT to create your own patch, the task of creating a key zone for each sample can be tedious. With the NN-XT you can automatically create a key zone for each sample.

To show you how this is done you'll need to begin with an empty NN-XT (no patch loaded). If you have a patch loaded, initialize the NN-XT before continuing.

First you will need to load all the samples you want to use. For this example you will load several samples that are included with Reason.

1 Click on the Load Sample icon. The Sample Browser window will appear.

2 Click on the Reason Factory Sound Bank in the Locations window.

3 Double-click on NN-XT Sampler Patches folder.

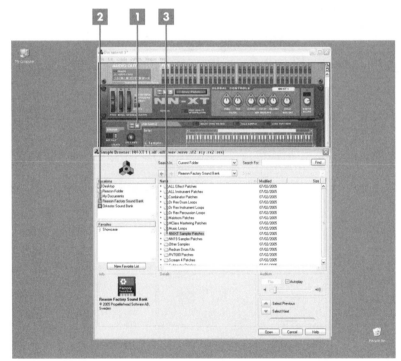

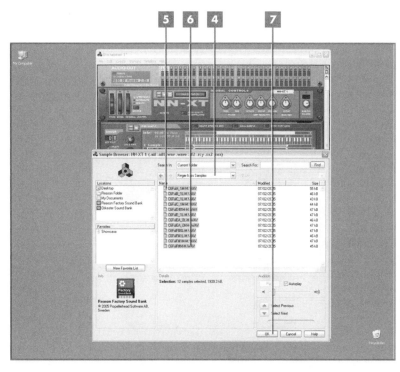

4 Navigate to the folder Bass: Finger Bass Samples.

5 Click on the file C6FulA_1M-M.wav. The file will become highlighted.

6 Shift-click on the file C6FulF#M-M.wav (at the bottom of the file list). All files in the file list will become highlighted.

7 Click OK. All the files will be loaded into the NN-XT.

All the samples will be loaded using the same key zone; however, you want to have every sample you loaded map to its own key zone.

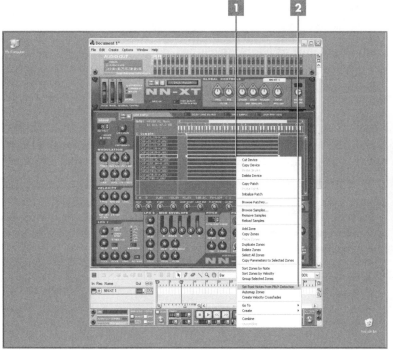

1 Right-click the selected key zones. The NN-XT's pop-up menu will appear.

❋ MAKE SURE TO SELECT SPECIFIC KEY ZONES

Right-clicking anywhere other than the selected samples or key zones will deselect the samples and key zones. If you do accidentally click elsewhere you can simply use the Ctrl-A key command (Command-C for Mac OS X users) to reselect all the zones.

2 Click on Set Root Notes from Pitch Detection.

3 Right-click on the NN-XT.
The NN-XT pop-up menu will
appear.

4 Click on Automap Zones.
Several new zones will be
created; each will be mapped
to one of the loaded samples.

❄ **AUTOMAPPING NON-INSTRUMENT SAMPLES**

If you try to use the Automap function on samples that contain several
pitches, such as vocals or drum loops,
automapping will create the same key
zone for each sample.

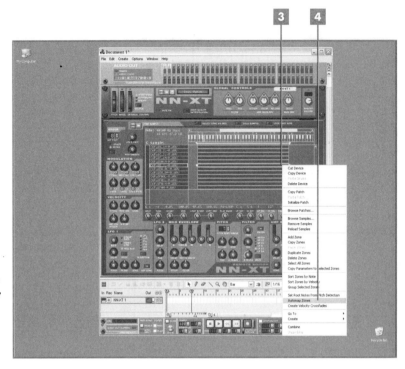

Global Controls

As mentioned earlier, each key zone in the NN-XT has its own
parameters such as filters, envelopes, and LFOs; however, there
are a few parameters that affect the NN-XT as a whole. The global
controls are located on the main body of the NN-XT

Filter

Use the filter on the main body to shape the tonal character of the
instrument as a whole.

❄ **GLOBAL PARAMETER KNOB AT TWELVE O'CLOCK**

When a global parameter's knob is in the center position, that parameter is not being applied to the NN-XT.

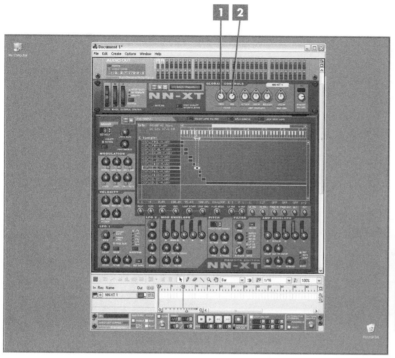

1 Turn the FREQ (frequency) knob to the left as you play your MIDI controller. The bass's sound will become darker. Turn the knob to the right and the sound becomes brighter.

2 Turn the RES (resonance) knob to the right. The bass's sound will become more synthetic.

✻ **USING FREQUENCY TO HEAR RESONANCE EFFECT**

To hear the effect of the resonance control, the frequency must be set to either a positive or a negative value.

Amp Envelope

The Amp Envelope controls the volume of the NN-XT, just as any other envelope; the difference is that this one has knobs instead of faders, and the sustain parameter has been removed.

1 Turn the Attack knob to the right while playing your MIDI controller. The time it takes for the notes to reach full volume will lengthen, and the notes will fade in.

❋ **NOT TOO MUCH ATTACK**

With some samples, increasing the attack parameter too much will cause the note to not even be produced when you play your MIDI keyboard.

2 Turn the Decay knob to left. The bass's notes will become shorter.

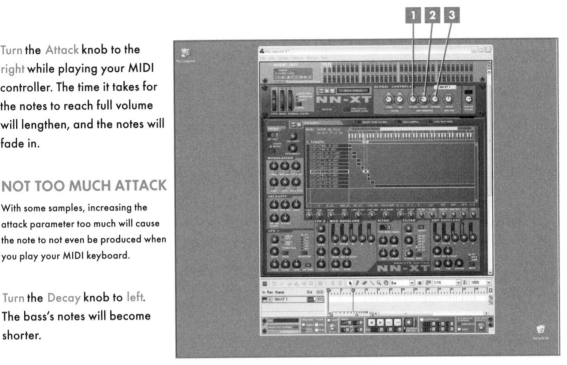

❋ **DECAY FOR PERCUSSIVE EFFECT**

Using a very short decay time is great for creating a percussive instrument effect.

3 Turn the Release knob to the right. The length of time it takes for the note to stop after you release the keys will be extended.

The last parameter in the Global Controls is the Decay control for the modulation filter. This parameter controls the decay time for any modulation applied to your samples. However, the bass samples you loaded above have no modulation applied, so in order to demonstrate this control's effect, you first need to apply some modulation.

❋ ❋ ❋

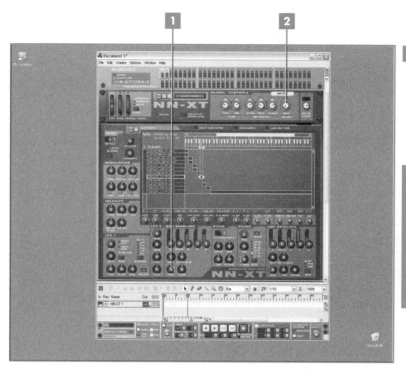

1 Turn the Pitch knob in the modulation envelope section up to its full value. The samples will now be playing at a much higher pitch.

❄ **PITCH FOR MODULATION EFFECT**

To demonstrate the use of the modulation you needed to raise the pitch in the modulation section. However, the modulation section itself is not a global parameter, and therefore this effect would be applied only to the selected key zones.

Next use the Global Mod Env Decay control so that the pitched modulation will be heard only when you first strike the key.

2 Turn the Decay knob all the way to the left. When you play a note from your MIDI controller, the higher pitched note will only be heard when the note is first played and will quickly fade away. The original bass sample will continue to play as normal.

Dr:rex Rex Loop Player

Rex files are sampled loops that have been prepared with Propellerheads' software application Recycle. The difference between a Rex file loop and a standard audio recording is that Recycle splices the loop into smaller pieces at the beat points, allowing you to change the tempo of a loop without affecting the pitch of the sample. Rex files can be purchased on sample CDs, or you can create your own if you have the Recycle application.

Loading Dr:rex

First you will need to add the Dr: rex device to your rack.

1 Click on the Create menu. The Create menu will appear.

2 Click on Dr:rex Loop Player. Dr:rex will be loaded into the rack.

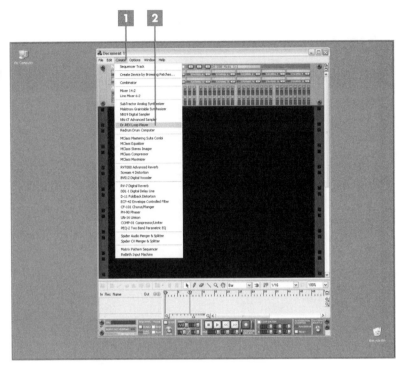

Loading a Rex File

To begin experimenting with the device, you need to load a Rex file into Dr:rex.

1 Click on the Browse Loop icon. The Rex File Browser window will appear.

2 Click on the Reason Factory Sound Bank.

3 Double-click on Dr:rex Drum Loops.

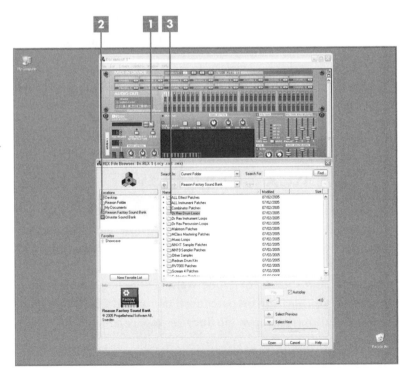

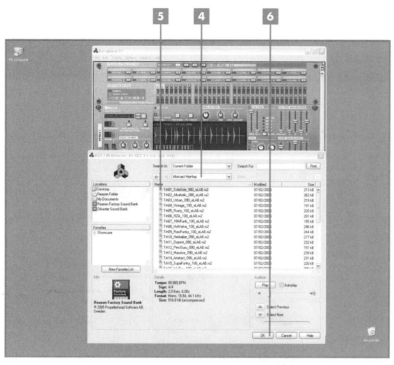

4 Navigate to **the folder**: Abstract HipHop.

5 Click **on the file** Trh01_SoleSide_080_eLab.rx2. **The file will become highlighted.**

6 Click OK. **The Rex file will be loaded into Dr:rex.**

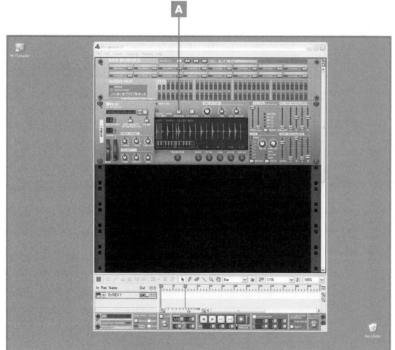

Previewing a Loop

With the previous instruments you've seen, you had to play notes from your keyboard to hear the effects of the changes you were making. With Dr:rex, you can use the preview function to start the loop's continuous playback to audition any changes you make.

A Preview. Click on the Preview button to start the loop's playback.

Tuning the Loop

As with all instrument devices in Reason, Dr:rex allows you to alter the tuning. The only difference with Dr:rex is that you are altering the tuning of a loop file.

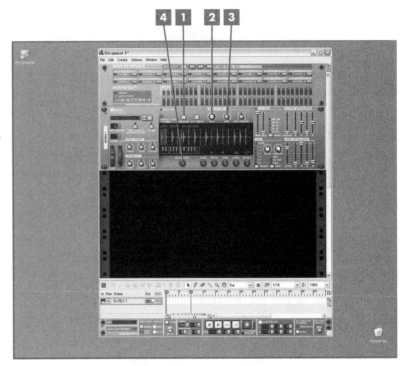

Tuning the Entire Loop

1. Click Preview. The loop file will begin playback.

2. Turn the OCT knob to the right. The pitch of the loop will rise in octave steps. Turn it to the left to decrease the tuning.

3. Turn the FINE knob to the right to increase the pitch in smaller amounts. Turn to the left to lower pitch.

4. Turn the Transpose knob to the right to increase the pitch in semi step. Turn the knob to the left to lower the pitch.

❄ THE TRANSPOSE KNOB

All loops in Dr:rex use middle C as their root key; this is indicated on the small red keyboard below the loop's display. As you turn the Transpose knob, the root note indication will move either up or down to reflect the changes.

Tuning an Individual Slice

As mentioned, a Rex loop file is sliced up into various parts. The slice points are where a drum beat takes place, and therefore each slice will be an individual hit of the drum loop. The tuning described above will be applied globally—in other words, to the entire loop; however, you can also alter the tuning of individual slices.

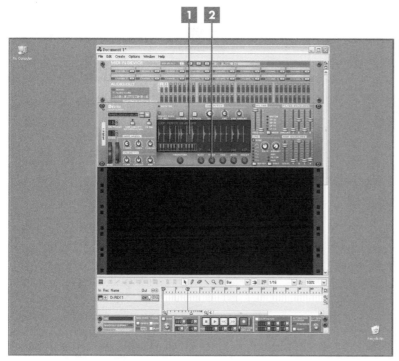

1 Click on the slice whose tuning you wish to alter. The slice will become highlighted in red.

2 Turn the Pitch knob to the right. The pitch of the slice will increase. Turn the knob to the left to lower the pitch.

Slice Controls

You can adjust certain parameters to customize the sound of the individual slices.

To control the volume of an individual slice:

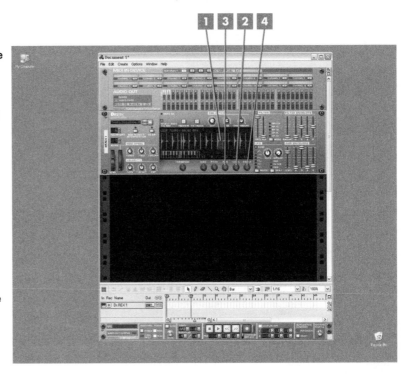

1 Click on the slice whose volume you wish to alter. The slice will become highlighted.

2 Turn the Level knob to the right to increase the slice's volume. Turn it to the left to decrease the volume.

The Pan control allows you to place a slice to the left, right, or in the center of the stereo field.

3 Turn the Pan knob to the left. The slice will move to the left side. Turn it to the right and the slice will be on the right.

The Decay knob controls the length of the slice.

4 Turn the Decay knob to the left. The slice will sound shorter. Turn it to the right. The slice will become longer.

❋ **WHERE TO FIND SLICE CONTROL VALUES**

All the slice control values are displayed in the LCD window directly above the Pitch, Pan, Level, and Decay knobs.

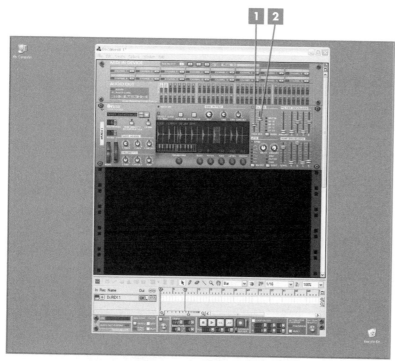

Filtering

Dr:rex also allows you to filter your loops.

1 Move the Freq (frequency) fader down. The loop will become darker and muffled.

2 Move the Res (Resonance) fader up. The loop will begin to sound more synthetic.

Auto Panning—LFO

With previous devices you saw how an LFO (Low Frequency Oscillator) can create a vibrato. Although it is possible to create the same effect with the LFO in Dr:rex, you will now use the LFO to make the loop automatically pan left to right in time with the song's tempo.

1 Click on the Sync button. This will make the panning follow the song's tempo.

2 Click on Pan. The LFO will now be set to alter the panning.

3 Turn the Amount knob to the right. The loop file will automatically pan between left and right.

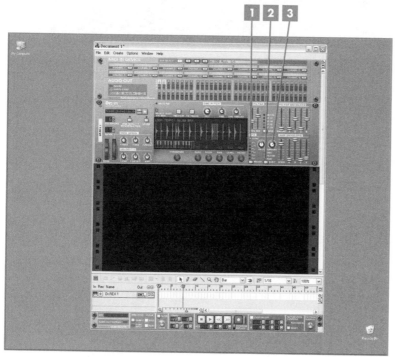

※ **FASTER AUTO PANNING**

If you want to increase the speed of the automatic panning, turn the Rate knob to the right; turn it to the left to decrease the speed.

Moving the Loop to a Sequencer Track

To play the loop in a song, you will need to send the loop information to a track.

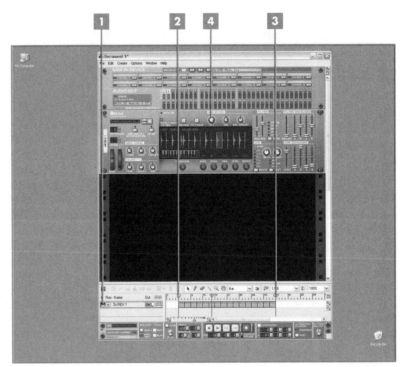

1 Click on the track to which you wish to send the loop information. The track will become highlighted.

2 Move the left locator to the position in the song where you want the loop to start.

3 Move the right locator to the position where you want the loop to end.

※ **MORE ON LOCATORS**

Locators will be covered in Chapter 7, "The Sequencer."

4 Click on the To Track button. The slice information will be sent to the selected track between the left and right locators.

5 } Effect Processors and Dynamics

Now that you've worked with most of Reason's sound modules and digital samplers, the next step is to learn how to add some effects to enhance and sweeten your mix. In this chapter, you'll learn how to

❋ Choose which type of effect to use.

❋ Route effects to the devices.

❋ Use reverb effects.

❋ Use distortion effects.

❋ Use modulation effects.

❋ Use delays and echoes.

❋ Control volumes and frequencies using dynamic tools.

❋ Create unique effects with the BV512 Vocoder.

Types of Effects

Before you can apply effects to the devices, it's a good idea to determine the type of effect you're trying to achieve. For example, if you want to make a drum loop appear as if it is being played in a large concert hall, you would use a reverb effect, as reverb is used to recreate the acoustical environment in which a sound is made. There are many types of effect devices in Reason; Table 5.1 briefly explains each type and describes typical uses.

Table 5.1   Common Uses for the Effect Devices

Effect	Description	Example of Use
Reverb	Reverbs are used to simulate the environments in which sounds are created. Each environment has its own unique sound, which is created by the reflections of an audio source on the surfaces (walls, etc.) of an environment. These reflections are referred to as "Reverberations."	Reverb is added to sounds to simulate the way an instrument or voice would sound in a particular acoustic environment (small room, large room, hall, etc.). You can also use reverb to control the perceived distance between the sound and the listener. Using a small amount of reverb will keep the sound source close to the front; adding more reverb will make the sound appear to be farther from the listener.
Distortion	Distortion occurs when a sound source is amplified to a level at which the sound begins to break up or overdrive the sound system or speakers.	Distortion is commonly used by rock 'n' roll guitarists to create a loud, thick guitar sound. A certain amount of distortion can be a welcome addition to a sound, adding extra bite and character. But be careful: too much distortion can be unpleasant.

Table 5.1 Common Uses for the Effect Devices (*continued*)

Effect	Description	Example of Use
Modulation Effects— Flanger, Chorus, and Phaser	Flangers, choruses, and phasers use oscillators like the ones found in the LFO sections of SubTractor to widen or thicken the sound.	Use these effects when you want to give a device a fuller, or fatter, sound.
Delays and Echoes	Delays and echo devices delay the audio signal a specified amount of time before playing (and repeating) it.	Use delays and echoes to create interesting timing or doubling effects that help to reinforce the sound.
Dynamics	Controls the amplitude levels of your sound source to make the level more consistent.	Use a compressor on a sound source with extreme changes in volume to make the signal more consistent. Use a limiter to control the maximum level of a sound source and avoid sudden peaks in the audio.
Equalization (EQ)	EQs control the amplitude levels of the different frequencies in a sound source.	Use an EQ when you want to increase or decrease the level of a frequency—e.g., to increase the bass of a sound module.
Vocoder	The vocoder is a unique effect that imposes the frequency characteristics of one device onto another.	Have you ever heard a song where it sounds as if a synthesizer was talking? This was most likely performed with a vocoder effect by imposing a synthesizer's frequency characteristics on a vocal recording.

Before you look at the effect devices, take a look at an important three-way function switch that is present on all effect devices. This switch acts more or less like the device's power switch.

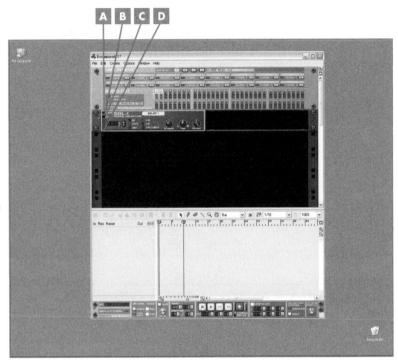

A Bypass. When the switch is in this position, audio is passing through the device, but no processing is taking place. This is a good way to perform an A/B comparison.

B On. This position will have the effect unit processing the audio.

C Off. The effect unit is off and no audio is being outputted from the device.

D VU meter. Directly under the three-way switch is a small VU meter that will display the output of the effect unit.

Routing the Effects

The first thing you must know is how you can connect the effects to a device in order to hear them. This section covers basic routing effects; more advanced routing is covered in Chapter 8, "Advanced Audio Routing with Effects."

Loading a Sound Source

To hear the effects, you'll need a sound source to which you can apply them. For example, use a simple drum loop produced by Dr:rex.

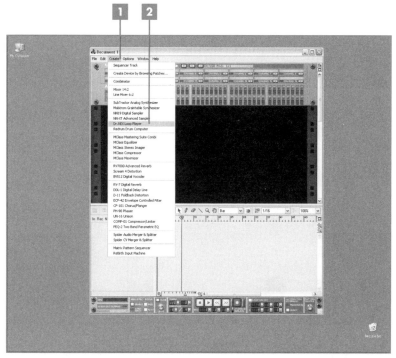

1 Click on the Create menu. The Create menu will appear.

2 Click on Dr:rex Loop Player. The device will appear in the rack.

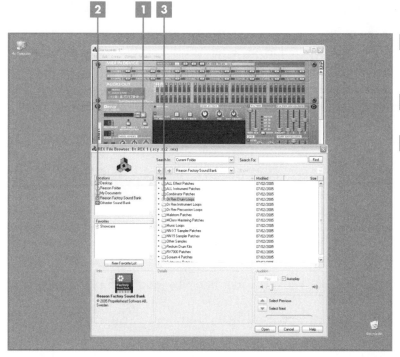

1 Click on the Browse Loop icon. The browse loop window will appear.

2 Click on Reason Factory Sound Bank in the Locations window.

3 Double-click on Dr Rex Drum Loops.

4 Navigate to **the folder** Abstract HipHop.

5 Click **on the file** Trh01_SoleSide_080_eLAB.rx2. **The file will become highlighted.**

6 Click **on** OK. **The file will be loaded into Dr:rex.**

Any time you want to audition any of the effects you're learning about, click the Dr:rex's Preview button to play the loop.

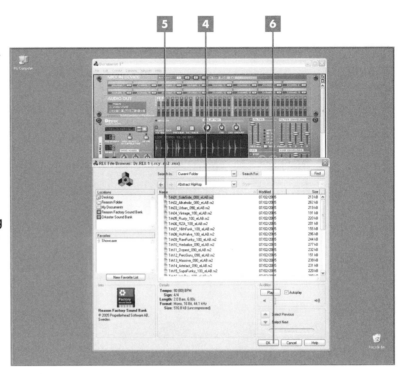

Loading Effect Devices and Automatic Routing

In the absence of a mixer in the rack, Dr:rex's outputs will automatically be routed to any effect processors that you place directly below it in the rack, and the effect processor's outputs will be routed to the output of your sound device. This is a simple form of audio routing that will enable you to get an idea of what each effect does.

 DELETE AN EFFECT BEFORE ADDING ANOTHER

After experimenting with each effect processor you should delete the effect device before moving on to the next one. This way your newly created effect device will also be automatically routed with the Dr:rex player. After you load an effect it might be helpful to flip the rack around and look at how Reason automatically routed the device.

To see how the routing works, begin by loading the RV-7 Reverb.

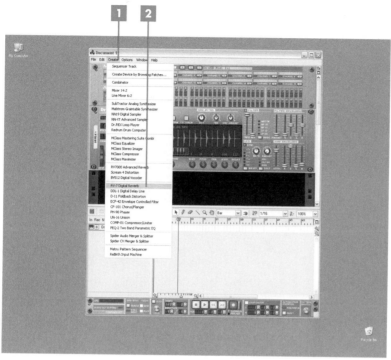

1 Click the Create menu. The Create menu will appear.

2 Click on RV-7 Digital Reverb. The RV-7 will be added to the rack.

3 Press the Tab key. The rack will flip around to show the rear view.

From the rear, you can see how Dr:rex automatically connects to the RV-7 and how the RV-7 is connected to the Audio In (which represents your audio interface's outputs).

Reverbs

Reverbs are the effect devices that you'll use when you want to recreate different acoustical environments. Since you have already loaded the RV-7 into the rack, begin by taking a look at reverb effects, and more specifically the RV-7.

❋ **AUDITIONING EFFECTS WITH DR:REX**

Remember, to audition the effects you apply you need to click on the Preview button of Dr:rex to start the playback of the loop.

RV-7 Digital Reverb

The RV-7 is an extremely simple reverb to use for recreating the natural reverberations of different environments.

Now, experiment with the RV-7.

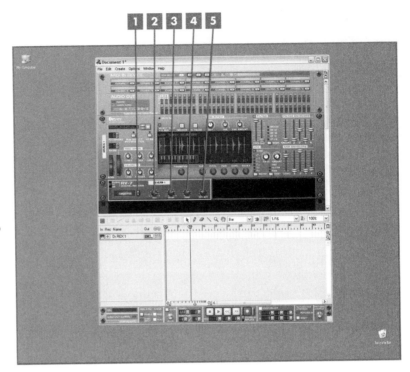

1 Click on the up arrow to scroll through the environment types. As you scroll through the environments, the loop will sound as if it is being played in that environment, such as a large hall.

2 Turn the Size knob to the right to enlarge the size of the environment. Turn to the left to decrease the size.

3 Turn the Decay knob to the right. The reverb will last longer. Turn to the left. The reverb will be shorter.

EASY ON THE REVERB

Making the length of the reverb too long can create an extremely muffled sound, so be careful when extending the reverb's length.

4 Turn the Damp knob to the right. The higher frequencies of the reverb will be reduced, producing a warmer-sounding reverb.

5 Turn the Dry/Wet knob to the left. The level of the reverb will be reduced.

DRY AND WET

When working with effects you will often see the terms "dry" and "wet." These words refer to the balance of the effect against the source. Dry is the audio source (the Rex loop in our example), and wet refers to the effect's level.

RV7000 Advanced Reverb

The RV7000 serves the same purpose as the RV-7—providing reverb to your mixes; however, the RV7000 gives you far more control over the sound of the reverb. The RV7000 is also modeled after classic outboard reverbs that have two panels to control the device, one being the reverb unit itself, which has only a few parameters to adjust, and the other being a remote unit that controls additional parameters.

REMOVING THE RV-7

Before loading the RV7000, be sure to delete the RV-7 from the rack. This way when you add the RV7000 the automatic routing of the device will be applied correctly in order for you to audition it.

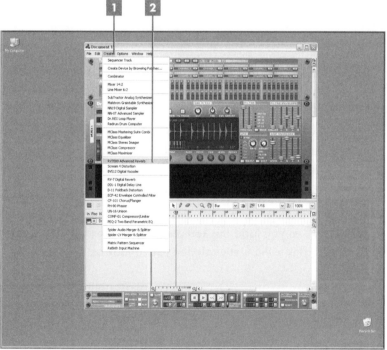

Adding the RV7000 to the Rack

1 Click on the Create menu. The Create menu will appear.

2 Click on RV7000 Advanced Reverb. The RV7000 will be loaded into the rack.

Now open the RV7000's Remote Programmer:

3 Click on the small arrow next to the Remote Programmer jack. The remote section will appear.

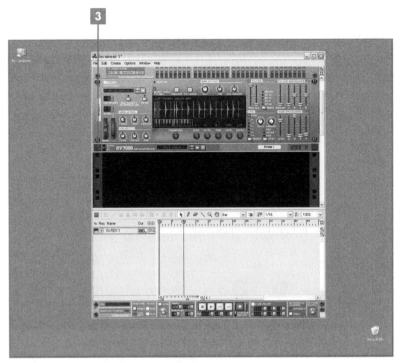

Setting the RV7000 Environment—Reverb Edit Mode

Compared with the R-7, the RV7000 gives you greater control over how the emulated environments sound. This section covers some of the basic functions for creating the desired environment.

The Remote Programmer has three edit pages: one to control the environment, another for the EQ, and a third for the reverb gate. By default, when you load the Remote Programmer the Edit Mode is displayed. This is the first mode for you to look at.

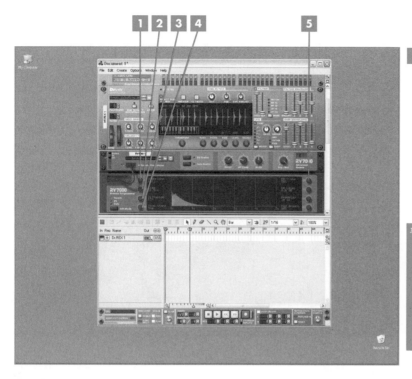

1 Turn the Algorithm knob to the right. The reverb will scroll through the various environments. If you start the Dr:rex loop, the sound of the loop will appear to be played in the currently selected environment.

❄ ALGORITHM

Reason uses the term *algorithm* to describe the environment, such as a small room or garage, the RV7000 is attempting to emulate. Just as each algorithm is different, so will the parameters be that you can affect on each of the eight knobs on Remote Editor.

2 Turn the Size knob to the right. The perceived size of your environment will increase.

❄ THE SIZE PARAMETER

Depending on the algorithm selected, the size parameter may or may not be available.

3 Turn the Diffusion knob to the left. The reverb will become brighter. Turn the knob to the right and the reverb will become softer and warmer.

4 Turn the Room Shape knob to the right. The reflections of the reverb will change to reproduce the new room shape. Listen to the different characteristics of each room shape.

5 Turn the ER -> Late knob to the right. The reverb will appear slightly further away.

WHAT IS REVERB?

Reverb is essentially created by the reflections of sound bouncing around a room. When trying to recreate these natural reverberations we often adjust what are called "early reflections" and "late reflections." Early reflections occur when the direct sound source (a voice, drum, etc.) first hits the walls or surfaces of the environment. Late reflections occur when the first (early) reflections are further reflected by other surfaces in the environment.

6 7

6 Turn the ER Level to the right. The early portions of the reverb will appear louder.

7 Turn the Predelay knob to the right. The reverb will appear larger because the predelay controls how far the surfaces in the environment are from the sound source (in this example, the drum loop).

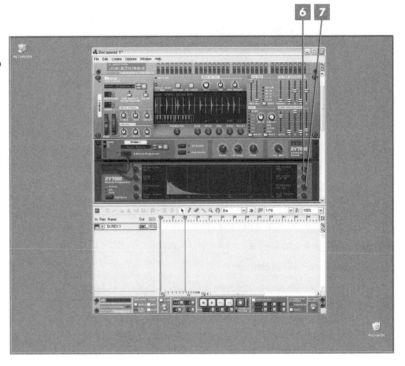

ENVIRONMENT PARAMETERS

The environment parameters demonstrated above are common controls; however, some of the algorithms have parameters that are uniquely their own. For more information on each of the parameters in all the algorithms, please refer to Reason's documentation.

THE REVERB EDIT WINDOW

The Reverb Edit window displays a waveform graphic showing the reverb's characteristics; this can be helpful in understanding how the reverb will sound.

Applying EQ to the Reverb—EQ Edit Mode

The RV7000 also comes equipped with a simple EQ that allows you to control the frequencies of the reverb itself. Take a quick look at how the EQ works.

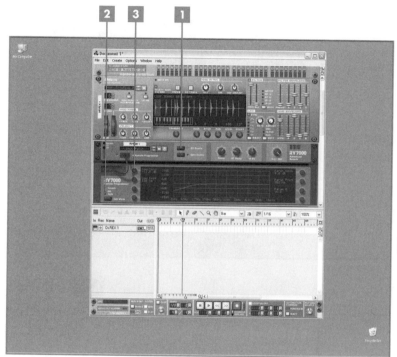

Turn on the EQ function.

1 Click on the EQ Enable button on the main body. The EQ section will become active.

2 Click on EQ. The Remote Programmer will reveal the EQ Edit page.

Use the EQ to reduce the low frequencies of the reverb.

3 Turn the Low Gain to the left. The low frequencies below 128 Hz will be gradually reduced. The EQ Edit window also gives you a visual representation of which frequencies are being affected by the EQ. Here you can see how turning the Low Gain to the left reduced the low-range frequencies.

Now change which low frequencies are reduced.

4 Turn the Low Freq knob to the right. The mid-frequencies will begin to be reduced. Here you can see the visual representation of the reduction to the midrange frequencies.

❄ RAISING AND LOWERING LOW FREQUENCIES

Move the Low Freq knob toward the left to reduce the levels of the lower frequencies. You can also turn the Low Gain toward the right to increase the low frequencies.

Now adjust the midrange and high-range frequencies.

5 Turn the Param (parametric) Gain knob to the right. A small amount of midrange frequencies will be increased. Turn the knob to the left to reduce the level of these frequencies. Note that increasing frequencies with the Parametric Gain knob will draw what appears to be a hill on the EQ graph.

6 Turn the Param Freq knob to the right. The frequencies affected by the Param Gain will increase to a higher range. Turn the knob to the left to lower the frequency range.

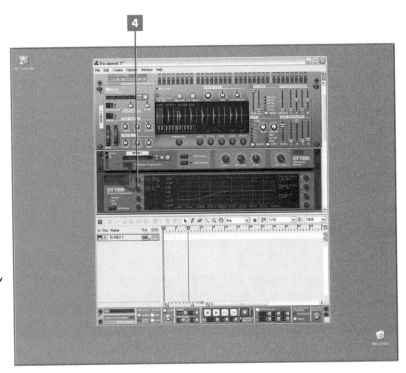

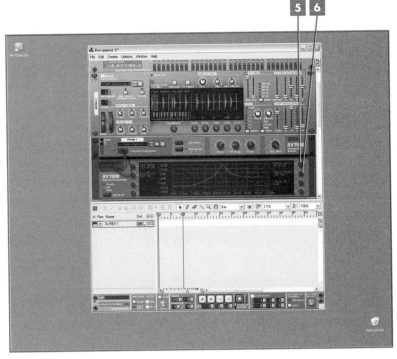

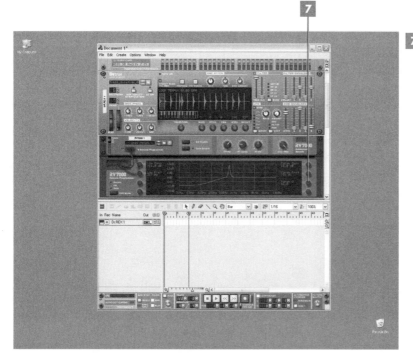

7 Turn the Param Q knob to the left. The range of the frequencies affected by the Param Gain will widen. Turn the knob to the right; the frequency range will be narrower. Notice that the width of the hill on the EQ graph changes as you adjust the Q knob.

Gating the Reverb—Gate Edit Mode

A gate basically sits in front of the reverb and opens when audio reaches a certain amplitude threshold. With that said, think of yourself physically opening a gate—how hard do you have to push before it opens? How fast will you open it? And how fast will it close? All these questions apply to the reverb gate as well, except that the audio opens the gate, not you.

Put the Remote Programmer into Gate Edit Mode.

1 Click on Gate Enable on the main body. The gate will become active.

2 Click on Gate. The edit window will change to the gate editor.

The first thing you want to set is how hard the audio will have to push before the gate opens. This is called the *threshold*.

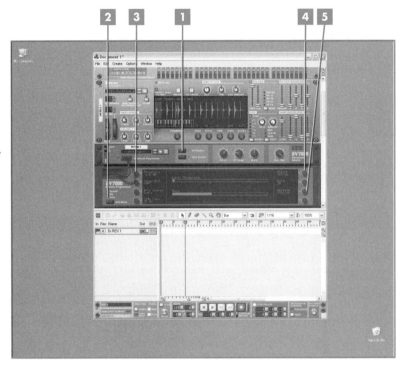

3 Turn the Threshold knob to the right. The reverb will become choppy because only the highest peaks in the loop are making it to the reverb. As you continue to turn the knob, the reverb (and audio source) will eventually disappear as the gate requires the audio to be louder than the threshold in order to open.

❋ TOO MUCH THRESHOLD

If you have turned the Threshold knob to the point at which you cannot hear the reverb, you have gone too far and the threshold must be lower. The idea here is that you want to hear the reverb, even if it is only on the high-level peaks.

4 Turn the Attack knob to the right. The reverb will have a small fade-in at the beginning. This is because the attack controls how fast the audio opens the gate.

5 Turn the Release knob to the right. The length of the reverb will be extended. The release controls how long the gate stays open before it begins to close.

TOO MUCH RELEASE

If you turn the release parameter up too far, the gate will have no time to close before the audio tries to open it again; thus the gate will remain open.

Global Controls

On the main body of the RV7000 are a few controls that will be applied globally.

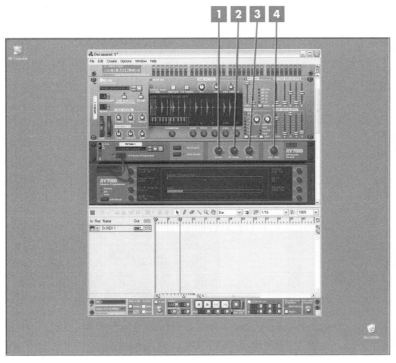

1 Turn the Decay knob to the right. The length of the reverb will increase. Turn the knob to the left. The reverb will become shorter.

2 Turn the HF Damp to the right. The reverbs will become warmer as the high frequencies are being reduced. Turn the knob to the left. The reverb will become brighter and clearer.

3 Turn the HI EQ knob to the right. The reverb will become brighter with an increase in the high frequencies.

4 Turn the Dry/Wet knob to the left. The level of the reverb will decrease, and you will hear more of the direct audio from the loop.

LOADING AND SAVING PATCHES

You can load and save RV7000 patches just as you can with Reason's sound modules.

Distortion

Distortion is generally thought of as the unpleasant sound we hear when we push analog equipment too hard to levels that exceed the device's tolerance threshold. So why would we want this in our music? Well, many believe that distortion can enhance sound by adding certain harmonics. Reason comes equipped with two distortion-creating devices.

D-11 Foldback Distortion

The D-11 is a perfect solution for when you want to quickly add some bite to your sounds. With only two parameters, the D-11 is a simple device to use.

1 Click on the Create menu. The Create menu will appear.

2 Click on D-11 Foldback Distortion. The D-11 will be added to the rack.

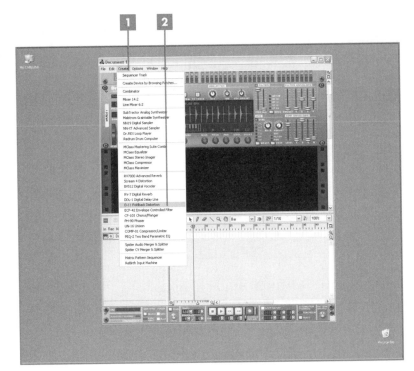

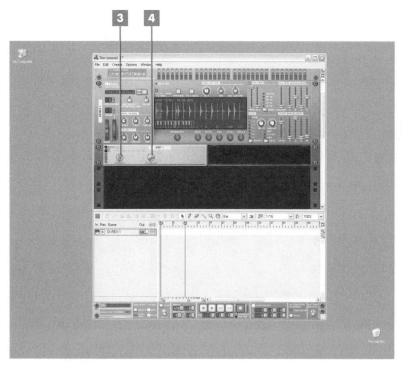

3 Turn the Amount knob to the right. The drum loop from the Dr:rex becomes slightly distorted.

4 Turn the Foldback knob to the right. The distortion becomes more severe the farther you turn.

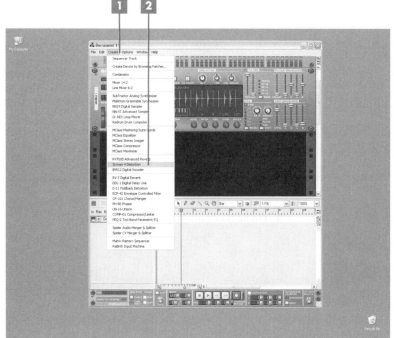

Scream 4 Distortion

The principle of the Scream 4 Distortion device is the same as that of the D-11; however, Scream gives you more control over the characteristics of the distortion.

Load Scream into the rack.

1 Click on the Create menu. The Create menu will appear.

2 Click on Scream 4 Distortion. Scream will be added to the rack.

Adding the Distortion

The Damage section of Scream is where you choose the distortion type and level.

1 Turn the Damage Control knob to the right. The level of distortion will increase.

2 Turn the Damage selector knob through the various distortion types. The distortion character will change to reflect the damage model.

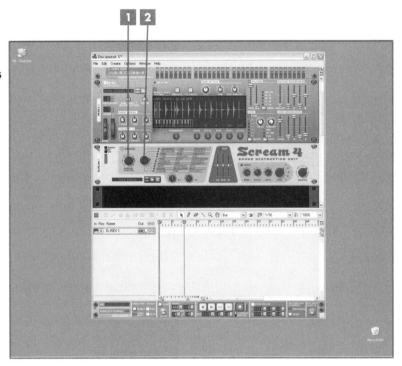

❄ P1 AND P2 KNOBS

Each distortion model has two additional parameters that are specific to each model and are available through the P1 and P2 knobs. For example, the Overdrive model has Tone and Presence parameters.

Filtering the Distortion

Scream is also equipped with a simple three-band filter that you can use to control the frequencies of the distortion.

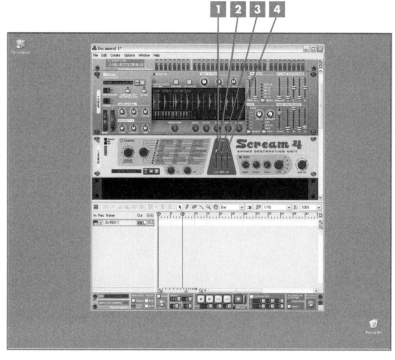

1 Click on the Cut button.
The filter will become active.

2 Move the Lo fader up.
The distortion will have a
heavier bass sound.

3 Move the Mid fader up.
The distortion will become
thinner sounding.

4 Move the Hi fader up.
The distortion will become
brighter sounding.

❋ FADERS IN MID POSITION

When the faders are in the middle position the filters are neither boosting nor cutting
their respective frequencies.

❋ MAKING SCREAM SCREAM

Moving the filter's faders up will increase the output level of Scream. Watch your
speakers, and keep your pointer on the Master Volume control!

Adjusting the Tone of the Distortion

The body section offers four more parameters that can be used to
further adjust the color and tone of the distortion.

1 Click on the body section power button. The body section will be activated.

2 Turn the Reso knob to the left. The distortion will become slightly warmer. Turn the knob to right. The distortion will sound more synthetic.

3 Turn the Scale knob to the left. The distortion will become duller and somewhat muffled.

4 Turn the Type selector knob. Listen to the different characteristics of each body type.

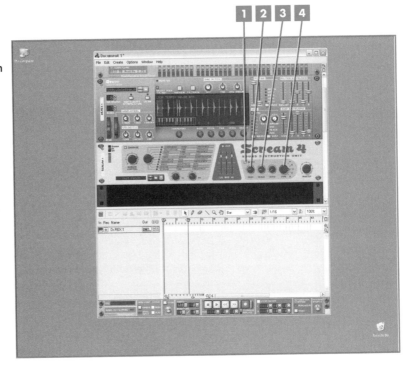

SAVING SCREAM PATCHES

Scream 4 distortion also supports saving patches. Click on the Save Patch icon (floppy disc icon) to save the patch to a location on your hard drive.

Modulation Effects

Modulation devices are often used to thicken or fatten the sound of a device. There are several devices that can perform such a task, all having their own unique effects on the sound.

CF-101 Chorus/Flanger

Chorus and flanger effects are used when you want to widen or thicken the sound. As the two effects share mostly a common set of parameters, both effects can be achieved using the same device.

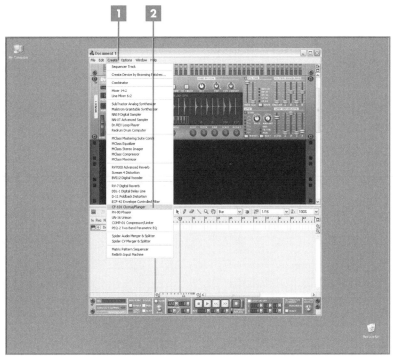

1 Click on the Create menu. The Create menu will appear.

2 Click on CF-101 Chorus/ Flanger. The device will be loaded into the rack.

When creating a chorus or flange, a delay is applied to the input, then the output is sent back to the effect's inputs (this is all done internally by the CF-101).

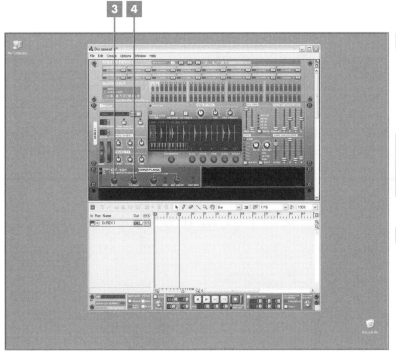

3 Turn the Delay knob to the right. The length of delay will be increased and will produce a wider, thicker sound.

❋ **FLANGE EFFECTS**

Shorter delay times are generally used to create a flange effect, while longer times are used for chorus.

4 Turn the Feedback knob to the right. The sound will begin to sound very robotic. The feedback controls how much of the delay is fed back into the input.

The CF-101 also uses an LFO to constantly change the delay times, which adds a sweeping sound to the chorus or flange.

5 Turn the Rate knob to the right. The sweeping speed of the chorus/flange will become faster.

❄ **THE SYNC BUTTON**

Clicking on the Sync button will synchronize the speed of the LFO to the song's tempo.

6 Turn the Mod Amount knob to the right. The amount of sweeping sound in the chorus/flange will increase.

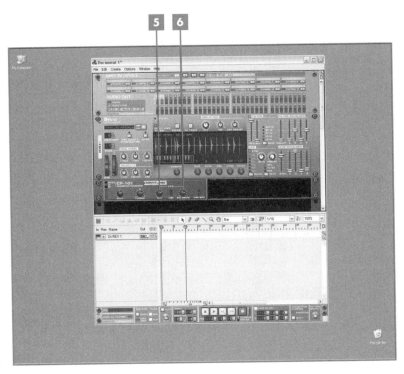

PH-90 Phaser

A *phaser* is yet another modulation effect that can add space and depth to your sound. A phaser effect works by routing the incoming audio through a notch filter, which is then routed internally back to the device's input. A notch filter simply removes all frequencies to which the filter is set. Audio that is run through the filter is "phase shifted" (hence the name of the effect) and when mixed back to the device's input, results in a tonal sweeping effect. The PH-90 uses four notch filters to give you more control over how the effect sounds.

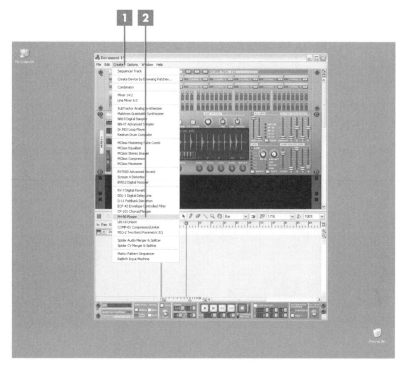

1 Click on the Create menu. The Create menu will appear.

2 Click on PH-90 Phaser. The PH-90 will be loaded into the rack.

Now take a look at the various parameters and the effect they have on the Dr:rex loop.

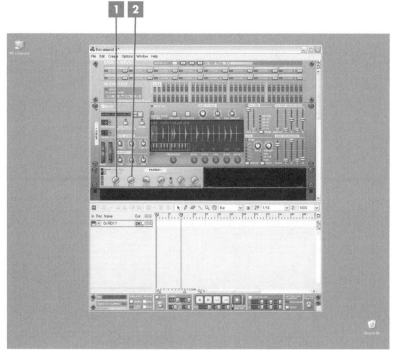

First, adjust the filters.

1 Turn the Freq knob to the right. As you turn, the sound will become thinner. Turn the knob to the left and the sound will become warmer and heavier.

Now adjust the space between the four filters.

2 Turn the Split knob to the right. The distance between the four notch filters will increase. Listen to the effect it has on the phaser.

145
❄ ❄ ❄

3 Turn the Width knob to the right. The width of the four filters will increase. The width determines the range of frequencies the notch filter will remove.

4 Turn the Rate knob to the right. The sweeping sound in the phaser will increase its speed.

5 Turn the F. Mod. The amount of the sweeping effect will change.

The Feedback knob controls how much of the four filter's outputs are returned to the PH-90's inputs (internally).

6 Turn the Feedback knob. The level of the phaser will change.

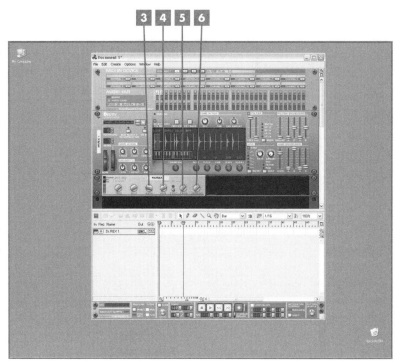

UN-16 Unison

The UN-16 is a tool that creates multiple portions of the audio, then detunes each one and mixes it back with the original. This is a useful way to create a fuller, bigger sound.

1 Click on the Create menu. The Create menu will appear.

2 Click on UN-16 Unison. The UN-16 will be loaded into the rack.

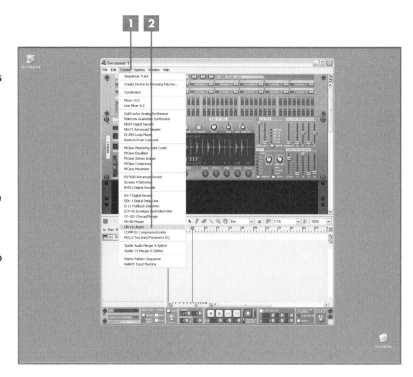

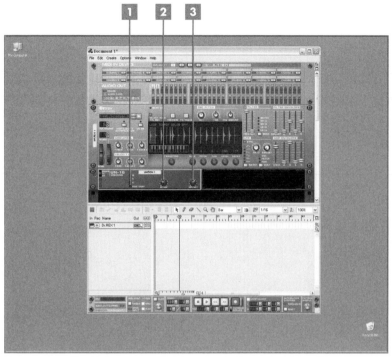

You can control how many parts the UN-16 splits the audio into.

1. Click on the Voice Count button. As you toggle through the amount you will notice that the higher numbers produce a thicker sound.

2. Turn the Detune knob to the left. The sound will become thinner as less detuning is applied.

3. Turn the Dry/Wet knob to balance the mix of the original signal and the effect.

❋ THICKENING THE SOUND

The amount of detuning applied by the UN-16 is slight—just enough to thicken the sound.

DDL-1 Digital Delay

The DDL-1 is a simple delay device you can use to add bounce to your drums, reinforce some of your samples, or even create spacey effects. A delay device works by simply recording a small segment of the audio and then playing it back at a predetermined delayed time.

1 Click on the Create menu. The Create menu will appear.

2 Click on DDL-1 Digital Delay Line. The DDL-1 will be loaded into the rack.

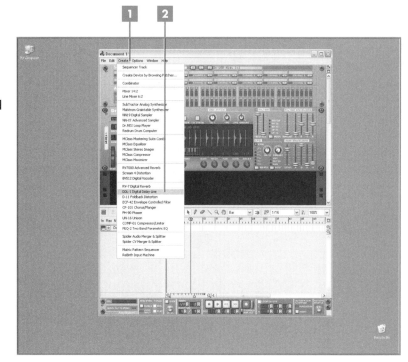

1 Click on the up arrow to increase the amount of steps. The delay time will increase.

❋ DELAY TIME MEASUREMENTS

There are two units that can be used when adjusting the delay time. By default the units are set to steps, which use note sizes and the tempo of the song to measure the delay time. The other unit is milliseconds (ms). This setting allows you to enter a millisecond value as a delay measurement, independent of the song's tempo.

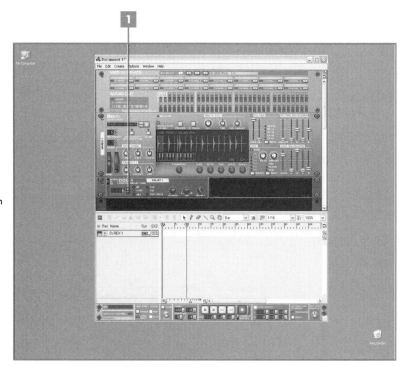

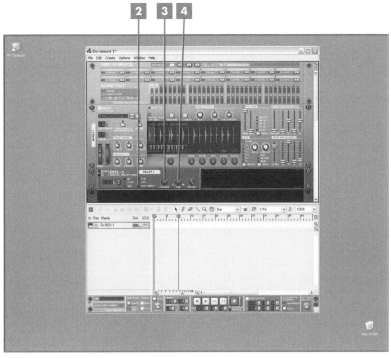

2 Click on the Step Length button to adjust the step size. The delay time is calculated from both the step amount and step size—for example, if you set the step amount to 2 and the step size to 1/16, then the delay time will be every second sixteenth note.

3 Turn the Feedback knob to the right. The delay repeats will be extended.

4 Turn the Pan knob to the right. The delay will be on the right side. Turn to the left. The delay will be on the left.

Compressors and Equalizers

Compressors work to control levels by automatically reducing the volume when it gets too high. Use EQ (equalizers) when you want to boost or reduce certain frequencies.

COMP-01

A compressor is useful for improving the consistency of a signal's volume—boosting quiet parts and pushing down loud parts in order to achieve a smoother, more balanced result.

1 Click on the Create menu.
   The Create menu will appear.

2 Click on COMP-01
   Compressor/Limiter. The
   COMP-01 will load into
   the rack.

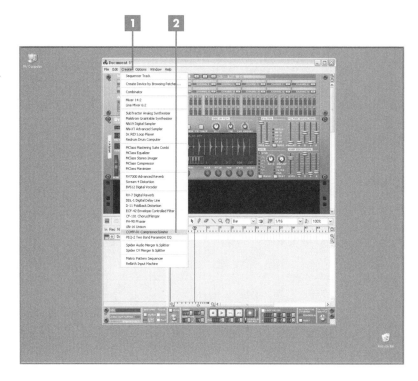

When using a compressor you
need to tell it at what level
you wish it to start reducing
the volume and how much to
reduce it by.

1 Turn the Ratio knob to the
   right. The loop will begin to
   sound heavier and begin to
   create a pumping feel on
   higher volumes. The pumping
   is a result of the compressor
   pushing the volume down and
   then returning to normal.

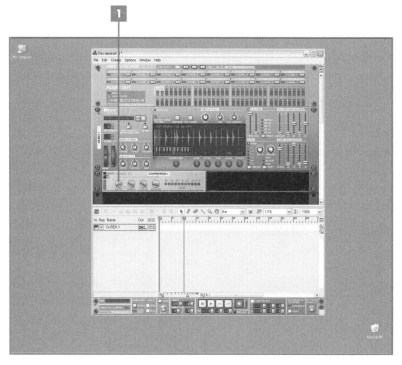

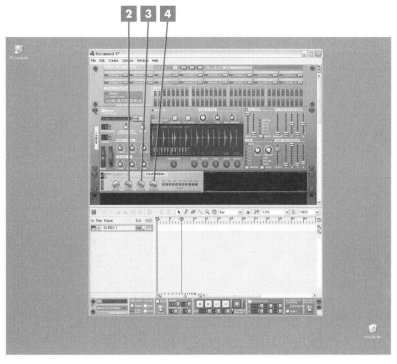

Before moving on, set the ratio so that there is pumping from the compressor. This will be useful to clearly see how the remaining parameters affect the sound.

2 Turn the Threshold knob to the left. The pumping effect will become less and less as you turn. Turning the knob to the right will increase the pumping effect. When the audio's level passes the level set by the threshold, the compressor will start reducing the volume. If the threshold is set too high the compressor will never reduce the volume.

3 Turn the Attack knob to the left. The pumping effect will become smoother. Turn the knob to the right and the pumping will become sharper and more apparent. The Attack setting controls how fast the compressor reduces the volume once it has passed the threshold level. If the compressor reduces the volume slowly, then the effect is less apparent and more natural, but if the compressor is too slow, the high-level passages will not be reduced quickly enough and will still appear too loud.

4 Turn the Release knob to the left to make the pumping of the compressor sharper or to the right to make the pumping duller. The release controls how fast the compressor returns to normal after reducing the volume. If this is set too fast, the pumping effect will be more drastic.

✳ GETTING A NATURAL SOUND FROM THE COMP-01

It can take some time to get the hang of using a compressor. Try to shoot for a natural sound (unless you are intentionally going for a unique effect). Set the threshold so that only the extremely high peaks are reduced. Also, try not to set the attack and release times too low; this will create the pumping effect. You'll find plenty of information on the Internet for tips on using a compressor.

PEQ-2

The PEQ-2 is a straightforward
two-band parametric equalizer.
The term "two band" essentially
means that there are two equalizers that can be used. Each
EQ is able to filter a different
frequency.

1. Click on the Create menu. The
Create menu will appear.

2. Click on PEQ-2 Two Band
Parametric EQ. The PEQ-2 will
be loaded into the rack.

Boosting Frequencies

With the Dr:rex loop playing:

1. Turn the Gain knob to the right.
The loop will become thinner;
sounding like it is being played
through a phone.

2. Turn the Freq knob to the right.
The sound becomes brighter
as you turn. As you turn to the
right you are instructing the
EQ to increase the levels of the
higher frequencies.

3. Turn the Freq knob to the left.
The sound will become darker
and have more of a bass
presence; this is because you
are now increasing the low-
range frequencies.

Reducing Frequencies

Now that you know how to increase frequency levels, look at how to reduce them. First, reset the Gain and Freq settings before proceeding to the following steps.

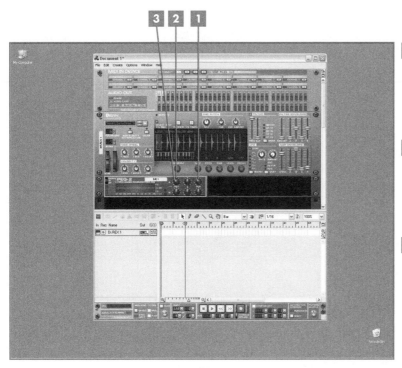

1 Turn the Gain knob to the left. The sound will become muffled because you have now removed most of the midrange frequencies.

2 Turn the Freq knob to the right. The sound will become heavier in the low range, as you are now removing the high-range frequencies.

3 Turn the Freq knob to the left. The low-range frequencies will start to disappear as you turn, and the high frequencies will become more dominant because you are now reducing the low-range frequencies.

Changing the Frequency Range

When you boost or reduce frequencies you are actually boosting or reducing a range of frequencies around a center frequency (the center frequency being that to which the Freq knob is set). You do have the ability to adjust the width of the frequency's band that is affected by the boost or reduction.

1 Turn the Gain knob to the right. On the EQ graph, the gain representation resembles a hill; the width of the hill at the bottom will be the range size.

2 Turn the Q knob to the right. The size of the frequency range will narrow.

3 Turn the Q knob to the left. The size of the range will widen.

❋ PEQ-2: A TWO-BAND EQUILIZER

As mentioned, the PEQ-2 has two bands of EQ: A and B. The parameters that control these bands are identical.

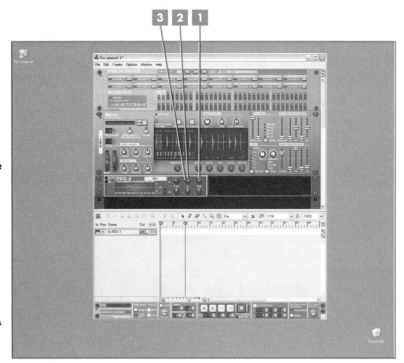

BV512 Digital Vocoder

The BV512 is in an effect category all on its own and perhaps one of the most unique effects found in Reason. The idea of the vocoder goes back to the late 1920s when telephone companies were trying to find new ways to push larger amounts of telephone information through the phone lines. Although the idea never really made it to prime time in the telephone market, today we can enjoy the interesting affect the vocoder has musically.

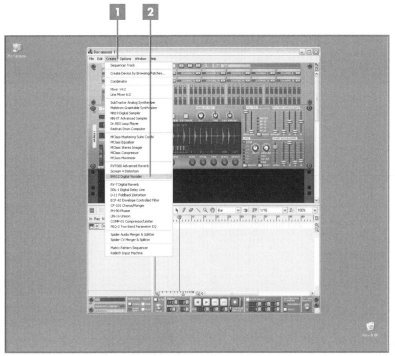

1 Click on the Create menu. The Create menu will appear.

2 Click on BV512 Digital Vocoder. The device will load into the rack.

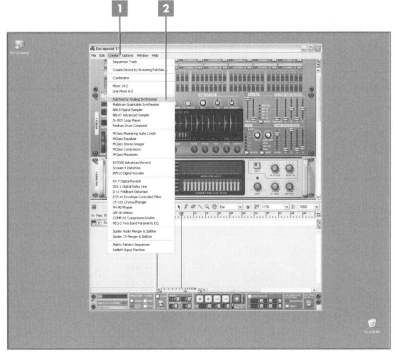

The BV512 works by analyzing an audio source referred to as the *modulator* to create a "blue print" of the different frequencies in that audio source. This blue print is then imposed on a second audio source, known as the *carrier*. The result is that the carrier wave can take on a synthetic and robotic sound.

1 Click on the Create menu. The Create menu will appear.

2 Click on SubTractor Analog Synthesizer. The SubTractor will be loaded into the rack.

Automatic Routing of the Carrier

Take a look at how the BV512 and the SubTractor are automatically routed.

3 Click on the Options menu. The Options menu will appear.

4 Click on Toggle Rack Front/ Rear. The rack will turn to the rear view.

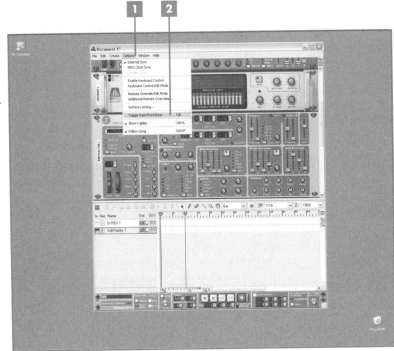

❊ Turning the rack around, you can see that the output of the Dr: rex Loop Player is automatically routed to the carrier input.

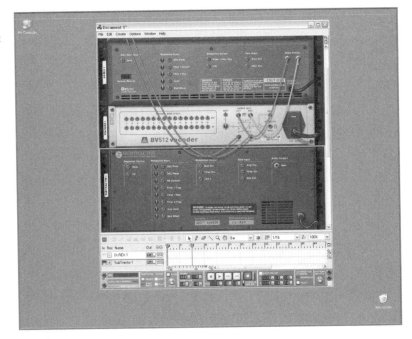

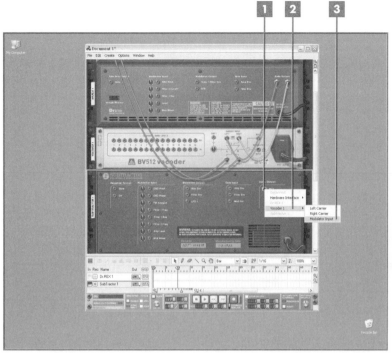

Routing a Modulator

With the Dr:rex loop being routed to the vocoder as the carrier source, you now need a modulator source. For the modulator source, load the SubTractor synthesizer to your rack.

❊ **A MODULATOR IS REQUIRED FOR BV512**

A modulator source must be present before the output of the carrier source can be heard.

1 Click on SubTractor's Audio Output. The connection menu will appear.

2 Click on Vocoder 1. The vocoder connections menu will appear.

3 Click on Modulator Input. A cable will appear connecting the SubTractor to the modulator input.

The Vocoder in Action

1 Click on Dr:rex's Preview button. The loop will begin playback.

❈ NO OUTPUT?

The output of the Dr:rex loop will not be audible because there is no modulator signal yet. Although you have connected the SubTractor to the modulator input, there will be no source until you actually play the SubTractor.

2 Click on the In column of the SubTractor track in the sequencer window. The track will become highlighted.

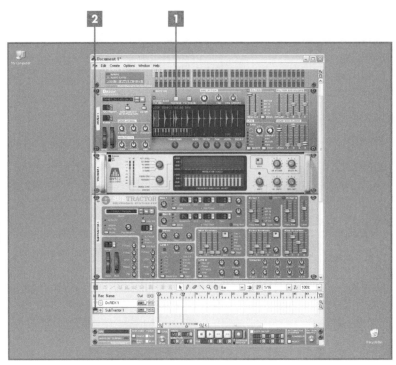

3 Play a few notes from your MIDI controller. You will be able to hear the loop. As you play different keys on your controller, the drum loop will sound as if it is being retuned instantly to match the note you are playing.

The Filter Bands

When the modulator source (the SubTractor in our example) is fed into the BV512, the device will analyze the frequencies to create a "blue print" that will then be used to alter the frequencies of the carrier input. The blue print will use several frequency filters to accomplish this; the number of filters used is selectable.

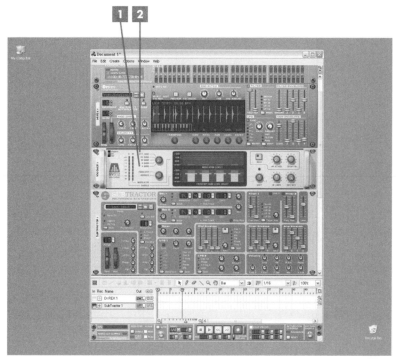

With the loop playing, and while holding down a key on your MIDI controller:

1 Turn the band selector switch to 4 Band. The sound will become fuller and have more bass. This is because the blue print is only using four filter bands and each band has a wider range.

2 Turn the band selector switch to 512 Band. The loop will begin to sound thinner and more synthetic. The blue print is now using 512 filters and can be more precise when trying to copy the frequency structure of the modulator source (the SubTractor in this example).

❊ FREQUENCY DISPLAY

The top half of the LCD screen on the BV512 displays the frequencies of the modulator source.

❊ ❊ ❊

Level Controls

Use the envelope to control how fast the carrier is altered by the modulator.

1 Turn the Attack knob to the right. The amount of time it takes for the vocoder to fully modulate the carrier source will extend. This is good for adding a sweeping effect to the carrier. It also makes the changes to the carrier smoother when playing from your MIDI controller.

2 Turn the Decay knob to the right. Play a note from your controller. After you release the key the vocoder will continue to process the loop. The farther right you turn the knob the longer the decay will be.

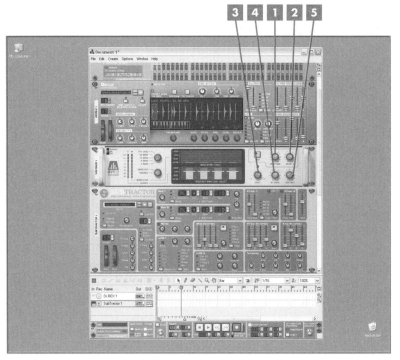

3 Turn the Shift knob to a positive value. The sound will become thin and tinny sounding. Turn the knob to a negative position and the sound will become heavier in the low frequencies.

4 Turn the HF Emph knob to the right. The High end frequencies will be boosted and the sound will become brighter.

5 Turn the Wet/Dry knob to the left. The sound of the SubTractor will become present and the level of the Dr:rex loop will drop.

❄ USING THE VOCODER AS AN EQUILIZER

The BV512 can also be used as a multi-band graphic EQ. For more information on how to do this, please refer to Reason's documentation.

6 } Pattern Sequencing Devices

In addition to Reason's sequencer, which you will learn about in Chapter 7, "The Sequencer," Reason offers a few other options for creating synthesizer lines and drum beats by using one of its pattern-sequencing devices. Patterns can be either synthesizer parts that have been programmed in the Matrix Pattern Sequencer and are played through a sound module device such as SubTractor or Malström, or drum beats programmed with the Redrum Drum Computer. By programming patterns and storing them in one of the device's preset banks, you can quickly recall a pattern at any point in the song. In this chapter, you'll learn how to

❋ Create drum patterns using the Redrum Drum Computer.

❋ Create synth lines with the Matrix Pattern Sequencer.

Redrum Drum Computer

If you are new to the world of sequencing and programming drums, the Redrum is a great way for you to get in the game. The Redrum allows you to store up to 32 different drum patterns that can be programmed to play up to 10 drum samples, and best of all it is very user friendly.

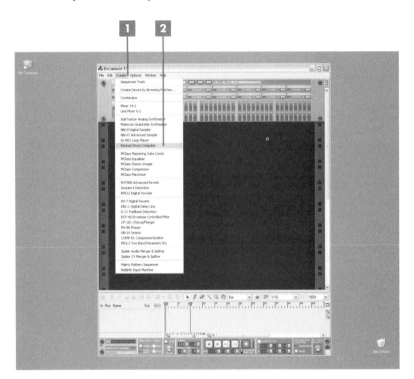

1 Click on the Create menu. The Create menu will appear.

2 Click on Redrum Drum Computer. The Redrum Drum Computer will be loaded into the rack.

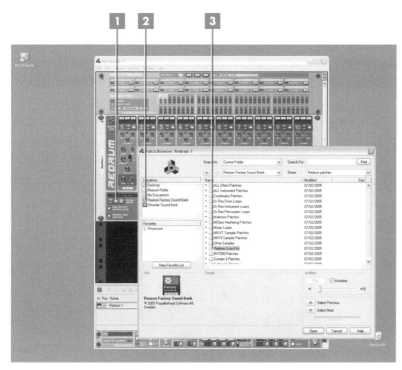

Loading Patches

Now load a drum kit into Redrum in order to dive into pattern programming.

1 Click on the Browse Patch icon. The Patch Browser window will appear.

2 Click the Reason Factory Sound Bank in the Locations window.

3 Double click on the Redrum Drum Kits folder in the main Patch Browser window.

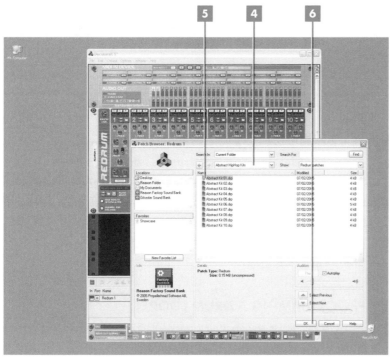

4 Navigate to the folder Abstract HipHop Kits.

5 Click on the patch Abstract Kit 01.drp. The patch will become highlighted.

6 Click OK. The kit will be loaded into the Redrum.

Once the patch is loaded you can see that various samples that make up the kit are loaded into each of the 10 drum channels.

Programming Patterns

With the drum kit loaded you can now get down to the task of programming a pattern into Redrum. This is actually a lot easier than it sounds; you can make a simple drum beat in a matter of minutes.

The Drum Pads

When programming these drum patterns you will use the 16 white pads on the front panel to program the triggers that will play the drum samples.

1 Click the Run button. Redrum's loop playback will begin.

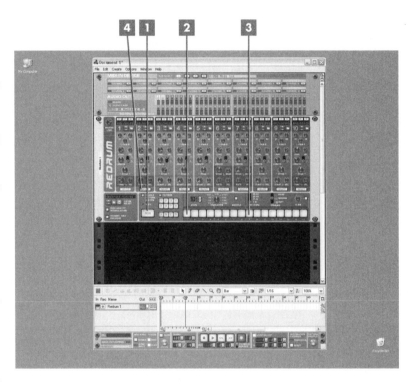

❄ **RUN STARTS AUTOMATICALLY**

When you start the playback of a Reason song that has pattern devices loaded, the Run button will automatically engage. If for some reason you don't want the pattern device to run automatically when you start the song's playback you must disable the pattern section of the device.

2 Click on pad 1 to enter a note on the first beat of the sample. The pad will highlight to reflect that a sample from drum Channel 1, which is a kick drum, will be triggered at the first beat of the pattern.

3 Click on pad 9. The pad will light up indicating a kick drum will be triggered at beat 3 of the 1-bar pattern.

4 Click the Select button of drum Channel 2. Drum Channel 2 will become selected.

❄ **PROGRAMMING A DRUM LOOP**

Whenever you want to program a particular drum sample in the loop, you must first select the drum channel in which the sample is loaded.

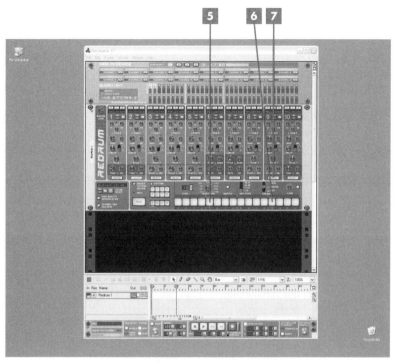

5 Click on pad 5. The pad will light up, indicating that a sample from drum Channel 2, a snare drum, will be triggered on beat 2.

6 Click on pad 13. The pad will light to show a snare will be played on beat 4. You will now hear a simple kick and snare beat.

7 Click the Select button of drum Channel 10. Drum Channel 10 will become selected.

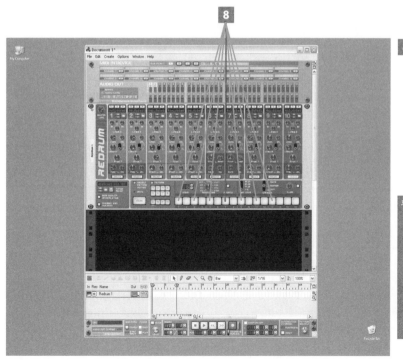

8 Click the pads 1, 3, 5, 7, 9, 11, 13, and 15. These pads will light up indicating a hi-hat sample to be played from drum Channel 10 on these beats. You should now have added a simple hi-hat to your kick snare combo.

❋ DEFAULT LOOP SETTINGS

You may notice that the pads are grouped into four; each group will count as one quarter note. As there are four groups you can assume that the loop is one bar. These are the default settings, which, of course, you can change. Later in this chapter I will explain how to change the length and beat structure of the loop.

Changing the Feel of the Beat

You've created a simple drum pattern. It might occur to you that, while this beat has perfect timing, it sounds a tad robotic and is missing some of that human feel. One of the reasons for this is that all the samples being played have the same level (velocity). Try giving the pattern a little of that human touch by altering the dynamic levels of the samples. To do this you need to program the trigger pads to play the samples at different velocities.

To demonstrate, change the hi-hat's velocity.

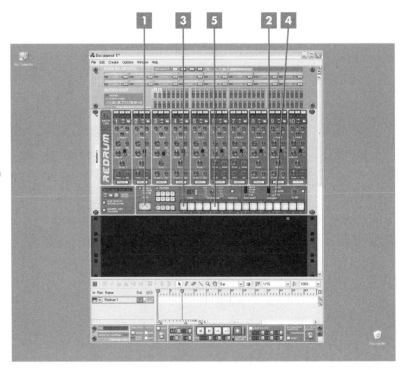

1 Click on the Run button to start the loop playback.

2 Toggle the Dynamic switch to the Hard position.

3 Click on pads 1 and 9. The pads' light will change from yellow to red. The hi-hat hits on beats 1 and 3 (pads 1 and 9) will be louder than the others.

4 Toggle the Dynamic switch to the Soft position.

5 Click on pads 5 and 13. The pads' light will change from yellow to green. The hi-hat hits on beats 2 and 4 (pads 5 and 13) will be softer than the others. The variation in dynamics gives the hi-hat a more natural swing.

❄ **HOW TO UNDO A PAD YOU'VE ACCIDENTALLY CLICKED ON**

If you accidentally click on a pad that you did not want to click on, or if you decide you wish to remove a trigger from the loop, you can simply click on the pad again to remove the trigger on that beat.

❄ ❄ ❄

Changing the Steps

Each trigger pad represents one step in the pattern. You can alter the number of steps that are available to program. By doing so you will effectively change the length of the pattern—for example, from one bar to two bars, etc.

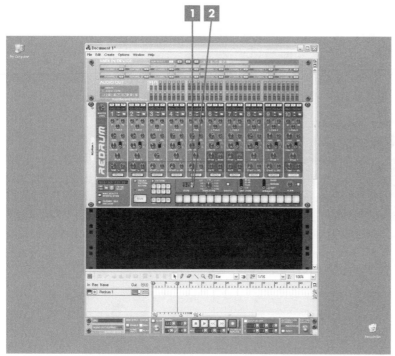

1 Click on the Steps up arrow and increase the value to 32. The pattern is now two bars long.

❄ **THE LENGTH OF YOUR PROGRAM**

Because you programmed only a one-bar pattern, when you extend the length to two bars the second bar will not be heard, since there is nothing yet programmed on it.

2 Click on the down arrow to decrease the value to 8. The pattern will now be only half a bar long.

❄ **MAXIMUM AND MINIMUM VALUES**

The maximum value of steps is 64, and the minimum value is 1.

Changing Step Size

Each step has been set by default to be a sixteenth note long. But you have the ability to change the step size to give you more control of your pattern.

1 Click on the Run button to engage the playback of the pattern.

2 Turn the Resolution knob to 1/8. The speed of the loop will slow down as the step size has increased.

3 Turn the Resolution knob to 1/32. The speed of the pattern will now increase as the step size has become smaller.

Flam

The flam feature lets you trigger a double shot of a sample, meaning the sample is played twice extremely close together to create an interesting effect.

1 Click Run to start the pattern's playback.

2 Click on the Flam power button to activate it.

3 Click on the small red light above pad 1. You will now hear the effect on the hi-hat at step 1.

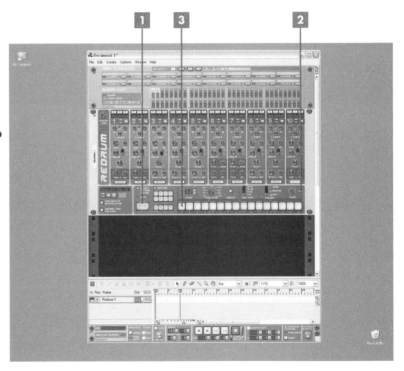

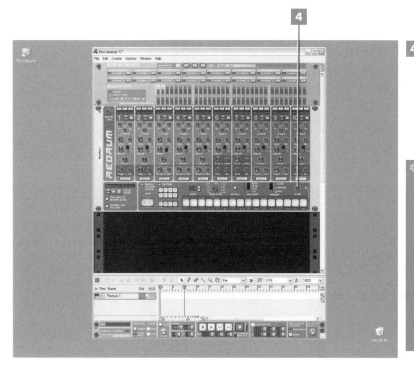

4 Turn the Flam knob to the right. The amount of delay between the original sample trigger and the double shot sample will increase.

❊ WHEN TO ACTIVATE FLAM

If the flam is active, when you activate any pad to trigger a sample, flam will automatically be placed on that beat. Clicking on the red light above a pad allows you to add flam to a pad that has already been set to trigger a sample. So if you do not wish to apply flam to your program then make sure that flam is not activated before programming the pads.

Shuffle

Earlier you saw how using varying levels helps when trying to create a human feel to the pattern. With the shuffle feature, Redrum will slightly alter the timing (adding a small amount of delay) of all the sixteenth notes that are between the eighth notes in the pattern to further enhance the human feel, since most drummers don't play in perfect time.

Now try the shuffle. In this pattern, the pads have a step size of 16; this would make pads 3, 7, 11, and 16 the eighth notes. Pads 2, 4, 6, 8, 10, 12, 14, and 16 are the sixteenth notes, and in this pattern these pads are not triggering any samples; therefore you would not be able to hear the effects of the shuffle. For this you'll need to add more notes to the pattern. (Before continuing, turn the flam function off and ensure that the resolution is set to 1/16)

1 Click on Run to start the playback of the pattern.

2 Click on Channel 10's Select button. The hi-hat channel will become selected.

3 Click on pads 2, 4, 6, 8, 10, 12, 14, and 16. The pattern will now be playing a hi-hat sample from every pad, and it will sound robotic.

4 Click on Shuffle. You will now hear the timing effects of the shuffle.

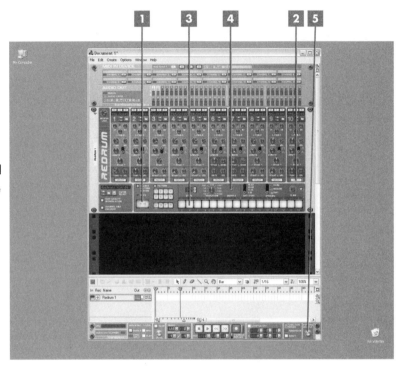

5 Turn the Pattern Shuffle on the transport panel to the right to increase the amount of shuffle. Turn it to the left to decrease the amount.

❋ SHUFFLE EFFECT

When adjusting the shuffle amount from the transport panel, all pattern devices loaded in the rack that have shuffle enabled will be affected.

Step Editing

If you count the number of trigger pads on the front of the Redrum, you'll find that there are only 16 pads, but as mentioned earlier you can have up to 64 steps to program to. To program the steps beyond 16, you need to tell Redrum which steps you wish to edit. This is done with the Edit Steps selector.

6 Toggle the Edit Steps button to 17-32. You can now program steps 17-32.

7 Toggle the Edit Steps button to 33-48. You can now program steps 33-48.

8 Toggle the Edit Steps button to 49-64. You can now program steps 49-64.

❋ CHECK THE EDIT STEP SWITCH

The pad numbers will not change when you change the Edit Steps value. The pads will always remain labeled as steps 1-16, so please double check the Edit Step switch to confirm you are editing the correct steps prior to performing any programming.

Drum Channels

Redrum is made up of 10 channels that hold the drum samples that will be triggered. Each channel has various parameters that are used to control the sound of the sample loaded on that channel. Here are a few of the common controls.

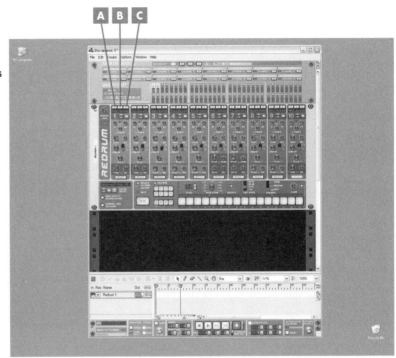

Mute, Solo, and Preview

A Mute. Clicking this button mutes the drum channel.

B Solo. Clicking this button solos the drum channel and mutes the other nine.

C Preview. This button allows you to preview the sample loaded in the channel.

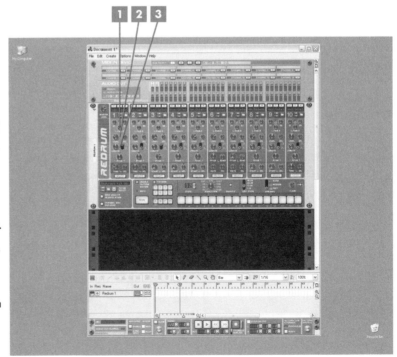

Sample Parameters

1 Turn the Pan knob to the left. The sample will be played on the left speaker. Turn the knob to the right, and the sample will be played on the right speaker.

2 Turn the Level knob to the left. The level of the sample will decrease. Turn the knob to the right and the level will increase.

3 Turn the Length knob to the left. The length of the sample will become shorter. Turn the knob to the right. The sample's length will extend.

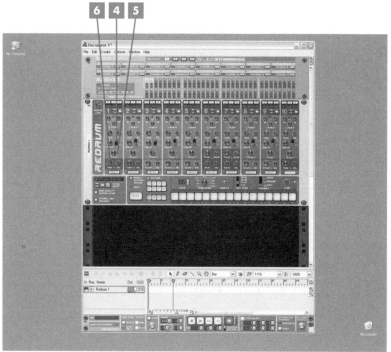

4 Choose the Decay Type by using the toggle switch to set the type of decay you want applied to the sample. When the switch is in the top position the sample's decay will be sudden; when in the bottom position the sample's decay will produce a smoother, fading decay.

5 Turn the Pitch knob to the left. The pitch of the sample will lower. Turn the knob to the right, and the sample's pitch will rise.

6 Turn the Tone knob to the left. The sample will have a darker tone. Turn the knob to the right, and the sample will sound brighter.

Getting Familiar with Patterns and Pattern Banks

The Redrum has four banks labeled A-D; each bank can store up to eight presets. When programming patterns, you will not be actually saving them, because you must select a pattern bank and preset before programming a pattern. All the programming you perform will be stored in that preset.

Copying a Pattern from One Bank to Another

In some situations you may want to copy the programmed pattern from one preset to another. One good example of when you may want to do this is if you have a basic drum beat that you want to add to, but you also want to keep the original beat. By copying the pattern to another preset number or to a preset in another bank, you can then add to it without altering the original.

❈ **PATTERN LAYOUT**

Each of Reason's pattern devices uses the same layout and design for storing its patterns—each has four banks with eight patterns per bank.

1 Right-click on the front panel. The Redrum pop-up menu will appear.

2 Select Copy Pattern. The patterns program will be copied to your computer's memory.

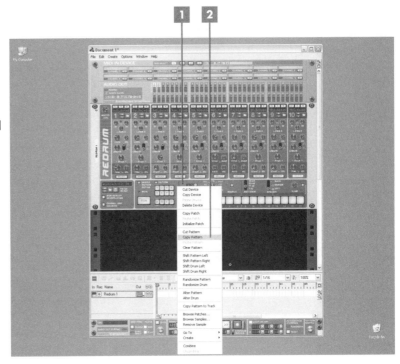

3 Click on preset 2. The pattern preset will become active.

4 Right-click on the front panel again. The Redrum pop-up menu will appear.

5 Click on Paste Pattern. The pattern from preset 1 will be pasted into preset 2.

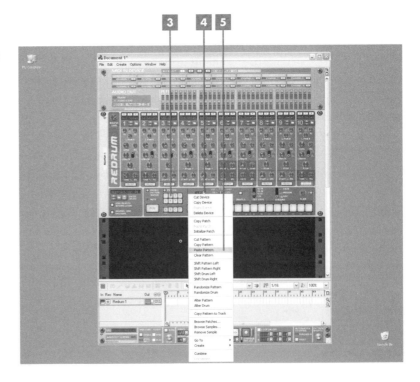

Global Parameters

There are a few parameters that you can adjust to control the
Redrum as a whole.

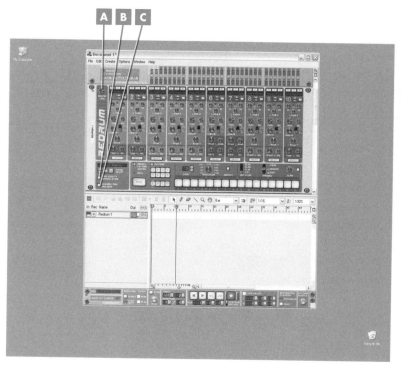

A Master Level. This is the master
volume control for the Redrum.

B High Quality Interpolation.
When this is activated, Redrum
will ensure the best possible
sound quality from the samples.
Turning off this setting may
reduce some of the pressure on
your CPU, but it will lower the
quality of sound.

C Channel 8 & 9 Exclusive. When this option is enabled, samples
on Channels 8 and 9 will be unable to play a sample at the same
time. For example, if Channel 8 is playing a sample when Channel
9 begins to play, Channel 8 will automatically stop playing. This is
helpful with instruments on which two sounds cannot be physically
played at once, such as an open hi-hat and a closed hi-hat.

The Matrix Pattern Sequencer

The Matrix works similarly to the Redrum; however, the Matrix is
used to create patterns that play sound modules devices, such as
SubTractor and Malström.

Loading the Necessary Devices

Since the Matrix is used to play sound modules, you will need to load at least one sound module to hear the Matrix's magic. For this exercise, you'll use the SubTractor. (Before loading the devices, remove the Redrum from the rack.)

1 Click on the Create menu. The Create menu will appear.

2 Click on SubTractor Analog Synthesizer. The device will be loaded into the rack.

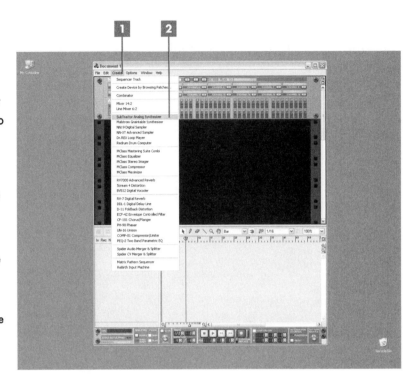

3 Click on the Create menu. The Create menu will appear.

4 Click on Matrix Pattern Sequencer. The Matrix device will be loaded into the rack.

5 Press the Tab key. The rack will flip to the rear view.

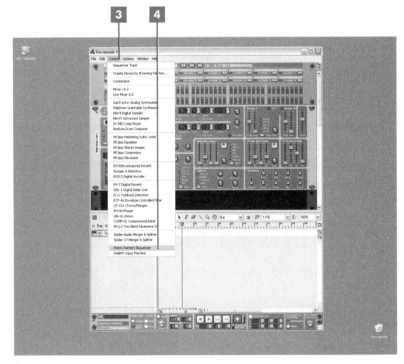

✳ Auto Routing. The Matrix will be automatically connected to the SubTractor via the Note CV and Gate CV connections. The Matrix plays the SubTractor with these connections.

✳ LOAD THE SUBTRACTOR FIRST

For the proper connection to be set up automatically, the SubTractor must be loaded into the rack before the Matrix.

Programming Patterns

Just like the Redrum, the Matrix allows you to program patterns that can be saved in one of its 32 presets (four banks of eight patterns). Take a look at how to program patterns with the Matrix.

Pattern Triggers

With the Redrum, you used the white pads to trigger the drum samples; with the Matrix, there are two separate triggers that need to be programmed to play the sound module.

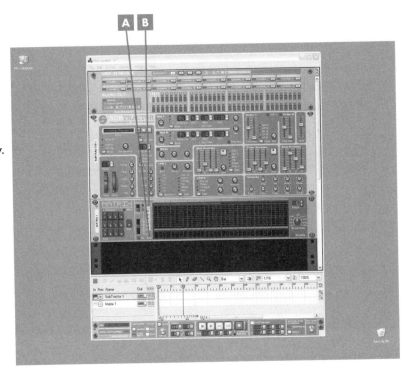

A Gate trigger. This area is where you enter gate trigger information. This trigger is responsible for telling the instrument to play a note; it does not tell which note to play.

B Note trigger. This trigger is used to tell the sound module which notes to play.

Programming the Triggers

Next you can program a very simple synthesizer line that will be played by the SubTractor.

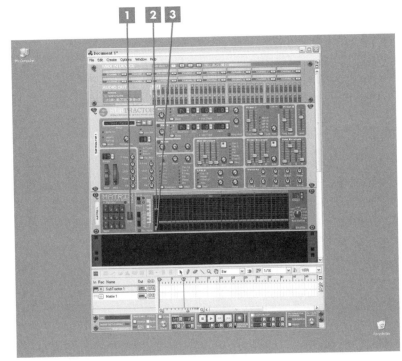

1 Click the Run button. The pattern will begin to play.

2 Click and drag the first step to a G note. Use the keyboard diagram on the left side to guide you to the correct note.

3 Click on the Gate trigger area on the first step. A parallel red line will appear in the Gate trigger. You will hear a G sixteenth note being played from the SubTractor at the beginning of the pattern.

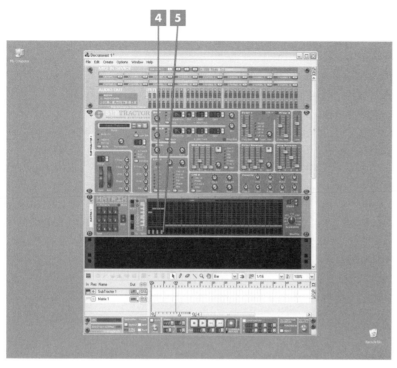

4 Click and drag **the** next three steps to an A note.

5 Click **on the** Gate trigger area for the next three steps. You will hear four A notes following the G notes.

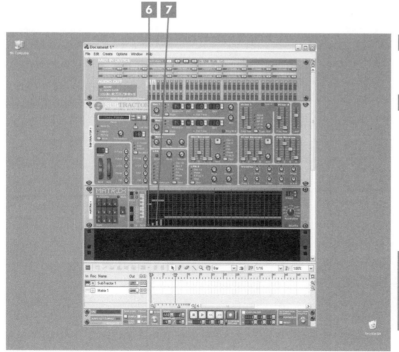

6 Click and drag **the** Gate trigger line in step 1 so that it's just above the bottom point.

7 Starting on step 2, re-size all of the Gate trigger's height so that each line is slightly higher than the one before it. The pattern will now start with a low level and slowly increase as it moves through the pattern.

❋ **GATE TRIGGER AND VELOCITY**

The height of the red lines in the Gate trigger reflects the velocity level of the note to be played.

Octave Edit

You can edit notes in different octaves with the Octave selector.

A Octave selector. The note trigger programming window allows you to edit notes in a single octave at a time. If you wish to program notes in a different octave, use this selector to choose the desired octave.

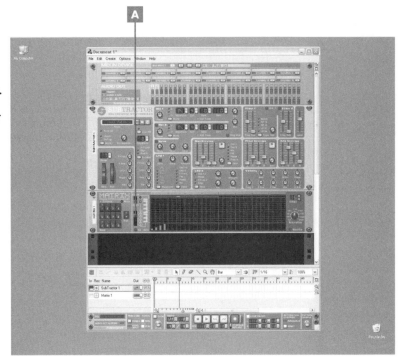

❄ MORE MATRIX CONTROLS

The Matrix is equipped with controls that allow you to alter the step size and number of steps in the pattern. Additionally, you can apply shuffle to the Matrix's patterns. Remember that the shuffle amount is located on the transport panel and will control the amount of shuffle on all loaded pattern devices.

❄ THE RED LINE

Along the top of the pattern's grid, a red line indicates the length of the pattern. If you increase the step value you will see this line extending.

7 } The Sequencer

By this point you're probably ready to start producing a Reason song of your own. For this you'll need a device that will record your performances; this is the job of the sequencer. The sequencer works something like a multi-track tape recorder, recording the performance of each Reason device on a separate sequencer track. Unlike a tape machine, however, the sequencer records digital data (MIDI) instead of audio. This data basically consists of commands that tell Reason's devices what to do and when to do it. In addition to recording and playing back performances, the sequencer allows you to edit your performances. In this chapter, you'll learn how to

❊ Record your performance to the sequencer.

❊ Record device automation.

❊ Perform edits in the Arrange Mode.

❊ Perform edits in the Edit Mode.

❊ Detach and resize the sequencer windows.

Recording to the Sequencer

Before you can record anything to the sequencer, you will need at least one device loaded in the rack. In this chapter, you will use the SubTractor synthesizer as the device with which to record.

1 Click on the Create menu. The Create menu will appear.

2 Click on SubTractor Analog Synthesizer. The SubTractor will be loaded into the rack.

❋ DEVICES AND TRACKS

When a device is loaded into the rack, a track will be automatically created in the sequencer for that device. However, if that device is deleted from the rack, the track that was created for it will remain.

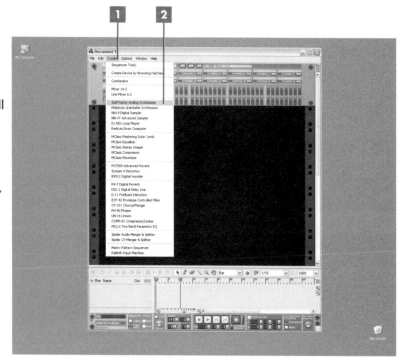

Track Information

Before getting into recording your performance, there are a few areas you should get familiar with to make your workflow easier. For every track in the sequencer there is a section in which information pertaining to that track is displayed. The information is divided into columns.

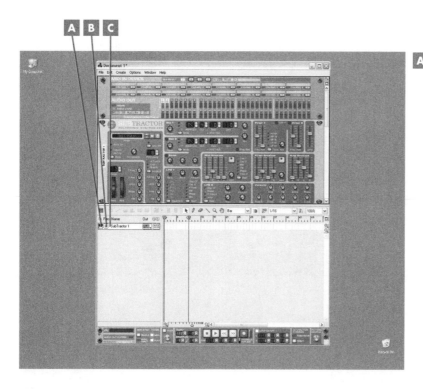

A In. This column indicates which track you will be recording to from your MIDI controller. Clicking on the keyboard icon in this column activates and deactivates the input for the track. Whenever you hit a key on your keyboard, a built-in VU meter above the keyboard will light up.

❋ MIDI THRU

The In column also controls MIDI Thru. MIDI Thru allows you to determine which device to play through when you play from your MIDI controller. If you have several sound devices loaded in the rack, you must enable the In column on the track connected to the device you wish to hear as you play.

❋ MAKE SURE THE CORRECT TRACK IS ENABLED

The In device is indicated by a small Keyboard icon in the In column. When recording, be sure that this icon appears on the track to which you wish to record. If the In is enabled on another track, the performance will not be recorded to the correct track.

B Rec. This column indicates that the track is enabled and ready to record.

C Name. This column is where you name the track. To name a track, double-click on the current name, type in the desired name, and press Return.

CHANGING THE TRACK NAME

Changing the name of the track will also change the name of the device the track is connected to.

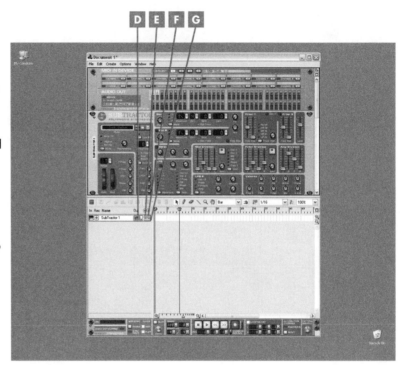

D Out. In this column you choose the device to which you want to connect the track. To change the connected device, click on the arrow, and a pop-up menu will appear displaying all the loaded devices. Select the desired device from this list.

E Mute Button. Click this button to mute the track.

F Solo Button. Click this button to solo the track

G VU Meter. Shows you the amount of volume when you play back recorded notes on the track.

OUT DEVICE

In the Out column there is also a small icon that resembles the device that the track is connected to. This will help you with a quick visual representation of the current connected device.

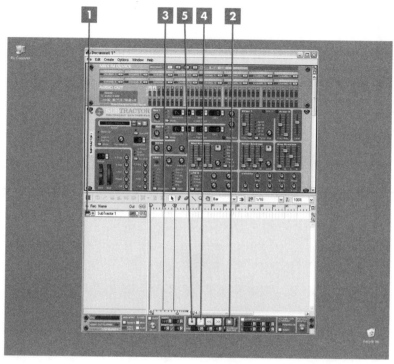

Recording

Next you'll learn how to record your performance to the track.

1 Click on the In column of the track you wish to record to. The MIDI icon will appear in the column, and the track will become highlighted.

2 Click on the Record button in the transport panel to arm Reason for recording. The Record button will light up indicating that Reason is ready to record.

3 Move the playback cursor to the point in the song at which you wish start recording.

4 Click the Play button to begin recording. While the song is recording, play a small performance on your MIDI controller keyboard.

5 Click the Stop button when you have finished performing. Reason will stop the song and stop recording to the track.

❄ TURNING OFF RECORD

If you wish to stop recording but keep playing the song, just click the Record button a second time.

When you have finished recording, you will notice that small colored lines have appeared on the SubTractor track in the sequencer. These lines represent your performance's MIDI information.

❈ **RECORDING KEYBOARD ENTERED NOTES**

If no key was played during recording, the track will remain empty. If you did play the keyboard but find that the track is empty after recording, refer back to "Track Information" earlier in this chapter to ensure that you have prepared the track correctly for recording. If the track is correctly set, refer back to "Configuring MIDI" in Chapter 1, "Setting Up Your Computer to Run Reason 3.0," to confirm that your MIDI connections are set up appropriately.

❈ **RECORDING STARTS AT THE PLAYBACK CURSOR**

Recording will automatically begin at the playback cursor. If you wish to start your performance at bar 5, for example, set the playback cursor to bar 4 or 3. This will give you some time to start the recording and prepare to play your performance at the start of bar 5.

Locators and Loop Recording

The locators perform various functions in Reason; however, they are most commonly used when performing loop recording. When loop recording, the portion of the song between the L and R locators will play over and over until recording is stopped.

Loop recording records in a continuous loop between the locators until you have stopped the recording.

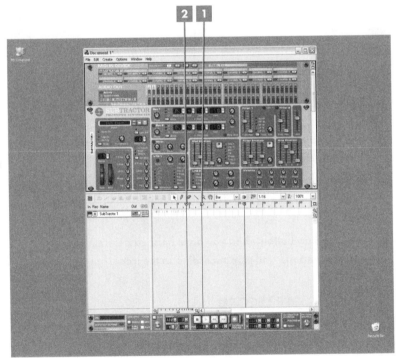

1 Drag the left locator to the point in the song at which you want the recording to begin.

2 Drag the playback cursor to one bar before the left locator. This will give you some time to start the recording and get ready to play the performance.

❈ ❈ ❈

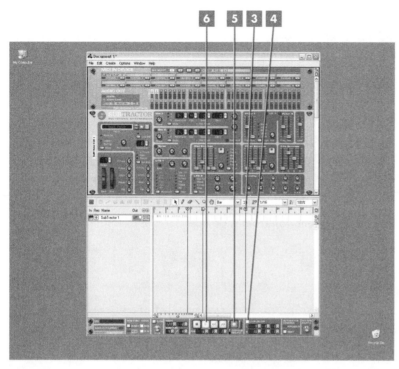

3 Drag the right locator to the point at which you want the recording to end.

4 Click on Loop On/Off to activate the loop function. The loop light will engage.

5 Click on the Record button. The sequencer will become armed for recording.

6 Click on Play to begin recording.

When the playback cursor has reached the right locator it will automatically jump back to the left locator while continuing to record.

Overdub or Replace

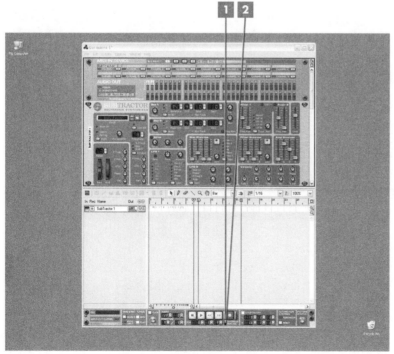

When recording in Loop Mode you can choose whether you'd like to have your performance *replace* data that was recorded on the previous pass or be *added* to that data.

1 Toggle the Record mode switch to Replace to have the performance replace any of the information that was already recorded.

2 Toggle the Record mode switch to Overdub to have the new performance added to the old.

RECORD MODES

The Overdub and Replace recording modes apply to all recordings, whether they're recording in Loop Mode or Standard Mode.

Device Automation

As you have discovered in earlier chapters, each device in Reason has plenty of knobs that can control a large number of parameters. With the sequencer you can record the movements of these parameters throughout the song; this is known as *automation*.

To record automation from a device:

1. Click in the In column of the track connected to the device you wish to automate.

2. Click the Record button. Reason will be armed for recording.

3. Click the Play button. Reason will begin recording.

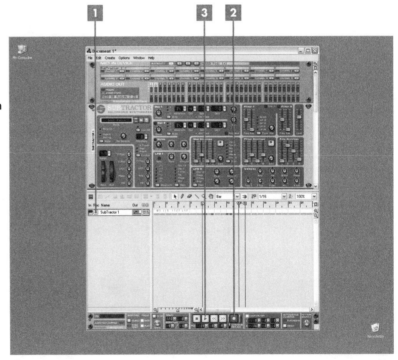

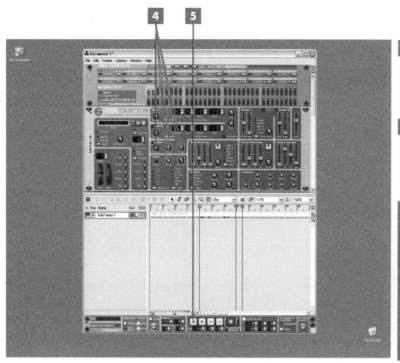

4 Adjust the parameters of the device that you wish to automate. The sequencer will record these movements.

5 Click Stop after you have recorded your automation. Reason will stop recording.

❄ **AUTOMATION INDICATOR**

When you've stopped recording automation, the parameters of the device you automated will have green boxes around them indicating that automation has been recorded for them. If you don't wish to see these, uncheck the box next to Show Automation Indication in General Preferences.

Editing in Arrange Mode

The sequencer has two modes with which to edit your performance: Arrange Mode and Edit Mode. The Arrange Mode is the default mode, and it's where you will edit the arrangement of your song by working with groups that hold MIDI information. Groups can be copied, cut, and pasted throughout the song. In general, the Arrange Mode will be used when you want to make large edits to rearrange the song.

Working with Groups

Groups allow you to create building blocks on the tracks. These blocks can be moved as well as copied anywhere in the song, allowing you to build your song in minutes.

Creating a Group

Before you can begin to work with groups you must create a group and add the MIDI information to it.

1 Click and drag **the** lower portion of the track, **just to the left of the MIDI information, to draw a box over all the MIDI data to highlight it.**

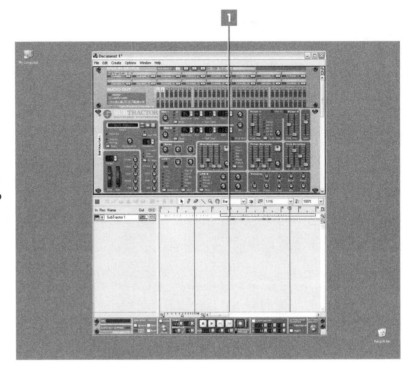

2 Click on the Edit menu. The Edit menu will appear.

3 Click on Group. **A colored box will appear over the MIDI information. This is the group.**

SELECTING TRACKS AND DEVICES

Because each track is routed to a device in the rack, selecting a track will also select the device in the rack and position your rack view to center on that device. And if you select a device in the rack, that device's track will also become selected on the arrange window.

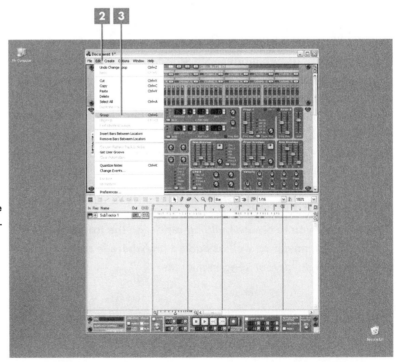

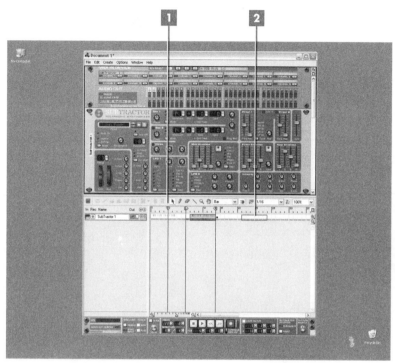

Moving Groups

You can quickly move a group to any position in the song.

1 Click on the Selection tool from the toolbar. The mouse cursor will change to an arrow.

❈ **CHOOSING THE SELECTION TOOL**

The Selection tool is set by default as the current tool, but if a different tool was selected you will need to change the cursor back to the Selection tool.

2 Click and drag the group to the desired location in the song.

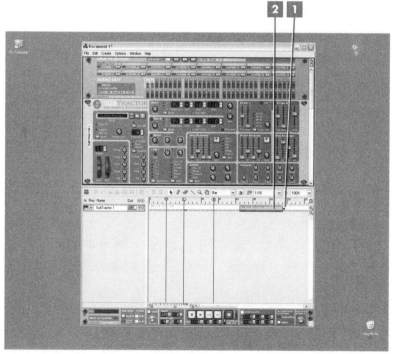

Resizing Groups

1 Click on the small black box on the right side of the group. The mouse cursor will become a small double-sided arrow.

2 Drag to the right to enlarge the group.

Drag **to the left** to shorten the group.

RESIZING ONE GROUP OVER ANOTHER

If you resize a group over the top of another group, those two groups will become one. This cannot be undone by resizing the group again. All edits will be applied to the newly created group.

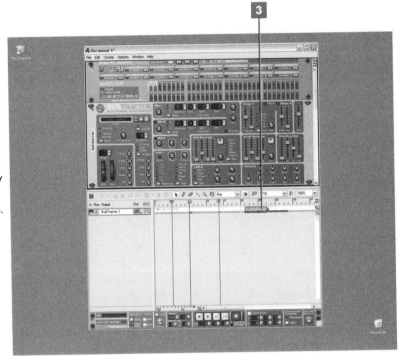

Move Groups with Snapping

When moving groups, you want to be sure that after the move, the group still fits the timing of the song. For this you use the Snap function. When repositioning a group, if the Snap function is on, you will be able to place the group only on a predetermined step of the grid, as opposed to being able to place it freely. The step size is set by the snapping value.

ENABLING SNAPPING

Snapping is enabled by default, but if you have disabled it you will need to enable it again.

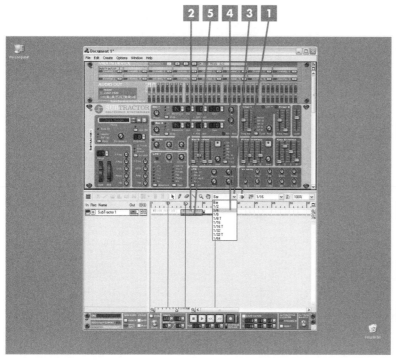

1. Click on the Snap to Grid icon. Snapping will be enabled.

By default, snapping is set to snap to every bar.

2. Click and drag the group to the next bar. You will see that the group will automatically line up at the beginning of the bar.

3. Click on the Snap Settings menu. The various snap settings will appear.

4. Click on 1/4. The snapping will be set to quarter note.

5. Click and drag the group again. The group will now snap on every quarter note.

Quantizing Your Performances

When you record your performance, chances are you won't play every note with perfect timing. Quantizing allows you to automatically correct these timing errors by moving them to the nearest predetermined beat subdivision.

Setting the Quantize Value

The quantize value determines how far the notes will move. For example, if you set the quantize value to 1/4, the notes will be moved to start at the closest quarter beat.

1 Click on the Quantize Value menu. The menu will appear.

2 Click on the desired quantize value. The value will be set.

Setting the Quantize Percentage

Before you apply any quantization you will need to set the quantizing strength. This will govern how far the note should be moved. If you set this to 100%, the notes will be moved closest to the quantize value; a setting of 50% will move the notes only halfway to the closest quantize point.

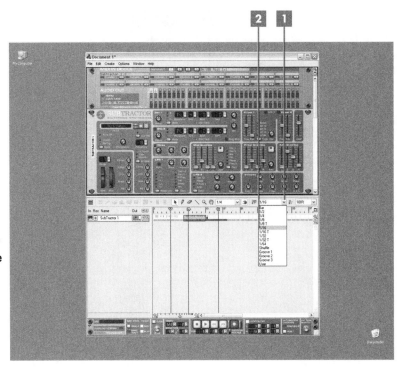

1 Click on the Quantize Percentage menu. The menu will appear.

2 Select the desired percentage. The percentage value will change to your selection.

❋ QUANTIZE VALUES

Typically the percentage of quantize you use depends on the style of music you are creating. A value of 100% will give you extremely tight timing that is most suited for dance and techno styles, while a lower setting of around 50% will be adequate for pop and rock music, in which a more human feel is desirable.

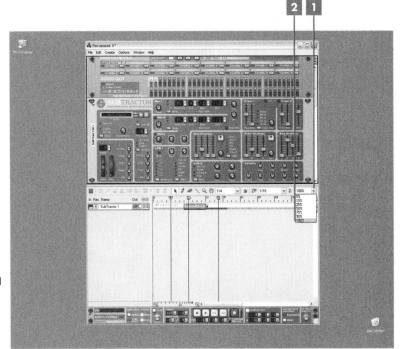

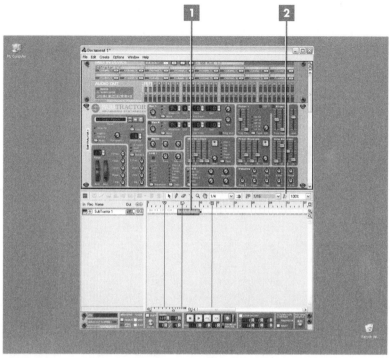

Applying Quantize

Once you have made your quantize settings you need to apply them to the performance.

1 Select the group to which you wish to apply quantizing.

2 Click on the Quantize Note icon. The notes within the group will be quantized.

 QUANTIZATION AND GROUPS

Quantization can be applied only to groups that have been selected. This holds true when you are working in Edit Mode as well. You must select the notes prior to applying quantization.

LISTEN TO QUANTIZATION CHANGES

After applying quantization it's a good idea to listen to the changes before moving on. That way, you can choose to undo the quantization if you don't like the results.

Quantize During Record

You could also have Reason automatically quantize your performance during recording. This method eliminates the need to quantize after recording; however, caution should be taken, since quantization that's applied during recording cannot be undone.

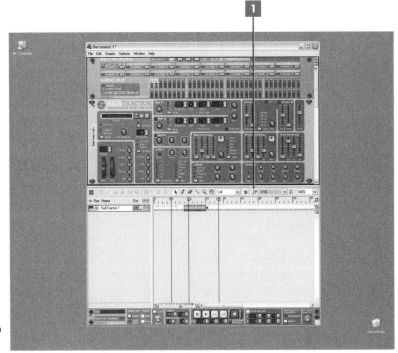

1 Click on the Quantize Notes During Recording icon. The option will be enabled.

Editing Tools

So far you have been using only the Selection tool to do all of your editing, and in most situations this is the only tool you need. There are times, however, when you will need additional tools to perform other tasks.

 EDIT TOOLS AND VIEW MODES

All the edit tools are available for both Arrange Mode and Edit Mode.

Deleting a Group

If you wish to completely remove a group from a track, follow these steps.

1 Click on the Eraser tool. The mouse arrow will be replaced with an eraser cursor.

2 Click on the group that you wish to delete from the track. The group will be removed.

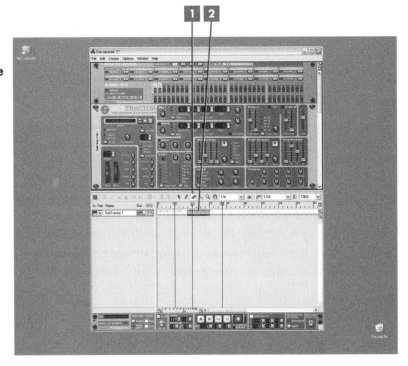

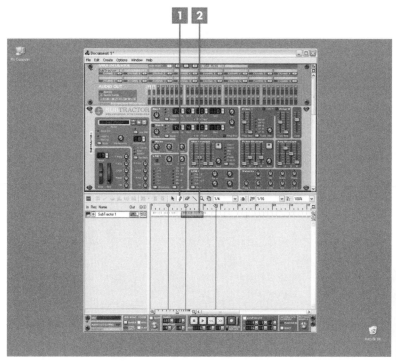

Drawing Groups on Tracks

You can also manually draw a group onto a track.

1. Click on the Pencil tool. The mouse cursor will become a pencil.

2. Click and drag the track area you want to draw a group on. A new group will appear on the track.

❋ USING THE ARRANGE PAGE

Although the Arrange page typically will be used for editing groups, it can also be used for editing single notes. By drawing a marquee over the top of a bunch of single notes, a new group will be created that contains them.

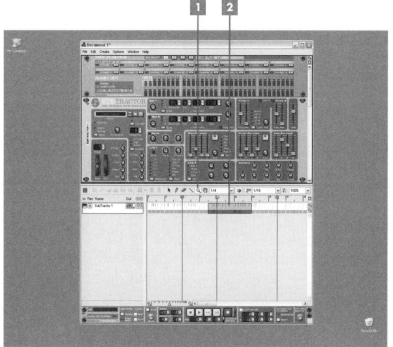

Zooming In and Out on Groups

Use the Magnify tool when you want to take a closer look at a group.

1. Click on the Magnify tool. The mouse cursor will become a magnifying glass.

2. Click on the group you wish to zoom in on. The group will appear larger.

The Magnify tool is also used when you want to zoom out.

1 Click on the Magnify tool.

2 Hold the Ctrl (PC)/Command (Mac) key The Magnify tool's mouse cursor will change from a + sign to a –sign.

3 Click on the group you wish to zoom out on.

Navigating the Arrangement

When working with larger songs, the Arrange window may become crowded, and you may find it difficult to move about the window. To make navigating the arrangement easier you can use the Hand tool.

1 Click on the Hand tool. The mouse cursor will become a hand.

2 Click and drag the hand anywhere in the arrangement. The entire arrangement will follow the position of the hand.

❄ **VERTICAL AND HORIZONTAL SCROLLING**

The Hand tool will move the arrangement both vertically and horizontally, allowing you to quickly access any part of the arrangement.

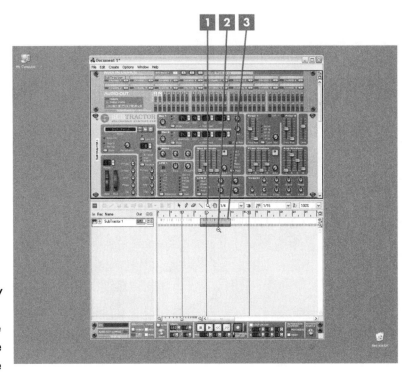

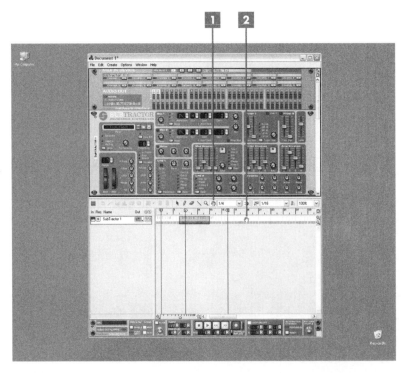

Editing in Edit Mode

The second edit mode for the sequencer, simply titled Edit Mode, gives a more precise way to edit your performances. The Arrange Mode is typically used for building arrangements out of groups, using them like building blocks. Edit Mode is primarily used when you want to edit the information within those blocks.

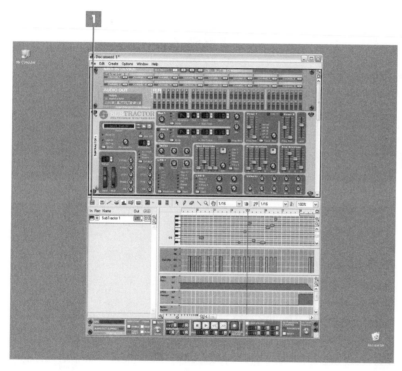

Putting the Sequencer in Edit Mode

To change the sequencer from its default Arrange Mode to Edit Mode:

1 Click on Edit Mode. The sequencer will change to Edit Mode.

Working with Lanes

Unlike the Arrange Mode, which shows an overview of the groups on all tracks, the Edit Mode shows only the information that is on the currently selected track. The track will be divided into separate lanes, each lane showing relevant information for the track, depending on which device it is connected to. Some lanes are used to edit a specific device—e.g., the Rex lane is used to edit a track connected to a Dr:rex Loop Player.

The Lanes

As mentioned, there are various types of lanes. Some are used for specific devices and some have several uses.

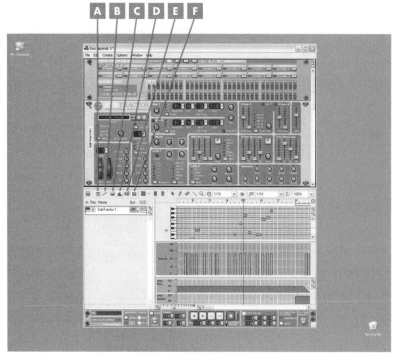

A Key lane. This lane is used to edit MIDI note information sent to sound module devices such as the Mälstrom and the NN-XT.

B Rex lane. This lane is used to edit the splices of a Rex file loaded in the Dr:rex Loop Player.

C Drum lane. This lane is specific to the Redrum device. It is used to edit notes being sent to Redrum slots.

D Velocity lane. This lane allows you to edit the velocity of note information. This lane is not specific to any one device.

E Pattern lane. Use this lane to edit the pattern changes of a pattern device.

F Controllers. This lane allows you to edit various MIDI controller messages used to automate various parameters of a connected device.

Enabling Lane Views

To view a lane, you must switch to Edit Mode, and then enable any
of the lanes you wish to see.

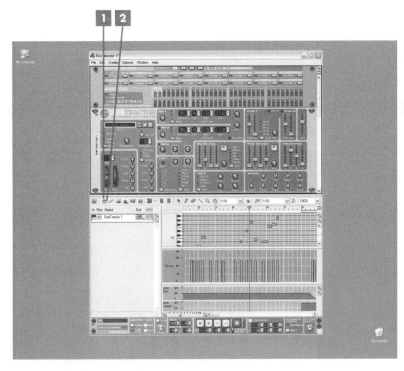

1 Click on the Show Key Lane
icon. The Key lane will appear
in the sequencer window.

2 Click on the Show Key Lane
icon again. The Key lane will
be removed.

❋ ENABLING OTHER LANE VIEWS

This exercise demonstrates how to enable the Key Lane view; however, the same
method is used to enable all other lane views. Click on the appropriate lane icon to
enable that lane's view.

❋ DEFAULT LANES FOR DEVICES

Each device has its own set of default lane views—for example, a track connected to
a Dr:rex device will show only the Dr:rex lane and the Velocity lane, since the others
are not relevant to the Dr:rex device.

Controller Lanes

The Controller lane allows you to edit the automation of a device that you may have recorded to a track.

To view the Controller lane:

1 Click on the Show Controller Lane icon. The lane will appear in the window.

Because each device has a different set of parameters that can be automated you will need to choose which controller you want to view and edit.

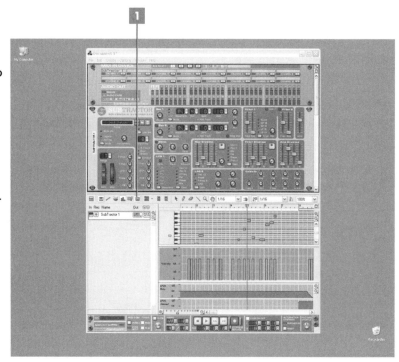

To view all controllers:

1 Click on the Show Device Controllers icon. All possible Controller lanes for that device will appear in the sequencer window.

To view only the Controller lanes containing recorded automation in the currently selected track:

2 Click on the Show Controllers in Track icon. The lanes for all controllers being used by that track will appear in the sequencer window.

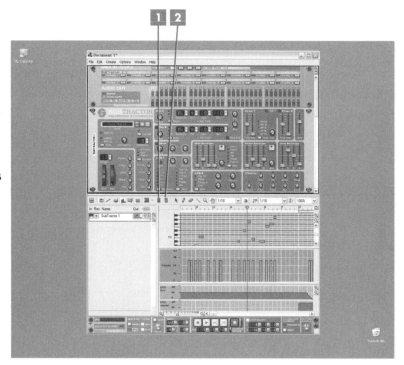

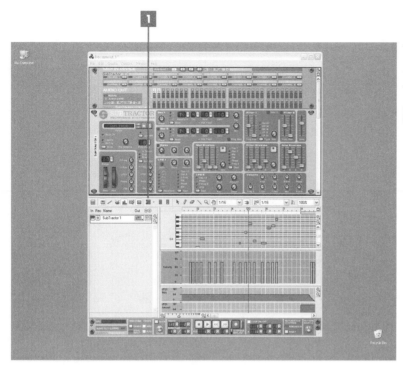

You can also select from a list the specific Controller lanes that you wish to view and edit.

1 Click on the Controllers icon. The Available Controller Lanes menu will appear.

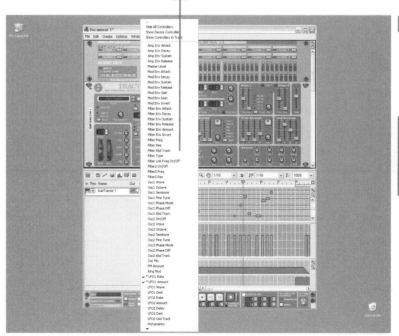

2 Click on the Controller lane you wish to view and edit. That Controller lane will appear in the sequencer window.

✳ CONTROLLERS

In the Available Controllers Lanes menu, an asterisk will be placed next to each Controller lane that is being used in the track.

203
✳ ✳ ✳

Setting the Lane's Grid

The Snap function can also be
used on information in Edit Mode.

Enabling Snapping

A Click on the Snap to Grid icon.
Snapping will be enabled.

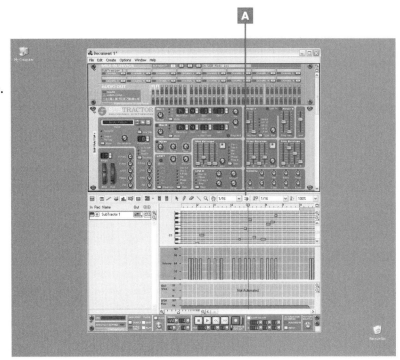

Changing the Grid Size

1 Click on the Grid size menu.
2 Click on the desired grid size.

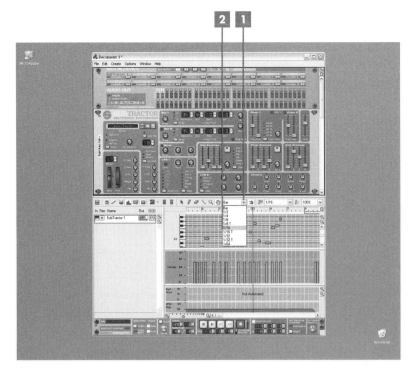

Editing the Tracks

Using the lanes, you can edit all the information on a track. You can even add or remove information manually.

Drawing Notes

In the lanes, you can use the Pencil tool to draw in note information.

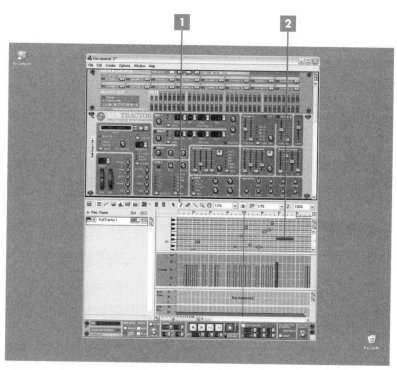

1 Click on the Pencil tool. Your mouse cursor will become the Pencil tool.

2 Click on the area of the Key lane where you wish to draw a note. A note will be drawn onto the track.

✻ **DISABLING UNNEEDED VIEWS**

With several lanes open at one time, the Edit Mode may become crowded; it's a good idea to disable all unneeded views.

✻ **NOTE LENGTH AND GRID SIZE SETTING**

The length of the note you draw depends on the value set in the grid size setting. To create a note longer than the size set by the grid, click and hold while dragging the mouse to draw a note. This way you can create a note of the desired length. The note will still snap to the grid value as you drag it.

Moving Notes

1 Click on the Selection tool icon. Your mouse cursor will become an arrow Selection tool.

2 Click and drag the note you wish to move to the desired position.

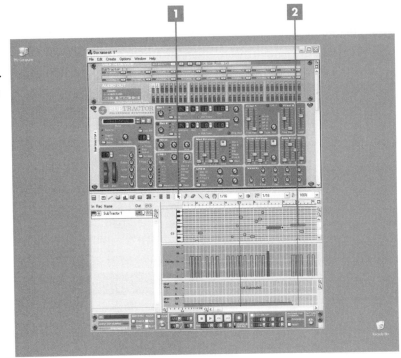

Changing Note Lengths

1 Select the note you wish to resize. The note will become highlighted.

2 Click on the small black box to the right of the note.

3 Drag the note to the right to make the note longer or to the left to shorten the note.

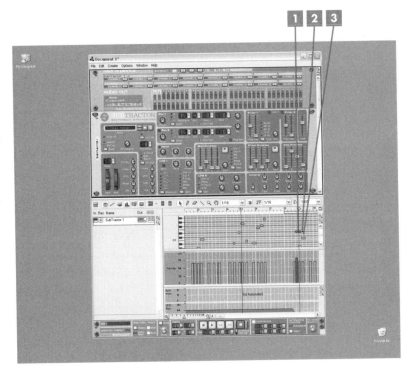

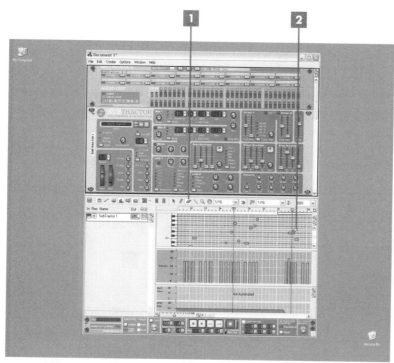

Deleting Notes

1 Click on the Eraser tool. The mouse cursor will become an Eraser tool.

2 Click on the note that you wish to erase. The note will be removed from the track.

❀ ABOUT EDITING NOTES

Editing note information—drawing, re-sizing, moving, and deleting—works the same way in the Key lane, the Rex lane, and the Drum lane.

Drawing Velocity Changes

You can also edit the note's velocity information. Velocity, you will recall, is the MIDI value that captures how hard you strike a note on your MIDI keyboard.

1 Click on the Show Velocity Lane icon. The Velocity lane will appear.

2 Click the note whose velocity you wish to edit. The note will become highlighted.

3 Click on the Pencil tool. The mouse cursor will become the Pencil tool.

4 Click and drag the note's Velocity setting to raise or lower the velocity.

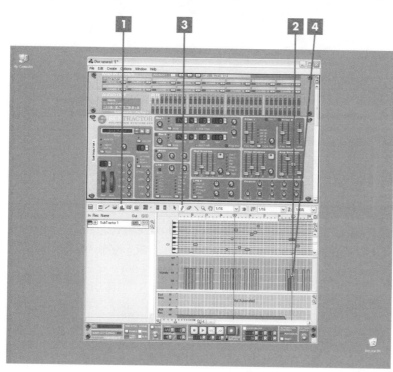

❀ ❀ ❀

Resizing the Sequencer Windows

When working with the sequencer, at times the screen can become a bit crowded, and you may wish to resize the sequencer window. Here you have a few options.

Changing the Sequencer Height

By default, the sequencer window will take up a small portion of the rack just above the transport controls. You can change the height of the sequencer to take up more of the rack.

1 Click and drag **the** dividing bar up **to increase the height of the** sequencer window.

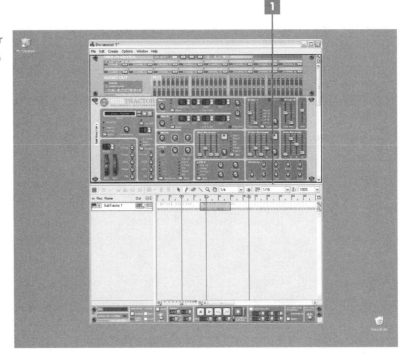

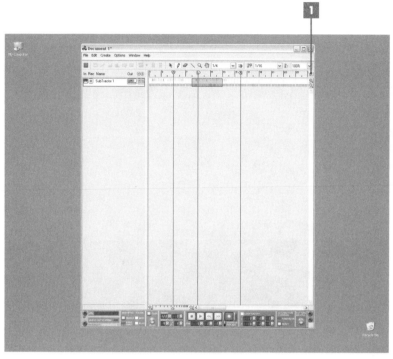

Sequencer Full Rack View

You can also have the sequencer fill the entire rack. This mode will cover all devices in the rack.

1 Click on the Full View button. The sequencer will expand to fill the entire rack.

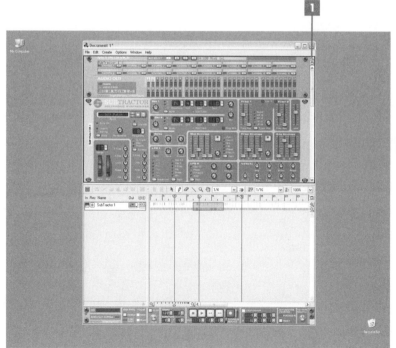

Detaching the Sequencer Window

You can actually detach the sequencer so that it will appear as a separate window.

1 Click the Detach Sequencer button. The sequencer will now be detached from the rack and will be in a window of its own.

Of course, you can also put the sequencer back into the rack.

1 Click the Detach Sequencer button. The sequencer will now be attached to the rack again.

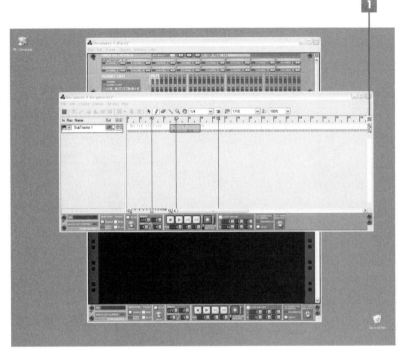

8 Advanced Audio Routing with Effects

In Chapter 2, "Fast Start," you learned to apply simple audio routing between the SubTractor and the Mixer 14:2. Since then, you've been introduced to Reason's other sound modules and effect devices. Some are equipped with only a single audio output, while others have several audio inputs and outputs. The routing possibilities among Reason's devices seem nearly endless, and making all those connections can be confusing. In this chapter, you will learn how to

❋ Connect effect devices as inserts.

❋ Connect effect devices as sends.

❋ Create chain effects.

❋ Chain mixer sends.

❋ Use the Spider to send audio to several effect devices.

Connecting Effects as Inserts

When you wish to apply effects to your sound module devices there are two possible routing methods: Insert mode and Send mode. I'll discuss Insert mode first. In this mode, the effect is "inserted" between the sound module and the mixer so that all the audio from the sound module passes through the effect device before being routed to the mixer. In this mode, the inserted effect will be applied only to the sound module to which it is connected.

Loading the Devices

To learn how to route audio to an effect using the insert, you'll first need to load some devices into an empty rack.

❄ STARTING WITH AN EMPTY RACK

As with the previous exercises, it is a good idea to start with an empty rack.

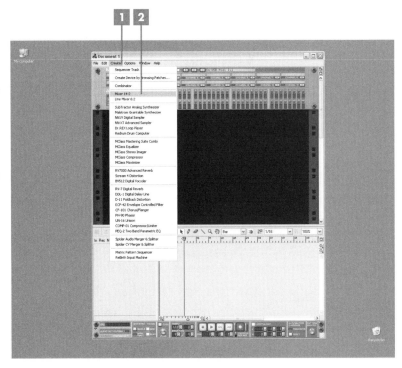

1 Click on the Create menu. The Create menu will appear.

2 Click on Mixer 14:2. The mixer will be loaded into the rack.

❄ LOAD THE MIXER FIRST

When you start a new song, loading a mixer into the rack first makes routing of subsequent devices easier.

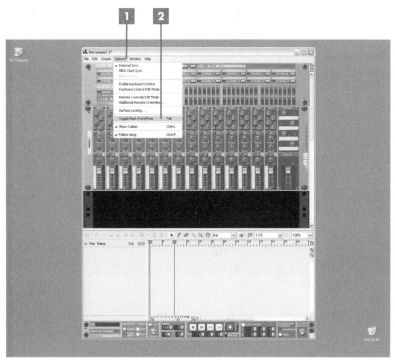

Next you'll need to check the default routing of the mixer.

1. **Click** on the **Options** menu. The Options menu will appear.

2. **Click** on **Toggle Rack Front/Rear.** The rear view of the rack will be displayed.

❋ **TOGGLE FRONT/BACK KEYBOARD SHORTCUT**

Remember that the Tab key will also toggle the rack between front and rear views.

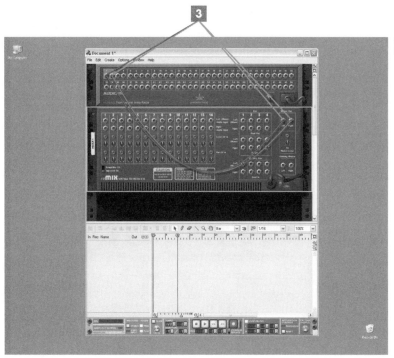

3. Check to be sure that the mixer's output is connected to the first two inputs of the Hardware Interface.

After the mixer is loaded, you will add a SubTractor synthesizer while still in the rear view mode.

1 Click on the Create menu. The Create menu will appear.

2 Click on SubTractor Analog Synthesizer. The SubTractor will be loaded into the rack.

❄ **ANOTHER WAY TO CREATE DEVICES**

By now you should be comfortable using the Create menu, and for all exercises you'll be using the same menu when adding devices; however, you can also add devices to the rack by right-clicking (Control-clicking on Mac) in an empty portion of the rack, then choosing the required device from the drop-down menu.

3 The mono audio output of the SubTractor should have automatically been connected to Channel 1 of the mixer.

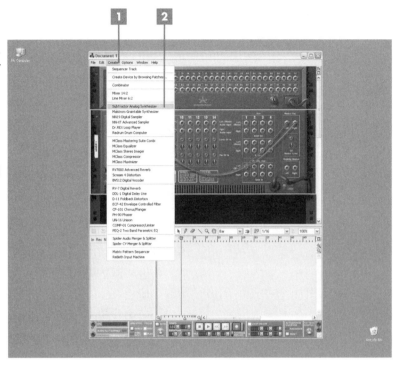

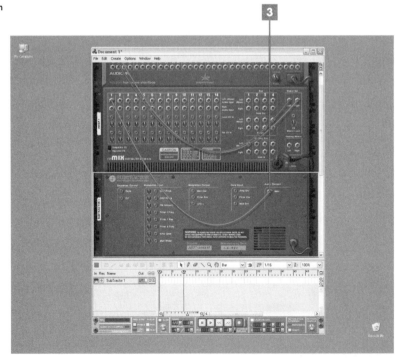

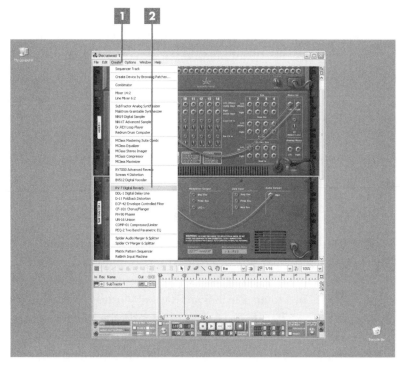

Inserting the Effects

While still in rear view mode, add the reverb effect to the rack.

1 Click on the Create menu. The Create menu will appear.

2 Click on RV-7 Digital Reverb. The RV-7 will be loaded into the rack.

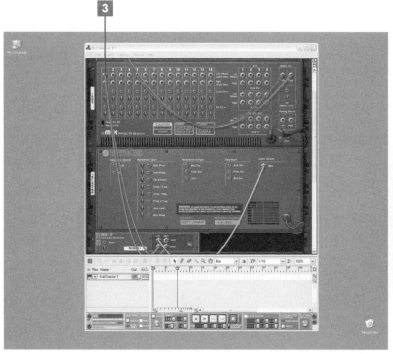

3 By default, the RV-7's inputs will be connected to the SubTractor's output, and the RV-7's output will be connected to Channel 1 of the mixer.

❋ INSERT EFFECT

When any effect device is loaded into the rack directly below a sound module, by default that effect device will be connected as an insert effect to the module above it. If a second effect device is added after the first, the two effect units will be connected to each other in Insert mode.

❋❋❋

In Insert mode, even though an effect unit is connected directly to a sound module device (or perhaps another effect device), it is possible to control the blend (mix) of the devices using the dry/wet parameter found on most of the effects.

DEVICES TO ROUTE AS INSERT EFFECTS

When using dynamic effect devices such as a compressor or EQ, it is best to route the audio as an insert in order to process all the audio of a device.

Connecting Effects as Sends

A *send* splits off a portion of the audio and sends that portion to its own destination, through a special "send" output to the effect device. The output is then returned to the mixer to one of its four stereo returns. This routing technique is usually used when you want to apply an effect to just a part of your device's audio signal, as opposed to the entire signal. Sends are also used when you want to share one effect device with more than one sound module.

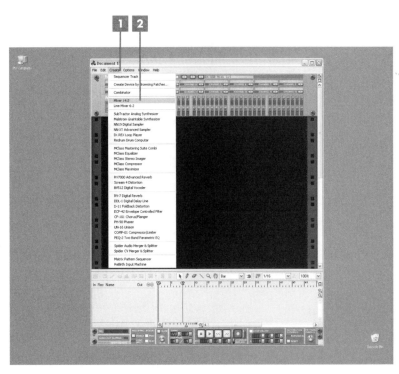

Setting up a Send

Again you want to start with an empty rack. This time, when you load devices into the rack, you're going to change the default routing.

Start with the mixer.

1. Click on the Create menu. The Create menu will appear.
2. Click on Mixer 14:2. The mixer will be loaded into the rack.

Now you need to add a sound module; load the Dr:rex.

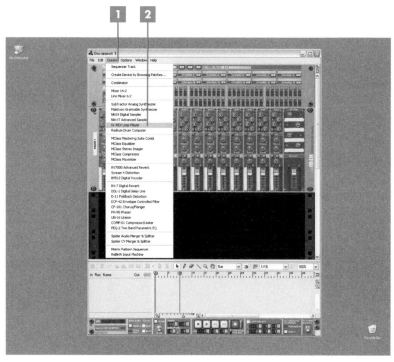

1. Click on the Create menu. The Create menu will appear.

2. Click on Dr. Rex Loop Player. The Dr. Rex Loop Player will be loaded into the rack.

Next you will need to load a loop into Dr:rex.

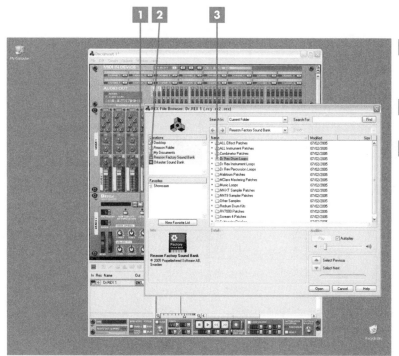

1. Click on the Loop Browser icon. The Browse Loop window will appear.

2. Click on Reason Factory Sound Bank.

3. Double-click on Dr Rex Drum Loops.

4 Navigate to the folder Electronic.

5 Click on the loop Elc04_ Autobahn_100_eLab.rx2. The loop will become highlighted.

6 Click on OK. The loop will be loaded into Dr:rex.

Next you will add the reverb just as you did in the insert section; however, you have to be careful that the reverb isn't connected as an insert by default.

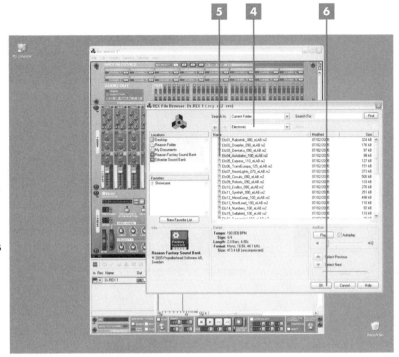

1 Click on the edge of the mixer. The mixer will become the highlighted device.

2 Click on the Create menu. The Create menu will appear.

3 Click on RV-7 Digital Reverb. The RV-7 will be loaded into the rack.

4 Press Tab. The rack will turn to the rear view.

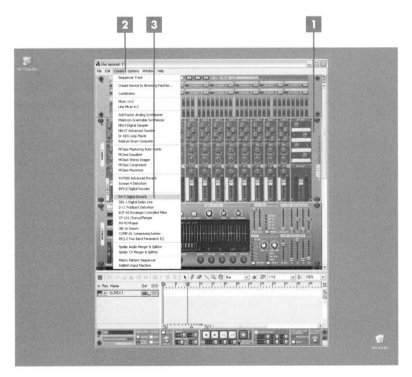

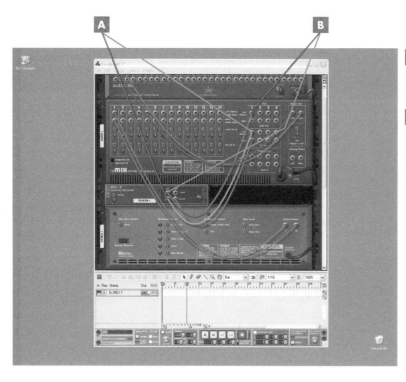

A By default, the inputs of the RV-7 will be connected to the Aux Sends 1 and 2 of the mixer.

B The outputs of the RV-7 will be connected to Returns 1 and 2 of the mixer.

5 Press Tab. The rack will return to the front view.

❈ WHY YOU NEED TO SELECT THE MIXER FIRST

If the mixer was not selected and highlighted before adding the RV-7, the RV-7 would be created under the Dr:rex Loop Player and would have been routed as an insert effect by default.

Sending Audio to the Effect

Now that you have your effect device patched in as an effect send, you need to actually send audio to it before you can hear any of the effect.

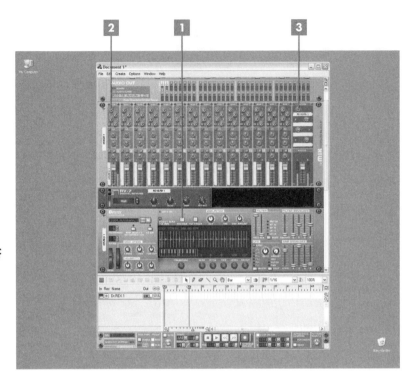

1 Click Preview on Dr:rex. The loop will begin to play.

2 Turn the Aux 1 knob on Channel 1 to the right. A portion of the Dr:rex loop will be sent to the reverb via the Aux output. You will now be able to hear the reverb that is being to sent to the loop.

3 Turn the Return 1 knob to the right to increase the volume of the reverb.

❋ **APPLYING THE RIGHT AMOUNT OF EFFECT**

The farther to the right you turn the Aux knob, the larger the portion of audio that will be sent to the effect connected to the send. This allows you to gauge how much of the effect you wish to apply.

Setting Up a Return

As suggested earlier, when you use the send option to apply effects, you will need a place to return the output of the effect device. You can do this by using the four stereo returns on the mixer.

As with the previous exercise, when any effect is added to a rack so that the default routing is set to Send mode, the returns will also be automatically routed. In the next exercise you will learn to set the return manually.

To begin you will need to disconnect the reverb's output from the mixer's returns so that you can follow the steps to reconnect it manually. This will help you in situations in which an effect device may not have been connected to the returns automatically.

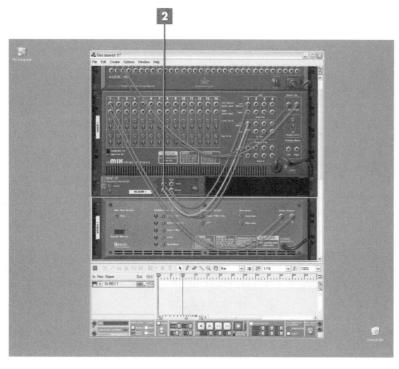

1 Press the Tab key. The rack will turn to the rear view.

2 Right-click on the Left Output of the RV-7. The connections pop-up menu will appear.

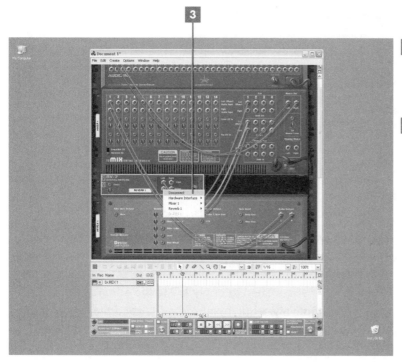

3 Click on Disconnect. The output of the reverb will be disconnected from the mixer's returns.

4 Again, right-click on the Left Output of the RV-7. The connections pop-up menu will appear.

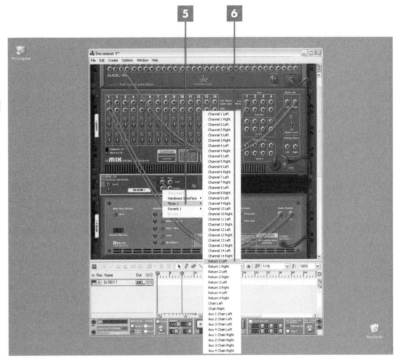

5 Click on Mixer 1. The mixer's connections menu will appear.

6 Click on Return 1 Left. The left and right output of the RV-7 will be connected to stereo Return 1 on the mixer.

❄ STEREO PAIRS CONNECTION

As demonstrated in this exercise, when you connect the output of a stereo pair, such as the RV-7's output, to a stereo paired input, such as the mixer's returns, when you connect the left cable, the right cable will be connected automatically as well. This also applies when disconnecting a stereo paired connection.

❄ CHOOSING ANOTHER RETURN

To assign the effect to a return other than Return 1, simply choose the return you wish to use from the mixer's connection menu in step 6.

Using Mixer Channels as Returns

Since the mixer has only four stereo sends, then four stereo returns should be sufficient; however, as you may have noticed, the returns allow you to control only the volume of the effect returning to the mixer. What if you wished to apply EQ to the effect's return? Or even more creatively, what if you wished to send the return of one effect to another effect—e.g., send a reverb's return to a chorus?

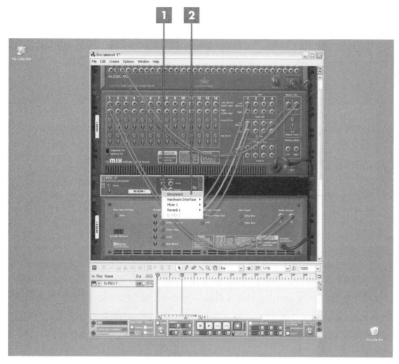

There is a way to do this.

1 Right-click on the Left Output of the RV-7. The connections pop-up menu will appear.

2 Click on Disconnect. The RV-7's output will be disconnected from Return 1.

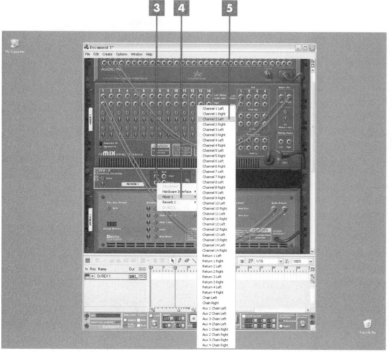

3 Again, right-click on the Left Output of RV-7. The connections menu will appear.

4 Click on Mixer 1. The mixer's connection menu will appear.

5 Click on Channel 2 Left. The RV-7's outputs will be connected to Channel 2 on the mixer.

WHY SELECT THE LEFT INPUT?

When connecting the output of the RV-7 to a channel on the mixer, it is important that you select the left input, not the right. If you choose left, both the RV-7's left and right outputs will be connected to the mixer's channels.

CONNECTING THE CORRECT OUTPUTS

In this exercise you could connect the outputs of the RV-7 to any channel other than Channel 1 (the SubTractor is already connected to Channel 1). You should check which channels are available prior to routing the outputs of any effect device to the mixer; if you choose a channel that is already occupied by another device, that device will automatically be removed from the mixer.

Chaining Effects

Another innovative way to work with effects is to create an effect chain. A *chain* is simply more than one effect connected in serial fashion. Chaining gives you a resourceful palette for creating your own unique effects or adding more character to existing effects.

Chaining Effects with Inserts

First, create an empty rack.

Once you have your empty rack in front of you, begin by adding a mixer.

1 Click on the Create menu. The Create menu will appear.

2 Click on Mixer 14:2. The mixer will be loaded into the rack.

Next you need a device as a sound source; this time load the Malström.

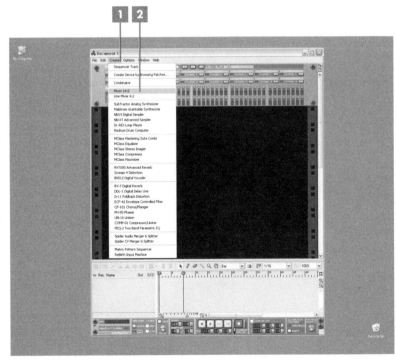

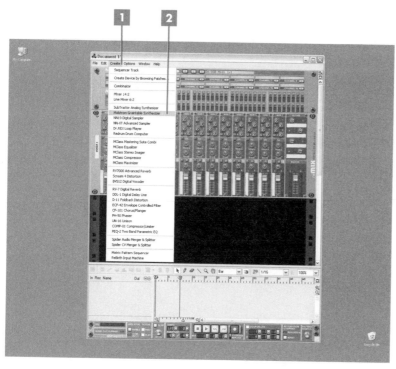

1 Click on the Create menu. The Create menu will appear.

2 Click on Malström Graintable Synthesizer. The Malström will be loaded into the rack.

Before adding any more devices, disconnect the Malström's default audio routing, which has the device's output connected to Channel 1 of the mixer.

Now you will load the first effect that will be used in your effect chain.

❄ VIEW THE BACK OF THE RACK

For the following exercise it is best to leave the rack view in the rear mode as you add the subsequent devices and rearrange the routing. Press the Tab key or choose Toggle Rack Front/Rear from the Options pull-down menu.

1. Click on the Create menu. The Create menu will appear.

2. Click on RV-7 Digital Reverb. The RV-7 will be loaded into the rack.

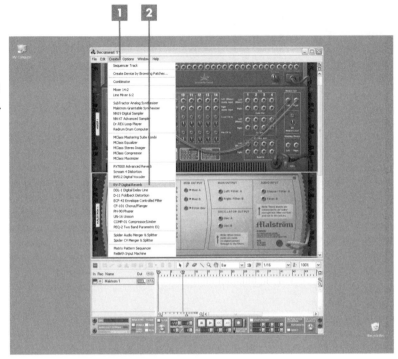

By default, the RV-7 will be placed under the Malström. The outputs of the Malström will be routed to the inputs of the RV-7, and the RV-7's outputs will be routed to Channel 1 of the mixer.

 CONNECTING THE RV-7

If the RV-7 did not load directly beneath the Malström, connected to the Malström's outputs, the Malström was not the selected device when you loaded the RV-7 into the rack. Remove the RV-7 and select the Malström before re-loading the RV-7.

Now you will add the second device to the effect chain.

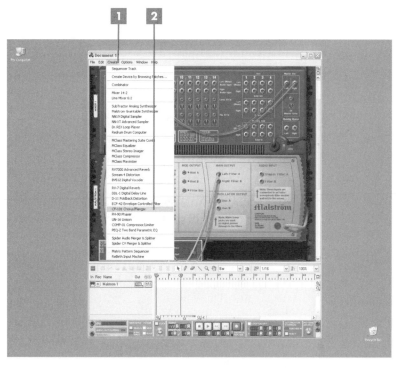

1 Click on the Create menu. The Create menu will appear.

2 Click on CF-101 Chorus/ Flanger. The CF-101 will be loaded into the rack.

By default, the output of the RV-7 is connected to the input of the CF-101, and the CF-101's outputs are connected to Channel 1 of the mixer. This is a simple example of an effect chain (in this case two effects are in the chain—the RV-7 and the CF-101). When playing the Malström, you will hear it processed through these two effects.

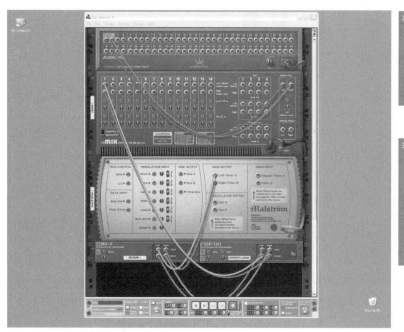

❋ **EXPANDING THE CHAIN**

To expand the chain with more effects, repeat the above exercise and choose another desired effect from the Create menu. The effect will be added to the chain.

❋ **ADDING MORE DEVICES TO THE CHAIN**

Remember, for any effect to be added to the chain you must first select the last effect device in the chain prior to adding the new effect. This will force Reason to load the effect into the chain by default.

Chain Effects as a Send

You can also create an effect chain that can be used in Send mode. The only major difference is the source of the audio. In the Insert mode exercise, the source was supplied directly by the instrument device (Malström). An effect chain that used as a send will use the Aux send of the mixer.

Once again, start with an empty rack before following these steps.

1 Click on the Create menu. The Create menu will appear.

2 Click on Mixer 14:2. The mixer will be loaded into the rack.

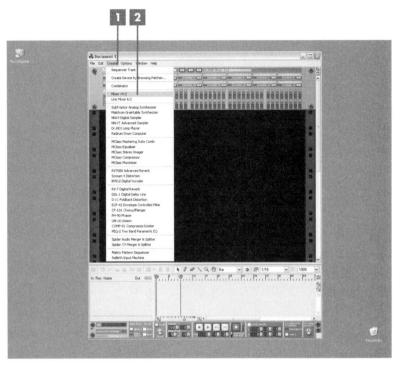

3 Click on the Create menu. The Create menu will appear.

4 Click on RV-7 Digital Reverb. The RV-7 will be loaded into the rack.

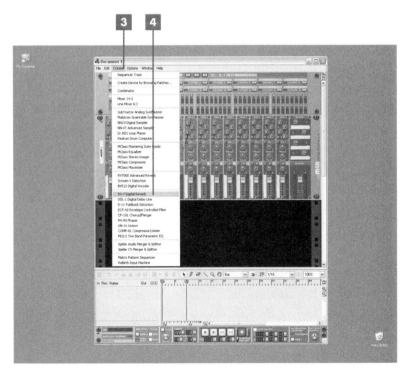

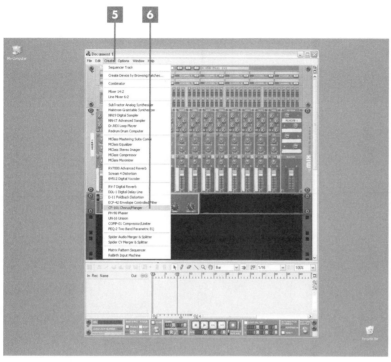

5 Click on the Create menu. The Create menu will appear.

6 Click on CF-101 Chorus/ Flanger. The CF-101 will appear in the rack.

7 Press the Tab key. The rack will turn to the rear view.

By default, the RV-7's left channel is connected to the left channel of Send 1 on the mixer, and the left channel of the CF-101 is connected to the left channel of Send 2. You need to disconnect the CF-101 from the mixer's send before you can add it to a chain.

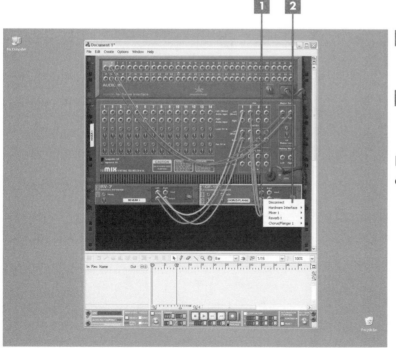

1 Right-click on the Left Output of the CF-101. The connections menu will appear.

2 Click on Disconnect. The CF-101 will be disconnected from the mixer.

Now set up a chain with the two effects devices.

1 Right-click on the Left Output of the RV-7. The connections menu will appear.

2 Click on Disconnect. The RV-7 will be disconnected from the mixer's return.

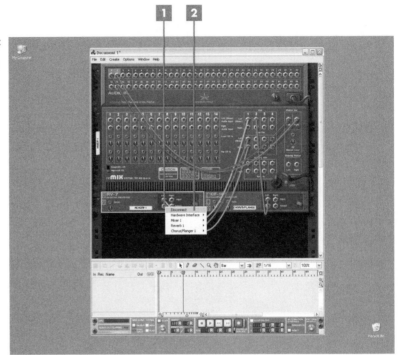

3 Again, click on the Left Output of the RV-7. The connections menu will appear.

4 Click on Chorus/Flanger 1. The CF-101 connection's menu will appear.

5 Click on Left. The left and right outputs of the RV-7 will be connected to the left inputs of CF-101.

Next change the return routing so that the effects will return to Return 1.

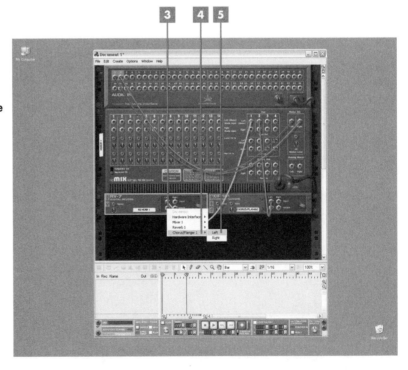

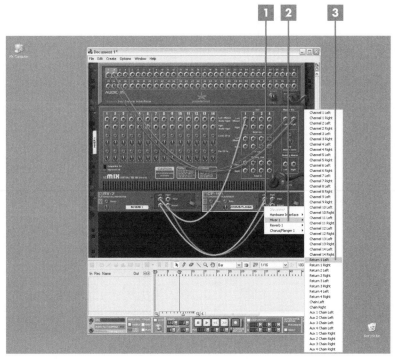

1 Right-click on the Left Output of the CF-101. The connections menu will appear.

2 Click on Mixer 1. The mixer connections menu will appear.

3 Click on Return 1 Left. The left and right channels will be connected to the left channel of Return 1.

Chaining Mixer Sends

There may be some situations in which the 14 channels on the mixer are not enough, so you may need to load two mixers. One issue you will come across when working with more than one mixer is managing the sends. For example, if you have a SubTractor connected to a channel of your first mixer, and a Dr:rex Loop Player connected to a channel on the second mixer, and you want to send both devices to the same effect (connected as a send), how would you do it?

In Reason, the mixers can be linked together; when you do this, the auxiliary sends are also linked. Therefore, connecting an effect device to Send 1 on one mixer would also connect the effect to the Send 1 of the second mixer.

Automatic Linking

To set up the link between mixers automatically:

1 Click on the Create menu. The Create menu will appear.

2 Click on Mixer 14:2. The mixer will appear in the rack.

Now add the second mixer.

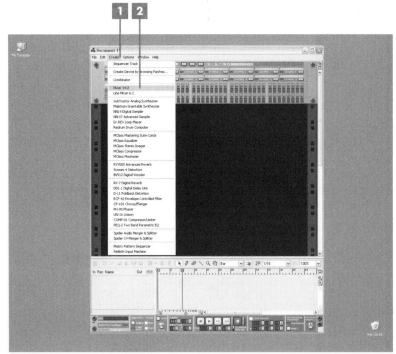

1 Click on the Create menu. The Create menu will appear.

2 Click on Mixer 14:2. The second mixer will appear.

3 Press Tab. The rack will turn to the rear view.

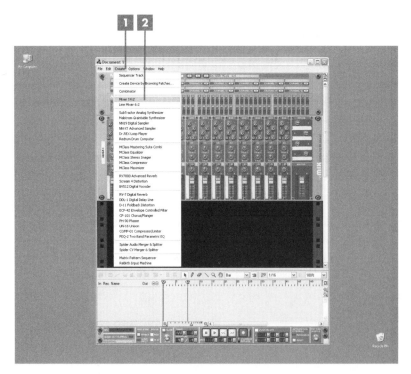

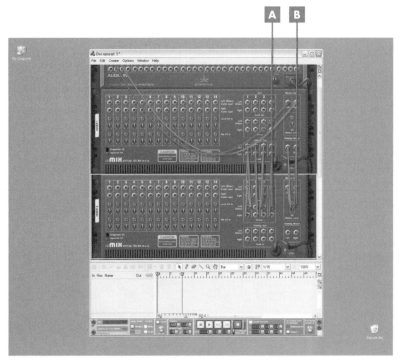

A All the stereo sends of the second mixer are connected to the Chaining Aux inputs of the first mixer. Any audio sent to the Aux Sends of mixer 2 will also feed the Aux Sends of mixer 1.

B The Master Section. The Master Output of the second mixer will be connected to the Chaining Master of the first mixer. This will allow the first mixer to control the master volume of the second mixer.

MASTER VOLUME CONTROL WITH TWO MIXERS

By connecting a second mixer(or more) to the Chaining Master of the main mixer, it will act as the Overall Master Mixer controlling the overall volume of all other connected mixers. However, the master volume fader on each of the other mixers will still control the master level for the devices connected to it.

MIXER POSITION

When adding a second mixer to the rack, the position of the mixer is irrelevant to the default routing. By default, automatic linking of mixers will take place whenever more than one mixer is added to the rack.

Manual Chaining

In most cases the automatic chaining of multiple mixers will be sufficient; however, there may be situations in which you want the second mixer's sends to connect to effects other than the ones connected to the first mixer.

Before you can reconnect the sends of mixer 2, you need to disconnect the automatic routing.

1 Right-click on the Left Chaining Aux 1 of Mixer 1. The connections menu will appear.

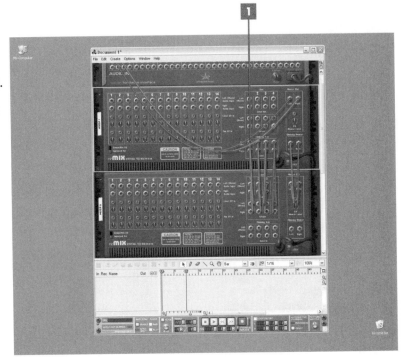

2 Click on Disconnect. The connection to the second mixer's Aux Send will be disconnected.

Now Mixer 2's Aux Sends are free to be connected to an effect device.

❋ CHAINING AUX CONNECTIONS

The above exercise demonstrates how to disconnect the automatic routing of Chaining Aux 1. Perform a similar operation to disconnect the routing from any of the other Chaining Aux connections.

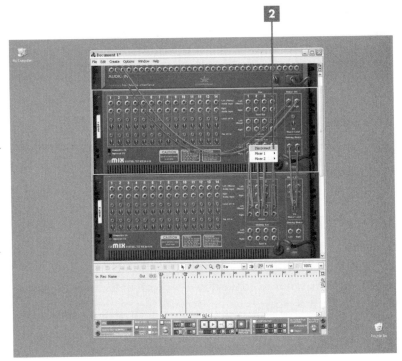

Splitting and Merging Effect Sends with the Spider

The Spider Merger/Splitter can be used creatively in the routing of effects. The following exercises show you how to use the Spider to add more than one effect to a mixer's send. Start with an empty rack and add a mixer to it.

✲ MERGING IS DIFFERENT THAN SENDING

Using the merge to send audio to more than one effect is not the same as using a chain effect as described earlier, since merged audio does not travel through one effect device to reach the next effect device. When using the Spider to split the send, each effect device's input is independent from the other's input.

First, load the Spider.

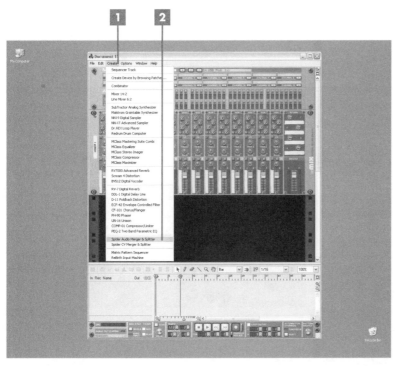

1 Click on the Create menu. The Create menu will appear.

2 Click on Spider Audio Merger & Splitter. The Spider will be loaded into the rack.

Next, add the effects.

1 Click on the Create menu. The Create menu will appear.

2 Click on PH-90 Phaser. The PH-90 will be loaded into the rack.

3 Press Tab. The rack will turn to the rear view.

By default, the PH-90 will be connected to the mixer's send and returns; before continuing you need to disconnect the default connections between the PH-90 Phaser and the mixer.

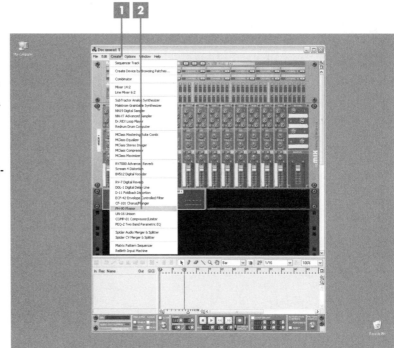

1 Right-click on the mixer's Left Aux Output 1. The connections menu will appear.

2 Click on Disconnect. The Aux connection to the PH-90 will be disconnected.

You will also need to disconnect the PH-90 from the mixer's returns.

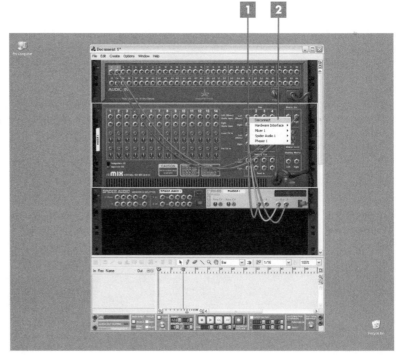

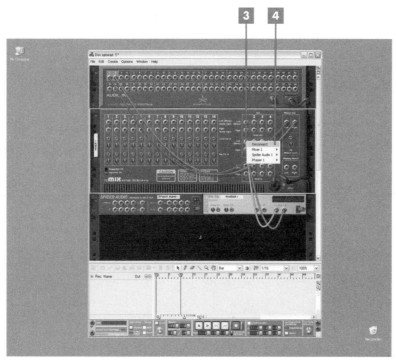

3 Right-click on the mixer's Left channel of Return 1. The connections menu will appear.

4 Click on Disconnect. The PH-90 will be disconnected from the mixer's returns.

Next you'll load the second effect device.

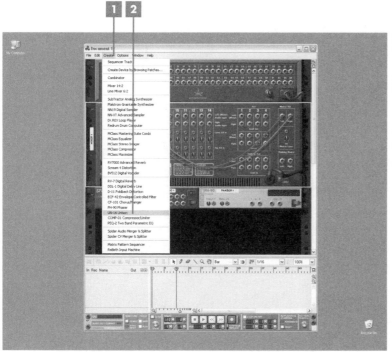

1 Click on the Create menu. The Create menu will appear.

2 Click on UN-16 Unison. The UN-16 will be loaded into the rack.

Again, the UN-16 will connect to the mixer's sends by default. You will need to disconnect this.

1. Right-click on the mixer's Left Aux Output 1. The connections menu will appear.

2. Click on Disconnect. The Aux connection to the UN-16 will be disconnected.

Now disconnect the UN-16's connection to the mixer's returns.

1. Right-click on the mixer's Left channel of Return 1. The connections menu will appear.

2. Click on Disconnect. The UN-16 will be disconnected from the mixer's returns.

Now you can connect the mixer's sends to the Spider.

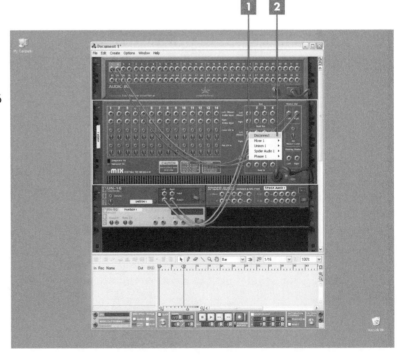

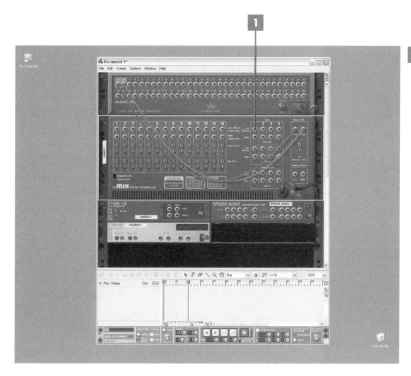

1 Right-click on the Left channel of Send 1 on the mixer. The connections menu will appear.

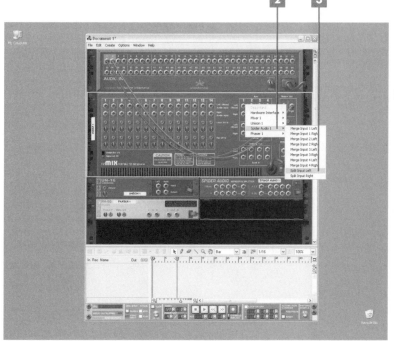

2 Click on Spider Audio 1. The Spider's connections menu will appear.

3 Click on Split Input Left. Both the left and right sends will be connected to the Spider's splitter section.

Now you need to connect the Spider's merger output to the mixer's returns.

1 Right-click **on the** Spider's Merger Left Output. **The connections menu will appear.**

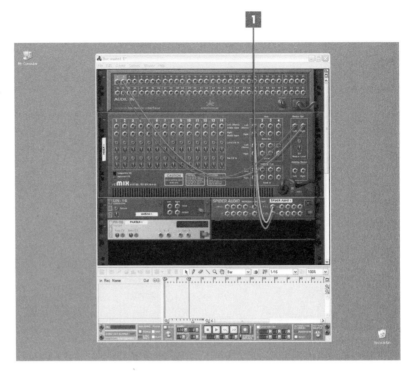

2 Click **on** Mixer 1. **The mixer's connections menu will appear.**

3 Click **on** Return 1 Left. **The Spider's left output will be connected to the left channel of Return 1.**

Now connect the right channel.

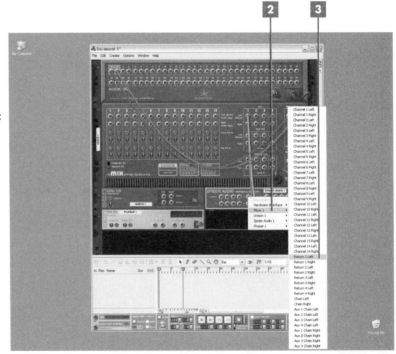

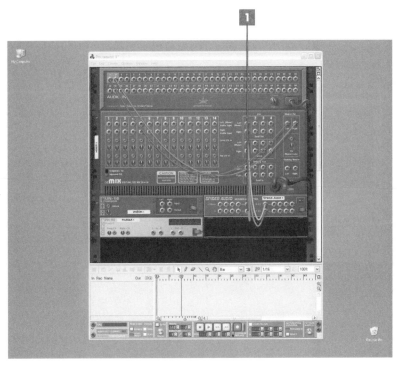

1 Right-click **on the** Spider's Merger Right Output. **The connections menu will appear.**

2 Click **on** Mixer 1. **The mixer's connections menu will appear.**

3 Click **on** Return 1 Right. **The Spider's right output will be connected to the right channel of Return 1.**

Next you will connect the Spider's split outputs to the effect device's inputs.

1 Right-click **on the** first Split Output Left. **The connections menu will appear.**

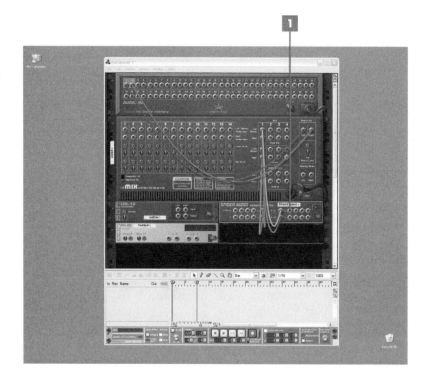

2 Click **on** Unison 1. **The Unison's connection menu will appear.**

3 Click **on** Left. **The Spider's first splitter output will be connected to the Unison.**

Both right and left channels will be connected to the Unison. Now connect the second splitter output to the PH-90

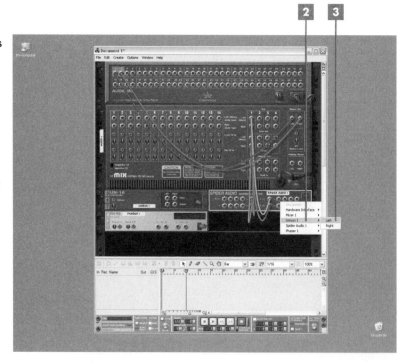

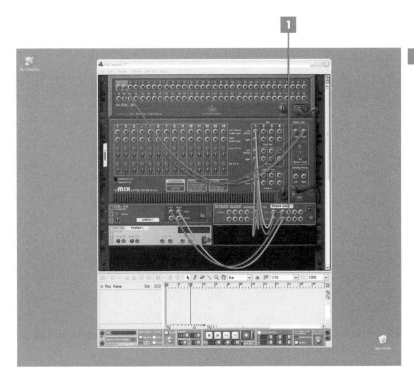

1 Right-click **on the** second Split Output Left. **The connections menu will appear.**

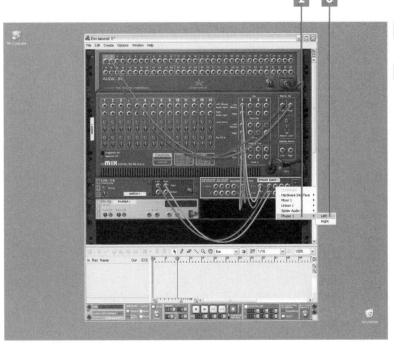

2 Click **on** Phaser 1. **The Phaser connections menu will appear.**

3 Click **on** Left. **The second split output will be connected to the PH-90.**

Both right and left channels will be connected to the Phaser. Now you need to return both effects to a single stereo return on the mixer.

1 Right-click on the Left Output of the UN-16. The connections menu will appear.

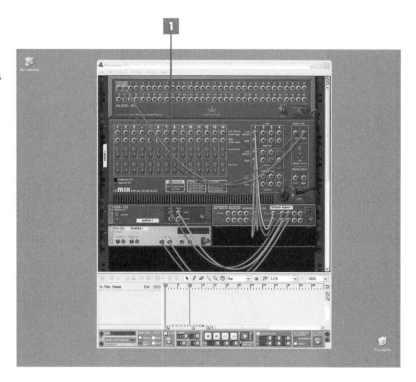

2 Click on Spider Audio 1. The Spider's connection menu will appear.

3 Click on Merge Input 1 Left. The left and right output of the UN-16 will be connected to the left channel of the Spider's Merger Input 1.

Connect the PH-90 to the Spider Merger.

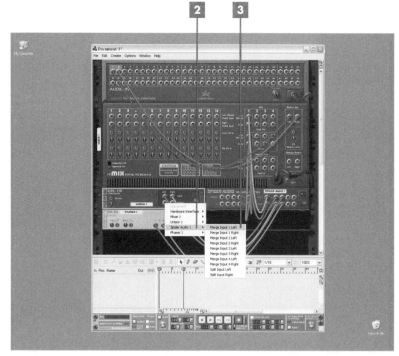

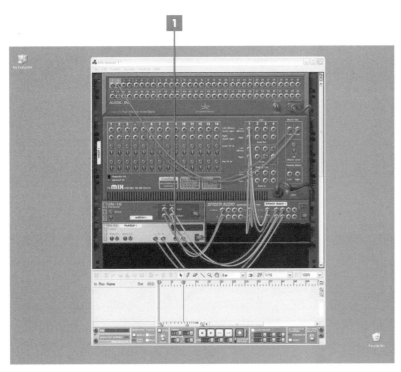

1 Right-click on the Left Output of the PH-90. The connections menu will appear.

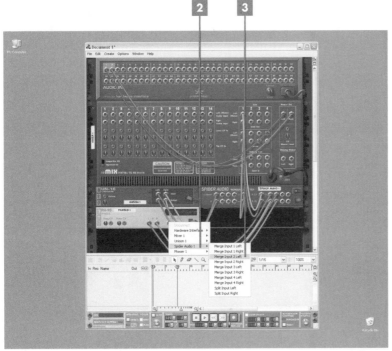

2 Click on Spider Audio 1. The Spider's connection menu will appear.

3 Click on Merge Input 2 Left. The left and right output of the PH-90 will be connected to the left channel of the Spider's Merger Input 2.

4 Press Tab. The rack will switch to the front view.

245
❊ ❊ ❊

5 Turn up the Aux Send on Channel 1 about halfway.

Now load a SubTractor and connect it to this effect send that you just created.

✹ MULTIPLE SPIDERS

Although the Spider can split and merge up to only four inputs and outputs, you can easily add another Spider to the rack to expand the number of inputs and outputs by chaining them together.

1 Click on either the right or left side of the mixer to select the device.

2 Click on the Create menu. The Create menu will appear.

3 Click on SubTractor Analog Synthesizer. The SubTractor will be loaded into the rack.

4 Play your MIDI controller. The default SubTractor patch will have a spacey effect to it.

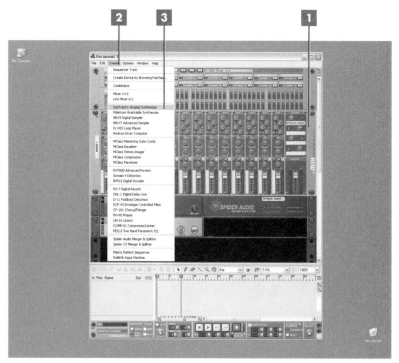

✹ ✹ ✹

9

External Control
of Reason

After looking at all the knobs, sliders, and faders of Reason's devices, you may be wondering if there is an easier way to control them, since it can be difficult to achieve precise control using a mouse. That's where external controllers come in. Reason offers MIDI control support, which allows you to use your MIDI controller to do more than just play notes—you can also use it to control some of those knobs, faders, and sliders. In addition, Reason's transport controls can be controlled from an external device (or even from another computer). In this chapter, you'll learn how to

❋ Enable remote control.

❋ Assign MIDI commands to control device parameters.

❋ Control Reason's transport from your MIDI controller.

❋ Synchronize Reason to another computer.

Enabling Remote Control

Remote control allows you to use your MIDI controller to control a device's parameters. Many MIDI controllers have been developed and marketed—most of them come equipped with various knobs and sliders designed for just such a task.

A Bit of MIDI Protocol Background

Before you venture into the land of remote control, there are a few basics you should know. Reason's remote control feature uses the MIDI protocol as its base of communication. Your MIDI controller sends various MIDI commands from all of its controls to Reason. Reason then receives and acts on those commands. The simplest example of this is triggering the sound modules from the keys on your MIDI controller. Some of these commands can be used for other things as well, such as controlling the parameters of a device or driving Reason's transport controls. As you discovered in Chapter 2, "Fast Start," when setting up control surfaces and keyboard preferences, Reason allows you to choose from a large variety of manufacturers and models of MIDI input devices. When you select a MIDI device, Reason assumes that certain commands can be received from it (e.g., from a keyboard, note information from the keys; pitch information from the pitch wheel, and so on). However, you need to tell Reason how to interpret these other kinds of MIDI commands.

 FIND OUT MORE ABOUT YOUR CONTROLLER

To learn more about the supported features of your MIDI controller, please consult your controller's documentation.

Mapping the Controls—Teaching Reason

Now you're ready to teach a device's parameter which MIDI controller commands to respond to. Since I don't know what controller you're working with or the type of controls you have available, for this example I will use the keys on a keyboard to control the Enable/Disable button of the EQ section on the RV7000 Advanced Reverb.

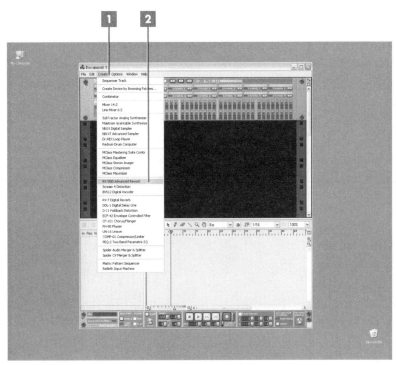

To learn how to remotely control the EQ of the RV7000, you'll need to load the device.

1 Click on the Create menu. The Create menu will appear.

2 Click on RV7000 Advanced Reverb. The RV7000 will appear in the rack.

Next you will map a key from your MIDI controller to turn on/off the RV7000's EQ.

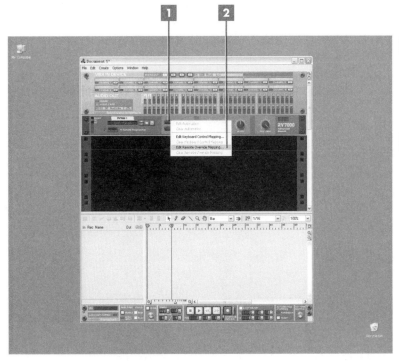

1 Right-click (Control-click for Mac users) on the EQ Enable button. The parameters pop-up menu will appear.

2 Click on Edit Remote Override Mapping. The Edit Remote Override Mapping window will appear.

3 Click **on the** Control Surface **drop-down menu and** select your keyboard.

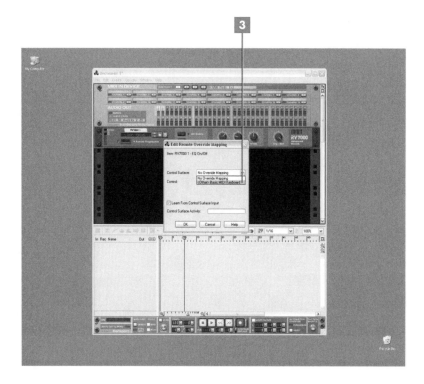

4 Click **on the** Control **drop-down menu and** select Keyboard.

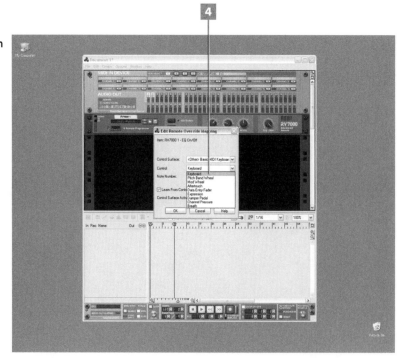

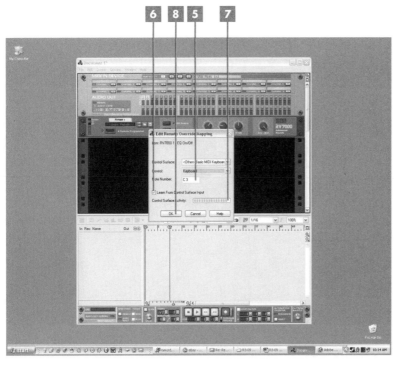

5 Enter C3 in the Note Number box.

6 Click the check box next to Learn From Control Surface Input.

7 Play the same C3 key from your MIDI controller. The EQ on the RV7000 will enable. Press it again, and the EQ will disable.

8 Click OK to accept these selections.

MIDI DEVICES WITH MORE CONTROL FEATURES

Here you used the keys of your MIDI controller to control only the on/off of the RV7000's EQ. Some MIDI controllers are equipped with controller knobs and/or faders that are perfect for controlling a Reason device's rotary knobs or faders.

ONE PARAMETER PER CONTROLLER KNOB OR KEY

Each key or controller knob on your MIDI controller can be mapped to only one parameter at a time. If you try to map the same key to a parameter twice, the first map will be overwritten.

Controlling the Transport

Next you'll learn how to use your MIDI controller to control Reason's transport. Unlike the reverb example above, you cannot simply right-click on the transport buttons to teach Reason which commands will control them; you must first put the remote control into Edit Mode.

1 Click on the Options menu. The Options menu will appear.

2 Click on Remote Override Edit Mode.

Once the remote is in Edit Mode, little blue arrows appear pointing to every parameter that can be controlled remotely.

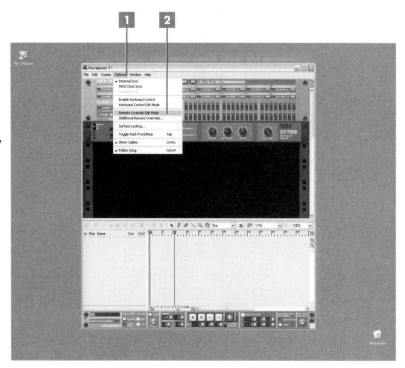

3 Click anywhere on the Transport Bar. It becomes highlighted in blue.

4 Right-click on the Play button. Choose Edit Remote Override Mapping from the menu. The Edit Remote Override Mapping window opens.

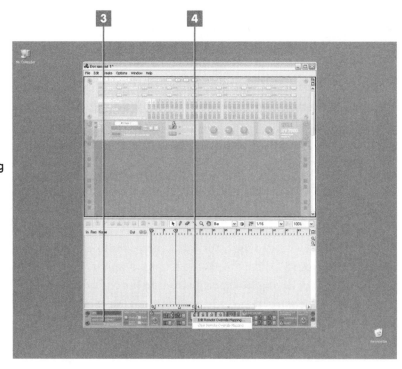

5

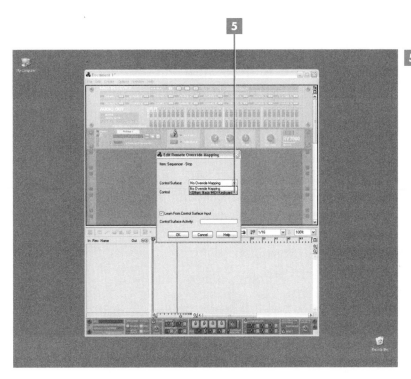

5 Click **in the** Control Surface **drop-down menu and** choose your keyboard.

6

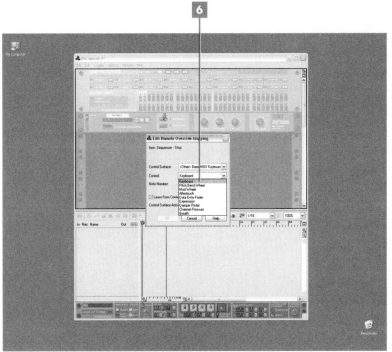

6 Click **in the** Control **drop-down menu and choose** Keyboard.

7 Enter D3 in the Note Number box.

8 Click the check box next to Learn From Control Surface Input.

9 Play the D3 key from your MIDI controller.

10 Click OK to accept these selections.

11 Play the D3 key from your MIDI controller. The song will begin playback.

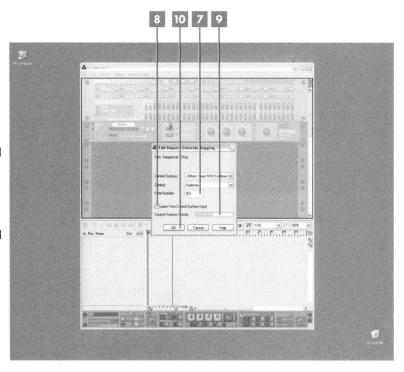

❄ GETTING OUT OF EDITING OVERRIDE MODE

To take Reason out of Edit Remote Override Mapping, go to the Options Menu and select Remote Override Edit Mode. (The check next to it will be removed and you will be back in Normal Mode).

❄ REMOTE CONTROL INDICATION

When a function has a remote control function enabled it will be indicated by a lightening bolt icon.

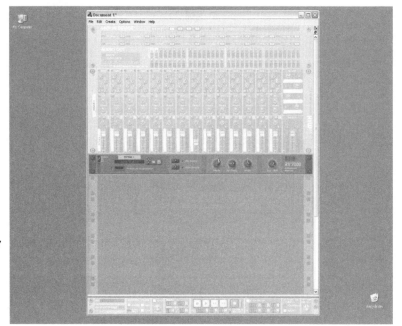

Synchronizing Reason to Another Computer

Another way Reason can be controlled externally is to have another computer tell Reason when to start and when to stop, otherwise known as *external synchronizing*. Why might you want to do this? Many people dedicate one computer for Reason and use a different computer to run their other music and recording software—such as Cubase SX or SONAR—for reasons of CPU efficiency, so that each application has all the computer resources it needs to run well. In these cases, it is possible to have the Cubase or SONAR computer control Reason on the second computer. Some users also work with video, and it's possible to have video equipment control the playback of Reason. In the next example, you'll learn how to set up Reason to slave to another computer.

Again, first walk through the steps to set up things properly.

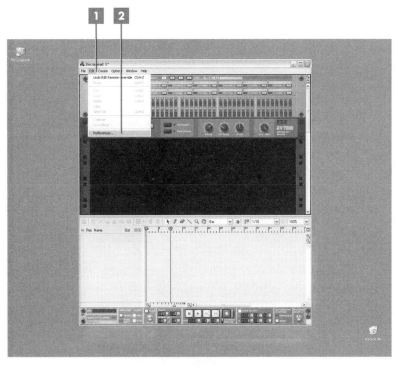

1 Click on the Edit menu. The Edit menu will appear.

2 Click on Preferences. The Preferences window will appear.

3 Click on the Page menu.
   The Page menu will appear.

4 Click on Advanced MIDI.
   The Advanced MIDI page
   will appear.

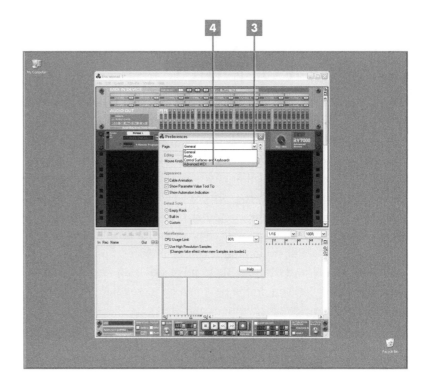

5 Click on the MIDI Clock Sync
   menu.

6 Select the MIDI interface
   that is connected to an
   external computer. Close the
   Preferences window.

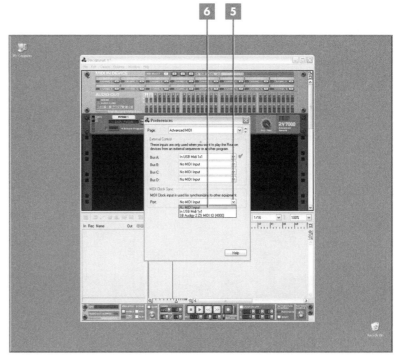

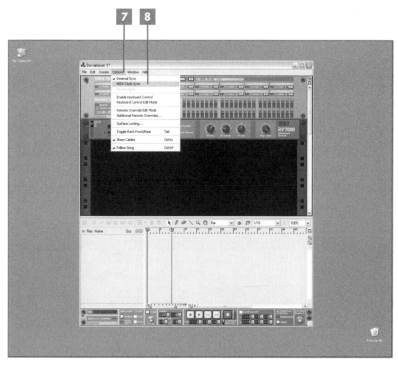

7 Click on the Options menu. The Options menu will appear.

8 Click on MIDI Clock Sync. Reason will now be set to start playing when an external computer tells it to.

❄ THE TRANSPORT WILL NOT FUNCTION

After setting Reason to follow synchronization from an external device, the transport panel will no longer be functional. You will need to start and stop the song from the external machine.

❄ CONTROLLING REASON FROM ANOTHER COMPUTER

If you decide to slave Reason to another computer, please consult the documentation of the application that will be used as the master for external synchronization.

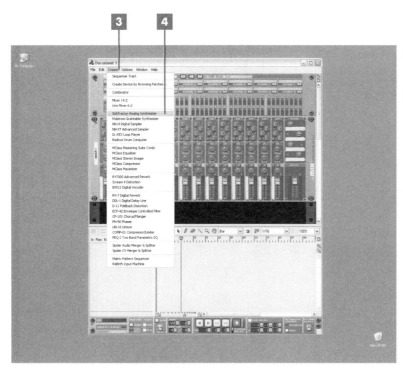

3 Click on the Create menu. The Create menu will appear.

4 Click on SubTractor Analog Synthesizer. The SubTractor will be loaded into the rack.

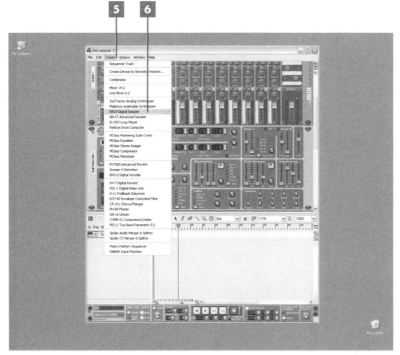

5 Click on the Create menu. The Create menu will appear.

6 Click on the NN19 Digital Sampler. The NN19 will be loaded into the rack.

Using CV to Create a Tremolo

Next, you need to load a patch into the NN19. You will create a tremolo in an NN19's Organ patch; however, you will not use any of the parameters on the NN19 to do so. You'll use the SubTractor's LFO1 section instead.

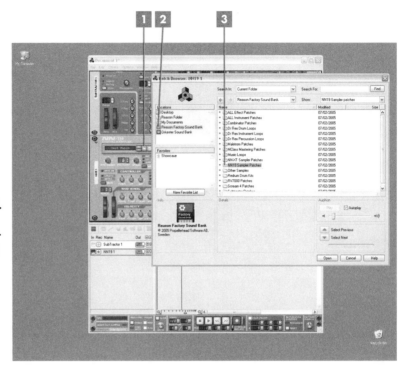

1 Click on the Browse Patch icon. The Patch Browser window will appear.

2 Click on the Reason Factory Sound Bank in the Locations window

3 Double-click on the NN-19 Sampler Patches folder.

4 Navigate to the folder called Organ.

5 Click on the patch ORGAN1. smp. The file will become highlighted.

6 Click OK. The Organ patch will be loaded into the NN19.

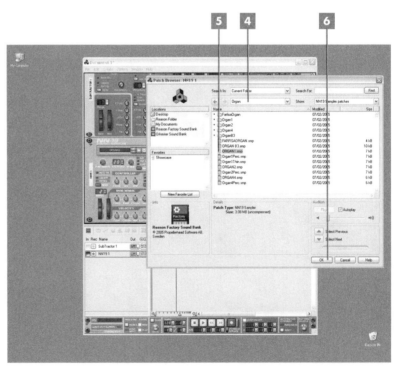

Play a few notes from your MIDI controller to familiarize yourself with the sound of the Organ patch.

Next, you'll make the connections that allow the SubTractor's LFO to control the NN19's volume.

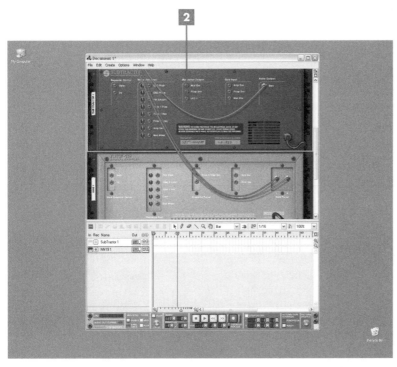

1. Press the Tab key. The rack will flip around to the rear view.

2. Right-click on the LFO1 Output of the SubTractor. The Connections menu will appear.

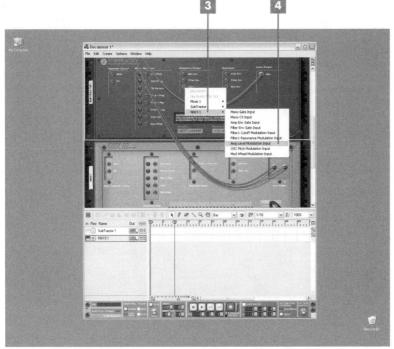

3. Click on NN19 1. The NN19's Connections menu will appear.

4. Click on Amp Level Modulation Input. A cable connecting SubTractor's LFO Output to the NN19 Level Modulation will appear.

5. Play your MIDI controller. The organ will now have a slight tremolo effect applied to it.

The tremolo effect is being created by the LFO1 on the SubTractor; therefore, to tweak the effect you need to adjust SubTractor's LFO 1 parameters.

263
❊ ❊ ❊

SUBTRACTOR LFO EFFECT ON THE NN-19

To control the amount of LFO sent to the NN19 you must use the Input Trim knob located next to the Level Input on the rear panel on the NN19 (not the LFO Amount knob).

Tremolo Reverb

Next I'll dig a little deeper into my Reason bag of tricks to demonstrate some of the more creative ways to combine the CV controls with effects. You will use the LFO section of the SubTractor to apply a tremolo to a reverb.

Begin by loading the RV-7 reverb device.

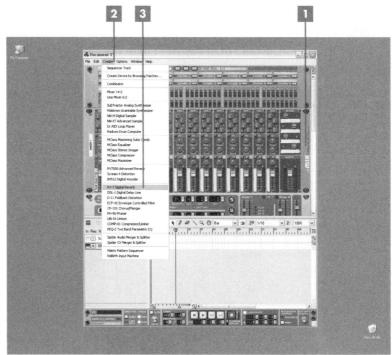

1 Click on either the left or right side of the mixer. The mixer will be selected.

SELECT THE MIXER FIRST

Selecting the mixer before loading the RV-7 is an important step in making certain that the RV-7 will be connected to the mixer by default.

2 Click on the Create menu. The Create menu will appear.

3 Click on RV-7 Digital Reverb. The RV-7 will appear in the rack.

4 Press the Tab key. The rack will flip to the rear view.

Next you will slightly alter the automatic routing between the RV-7 and the mixer.

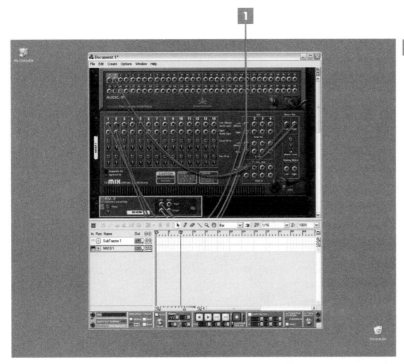

1 Right-click on the Left Return on the mixer. The Connections menu will appear.

2 Click on Disconnect. The mixer's returns will be disconnected from the RV-7.

3 Right-click on the RV-7's Left Output. **The Connections menu will appear.**

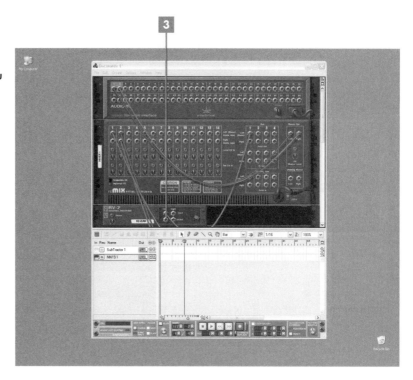

4 Click on Mixer 1. **The mixer's connections menu will appear.**

5 Click on Channel 3 Left. **Both left and right outputs of the RV-7 will be connected to Channel 3 on the menu.**

Next you connect the SubTractor's LFO to the Gate Input on Channel 3 of the mixer.

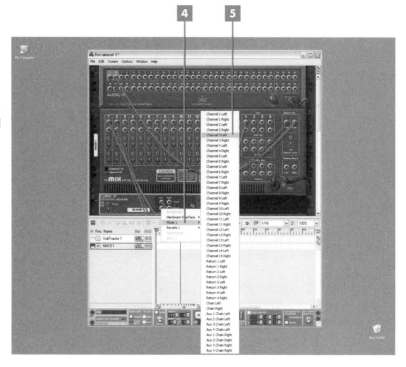

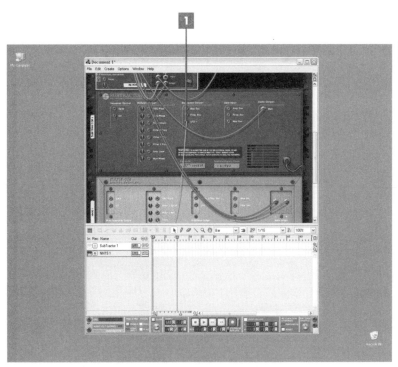

1 Right-click on the LFO 1 Modulation Output on the SubTractor. The connections menu will appear.

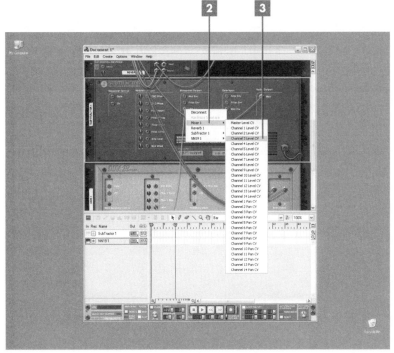

2 Click on Mixer 1. The mixer's connections menu will appear.

3 Click on Channel 3 Level CV. SubTractor's LFO will now be connected to the Level CV control on mixer Channel 3.

Now the LFO 1 on SubTractor will control the level of mixer Channel 3. And because the output of the reverb is connected to this channel, the level of the reverb will be affected.

Next you'll need to route the NN19's Organ patch to the reverb.

1. Press the Tab key. The rack will flip back to the front view.

2. Turn the AUX 1 Send knob on Channel 2 to the right. A value of about 50% will be enough to hear the effects.

3. Play a key on your MIDI controller and you will hear that the organ has a bit of reverb with a tremolo effect applied to it. The creative part of routing a reverb this way is that the LFO will affect the reverb only and not the Organ patch itself.

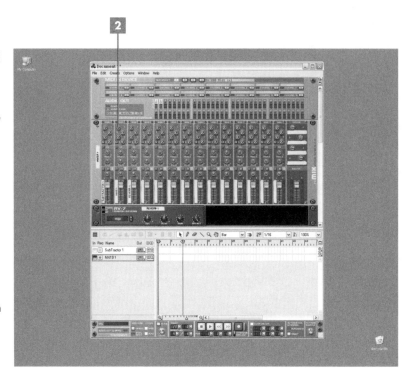

Controlling Effect Parameters

Next, use a device's parameter to control an effect device. In the previous exercise you didn't actually make any CV connections to the RV-7 directly; the connections were made to the mixer channel to which the reverb was also connected. In the following exercises, you'll control some of the effect's parameters directly.

You will need to start with an empty rack. You will use the LFO of an NN19 to control the panning on a DDL-1 Digital Delay Line.

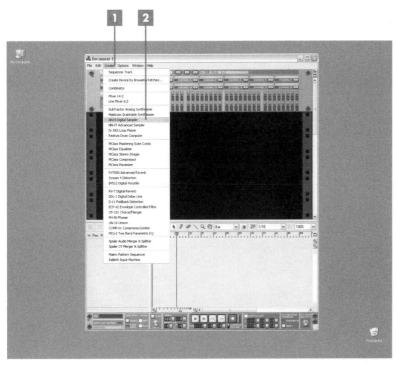

1 Click on the Create menu. The Create menu will appear.

2 Click on NN19 Digital Sampler. The NN19 will appear in the rack.

Next, load a Bright Piano patch into the NN19.

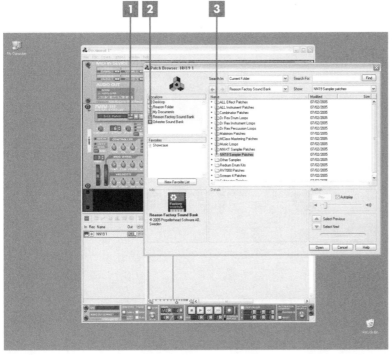

1 Click on the Browse Patch icon. The Patch Browser window will appear.

2 Click on Reason Factory Sound Bank in the Locations window.

3 Double-click on the NN19 Digital Sampler Patches folder.

4 Navigate to **the folder** Piano.

5 Click on the patch BRIGHTPIANO.smp. **The patch will become highlighted.**

6 Click OK. **The patch will be loaded into the NN19.**

Next add the digital delay device.

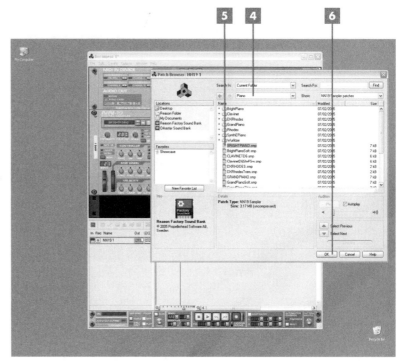

1 Click on the Create menu. **The Create menu will appear.**

2 Click on the DDL-1 Digital Delay Line. **The DDL-1 will be placed under the NN19 in the rack.**

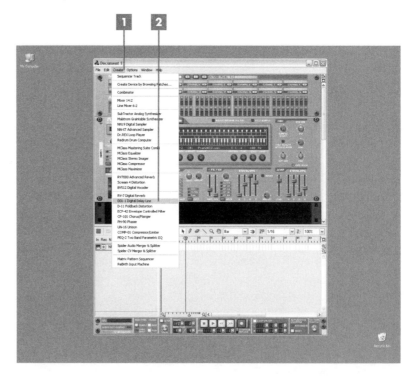

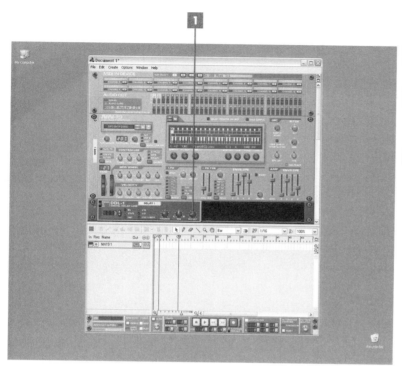

1 Turn the Dry/Wet knob to one quarter.

2 Play your MIDI controller to hear the delay being applied to the piano.

3 Press the Tab key to see the rear view of the rack.

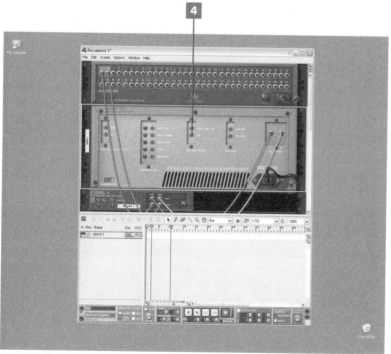

4 Right-click on the LFO Modulation Output on the NN19. The connections menu will appear.

❋ ❋ ❋

5 Click on Delay 1. The DDL-1's Connections menu will appear.

6 Click on Pan CV. The NN19's LFO output will be connected to the DDL-1's Pan CV control.

7 Play your MIDI controller. The piano's delay will automatically pan left and right.

Next, change the speed of the auto panning.

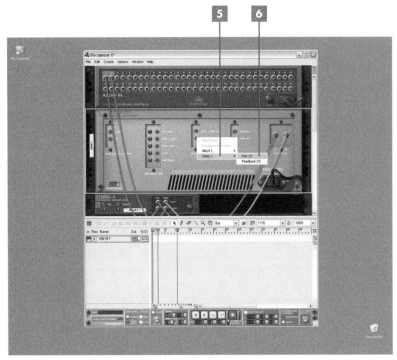

1 Turn the NN19's LFO Rate knob to the right. As you turn the Rate knob, play your MIDI controller. The speed of the pan will increase.

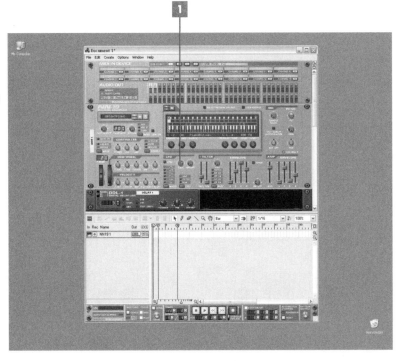

Expanding CV Routing with the Spider CV Merger & Splitter

In Chapter 8 you used the Spider Audio Merger & Splitter to perform some advanced audio routing. The Spider CV Merger & Splitter works exactly the same way, but with CV control instead of audio. In this section you will learn how to expand the CV-routing possibilities with the Spider to create some imaginative effects.

Routing Device Parameters to Several Devices

Perhaps one of the most obvious uses of the Spider CV is to split the CV control to several devices.

Starting with an empty rack, load the necessary devices. First up is the Spider.

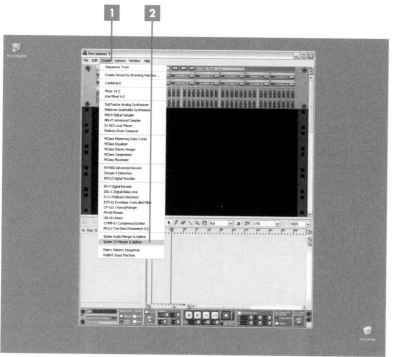

1 Click on the Create menu. The Create menu will appear.

2 Click on Spider CV Merger & Splitter. The Spider CV will be loaded.

Next load the SubTractor.

1 Click on the Create menu. The Create menu will appear.

2 Click on SubTractor Analog Synthesizer. The SubTractor will be loaded into the rack.

Now you will load two effect devices: the CF-101 Chorus/ Flanger and the PH-90 Phaser.

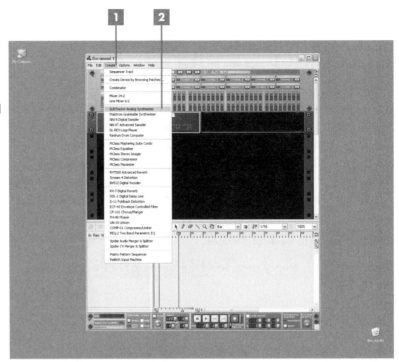

1 Click on the Create menu. The Create menu will appear.

2 Click on CF-101 Chorus/ Flanger. The CF-101 will appear in the rack.

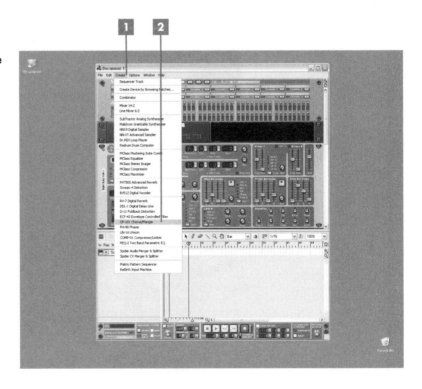

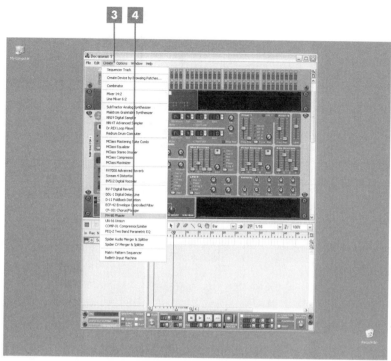

3 Click on the Create menu again. The Create menu will appear.

4 Click on PH-90 Phaser. The PH-90 will be loaded into the rack.

5 Press the Tab key. The rack will toggle to the rear view.

Next you need to make all the connections.

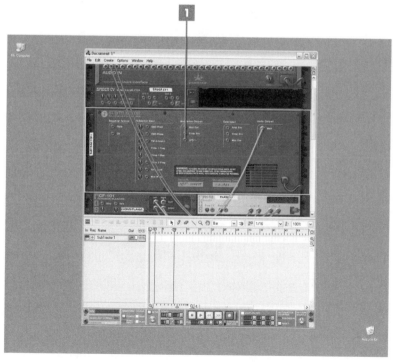

1 Right-click on the SubTractor's LFO 1 Output shown under the Modulation Output. The connections menu will appear.

2 Click on Spider CV 1. The Spider's connections menu will appear.

3 Click on Split A Input. The SubTractor's LFO will now be connected to the Spider's splitter input.

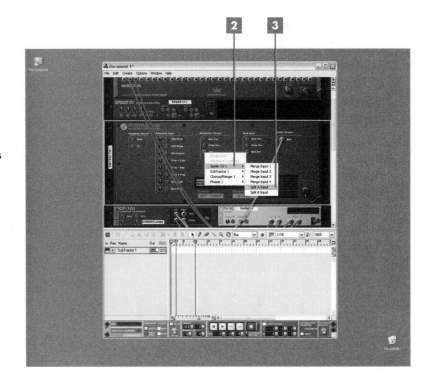

4 Right-click on the Spider's Split A Output 1. The connections menu will appear.

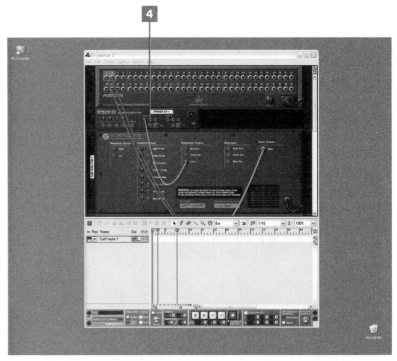

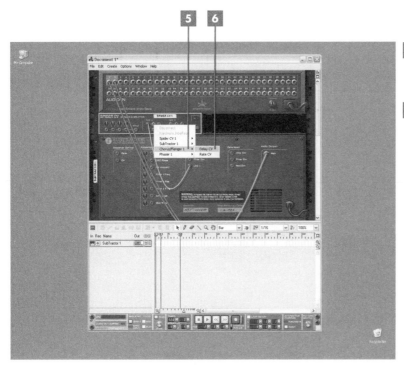

5 Click on Chorus/Flanger 1. The CF-101's connections menu will appear.

6 Click on Delay CV. The Spider's splitter Output 1 will be connected to the CF-101's Delay CV.

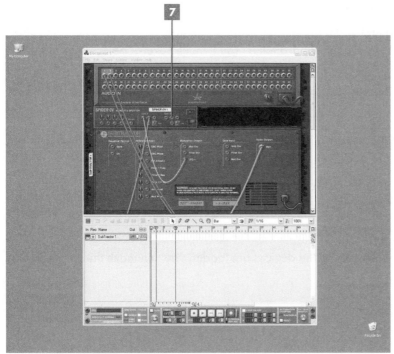

7 Right-click on the Spider's Split A Output 2. The Spider's connections menu will appear.

8 Click on Phaser 1. The PH-90's
   connections menu will appear.

9 Click on Freq CV. The Spider
   will now be connected to the
   PH-90's Frequency CV.

10 Play your MIDI controller. The
   SubTractor's LFO now controls
   both the CF-101's Delay
   parameter and the PH-90's
   Frequency parameter. The
   effects create a large sweeping
   sound in the SubTractor.

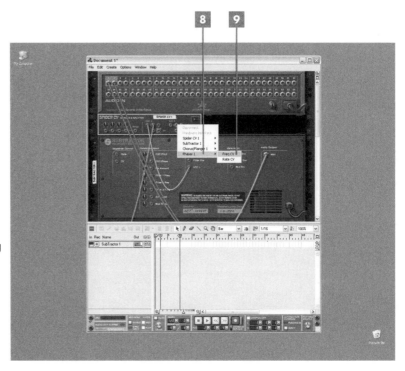

Merging CV to One Parameter

Next you'll use the Spider to let several device parameters control
just one other parameter. You'll make several devices control the
LFO of a CF-101.

Start this exercise with an empty rack. Using the Create menu, add
the following devices to the rack in the order in which they appear:

❋ **Mixer 14:2**

❋ **Spider CV Merger & Splitter**

❋ **SubTractor Analog Synthesizer**

❋ **Malström Graintable Synthesizer**

❋ **CF–101 Chorus/Flanger**

Now that all the devices are loaded you can make the connections.

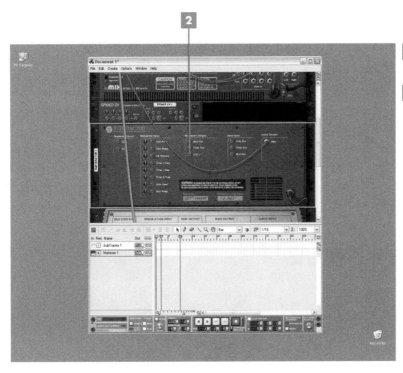

1 Press the Tab key to view the rear panel of the rack.

2 Right-click on SubTractor's LFO 1 Output. The connections menu will appear.

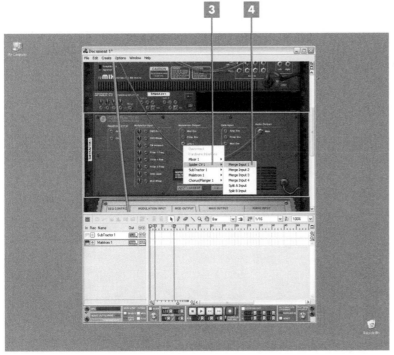

3 Click on Spider CV 1. The Spider's connections menu will appear.

4 Click on Merge Input 1. The LFO will be connected to the Spider.

279
❋❋❋

5 Right-click on Mod A Output from the Malström. The connections menu will appear.

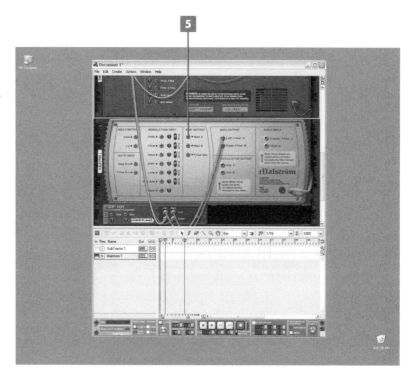

6 Click on Spider CV 1. The Spider's connections menu will appear.

7 Click on Merge Input 2. Mod A will be connected to Merge Input 2 on the Spider.

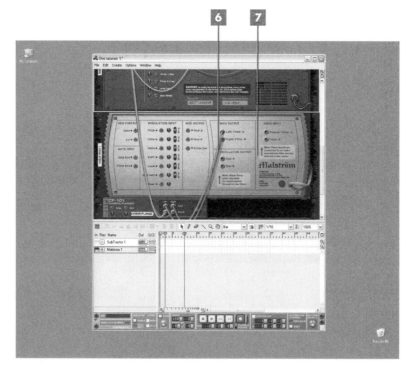

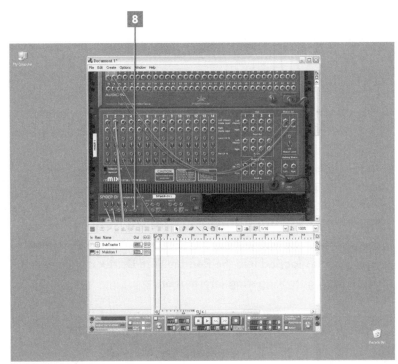

8 Right-click on Spider's Merge Output. The connections menu will appear.

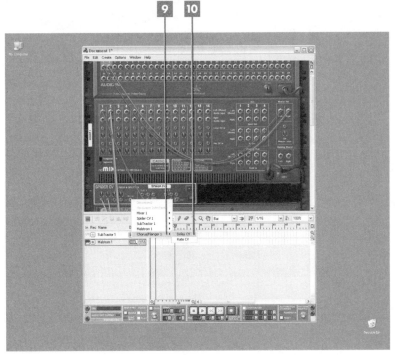

9 Click Chorus/Flanger 1. The CF-101's connections menu will appear.

10 Click on Delay CV. The Merge Output will be connected to the CF-101's Delay CV control.

11 Play your MIDI controller. The sound from the Malström is now choppy and swirling, much like the sound of a UFO in a low-budget Sci-Fi film.

This spacey effect is created by the LFO 1 on the SubTractor and the Mod A on the Malström altering the CF-101's Delay setting.

Triggering Notes with Gate Control

In Chapter 6, "Pattern Sequencing Devices," you learned about the Redrum Drum Computer, which allows you to build drum patterns by programming pads to trigger samples. The gate controls are also "triggering" devices. Any device with a gate output can be used to trigger notes on another device. When the level of the device reaches a certain point, it sends a trigger out the gate output.

Triggering Redrum Samples from Dr. Rex

In the next exercise you will use the gate output of the Dr:rex to trigger samples loaded into the Redrum. The Dr:rex device uses its slices to send gate-triggering information.

Again, starting with an empty rack, add the following devices in the order listed.

❋ **Mixer 14:2**

❋ **Dr:rex Loop Player**

❋ **Redrum Drum Computer**

Next you'll load a loop file into Dr:rex.

1 Click on the Browse Loop icon. The Browse Loop window will appear.

2 Click on Reason Factory Sound Bank in the Locations window.

3 Double-click on the folder Dr. Rex Drum Loops.

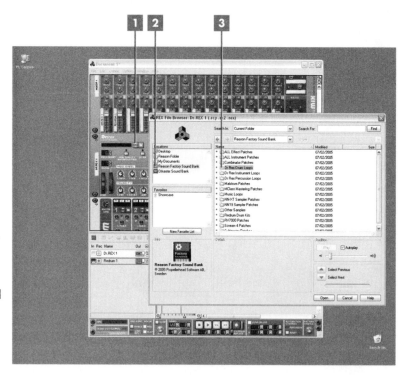

❋❋❋

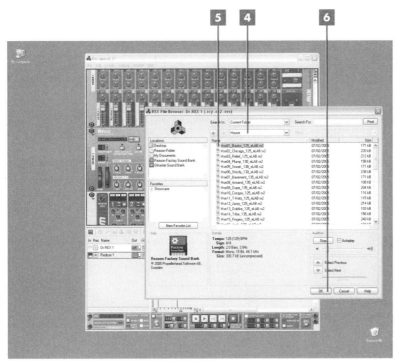

4 Navigate to the folder House.

5 Click on the loop Hse01_ Basics_125_eLAB.rx2. The file will become highlighted.

6 Click OK. The loop will be loaded into Dr:rex.

Next you'll load a drum kit into the Redrum.

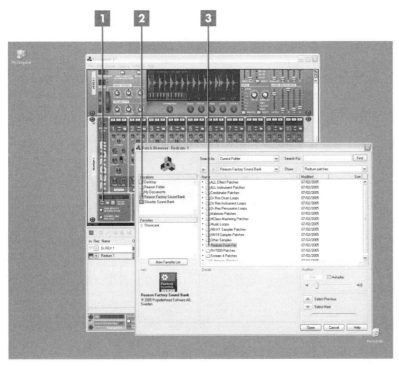

1 Click on the Browse Patch icon. The Patch Browser window will appear.

2 Click on Reason Factory Sound Bank in the Locations window

3 Double-click on the folder Redrum Drum Kits.

4 Navigate to **the folder** House Kits.

5 Click **on the kit** House Kit 01.drp. **The kit will become highlighted.**

6 Click OK. **The kit will be loaded into Redrum.**

Now make the connections so that the Dr:rex will trigger the kick drum on Channel 1 of the Redrum.

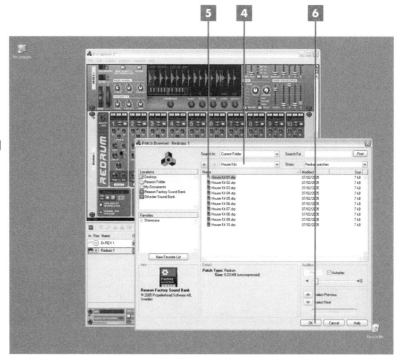

1 Press Tab. **The rear view of the rack will appear.**

2 Right-click **on the** gate output **of the Dr:rex device. The Connections menu will appear.**

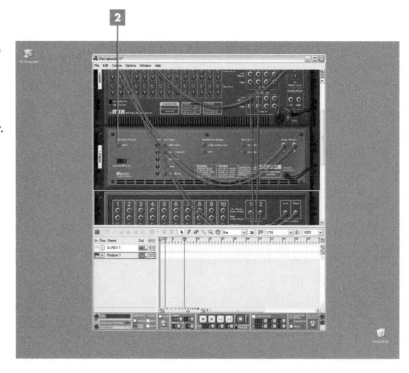

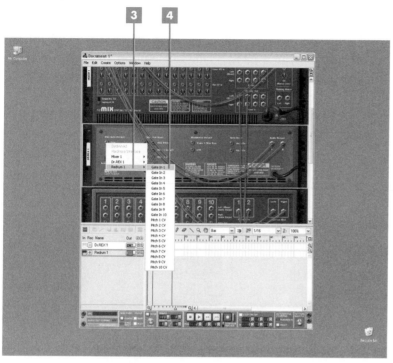

3 Click on Redrum 1. The Redrum's connections menu will appear.

4 Click on Gate In 1. The Dr:rex's gate output will be connected to the gate input on Channel 1 of the Redrum.

5 Press Tab. The rack will flip around to reveal the front panel.

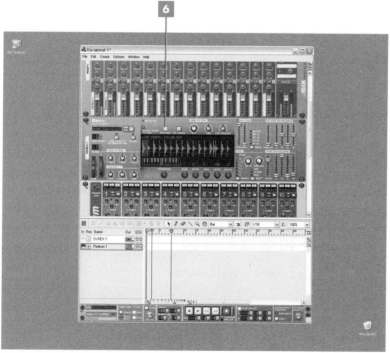

6 Click the Preview button. The loop will begin to play, and with every beat (slice) of the Dr: rex loop the kick drum on the Redrum will be triggered to play.

Expanding the Trigger

Next you will extend the trigger from the Dr:rex to play a SubTractor. Why would you want to do this? One good example would be to add some bottom end to a kick drum. If you have ever heard a car stereo blasting a really deep booming sound, chances are that a very low-range bass synthesizer was triggered by a kick drum to add that oomph that you hear.

First add the SubTractor.

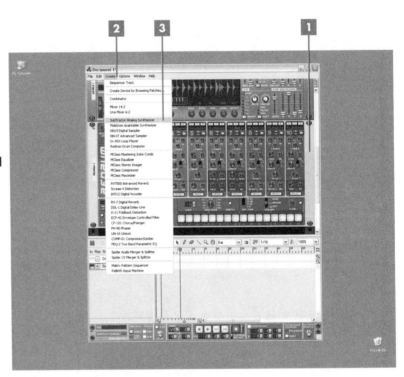

1 Click on the Redrum to select the device.

2 Click on the Create menu. The Create menu will appear.

3 Click on SubTractor Analog Synthesizer. The SubTractor will be loaded into the rack.

The Redrum not only provides a gate input on each channel, but there is also a gate output, which allows you to chain the triggering to another device equipped with a gate input. Using this connection, you will pass the triggering information to the SubTractor.

Connect the Redrum to the SubTractor.

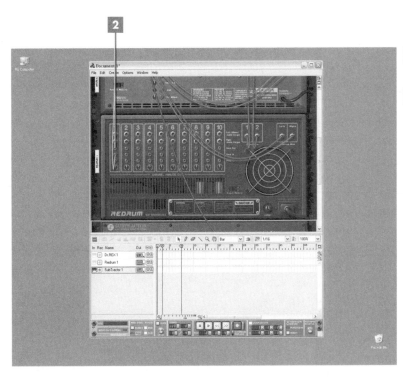

1. Press the Tab key. The rack will flip to the rear view.

2. Right-click on the gate output on Channel 1 of the Redrum. The connections menu will appear.

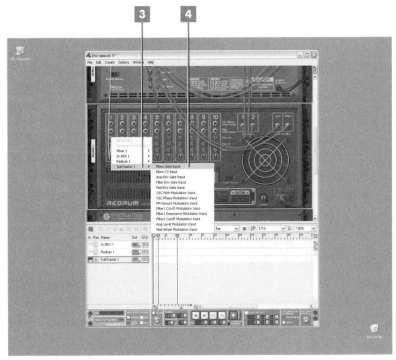

3. Click on SubTractor 1. The SubTractor's connections menu will appear.

4. Click on Mono Gate Input. The Redrum's gate output will be connected to the SubTractor.

Next you'll need to load a patch with plenty of low end into the SubTractor. Press the Tab key to toggle to the front view of the rack.

1 Click on the SubTractor's Browse Patch icon. The Patch Browser window will appear.

2 Click on the Reason Factory Sound Bank in the Locations window.

3 Double-click on the folder Subtractor Patches.

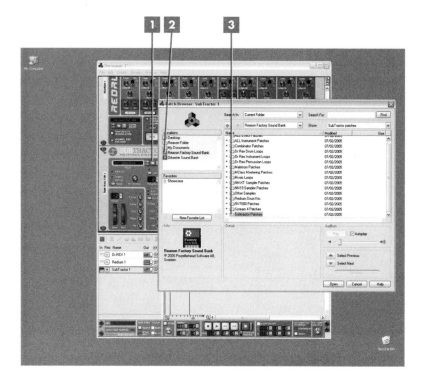

4 Navigate to the folder Bass.

5 Click on the patch DeepBass. zyp. The patch will become highlighted.

6 Click OK. The patch will load into the SubTractor.

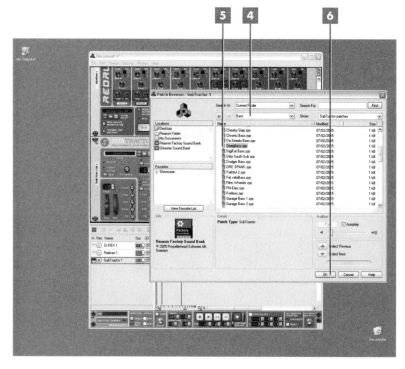

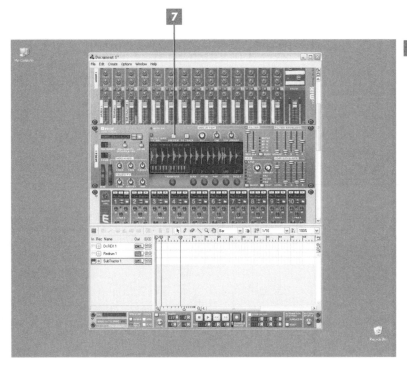

7 Click Preview on the Dr:rex Loop Player. The loop will begin playback, and you should hear the SubTractor patch being triggered by every slice on the Dr:rex.

❊ USING ONE DEVICE TO TRIGGER ANOTHER

In this example you used the Dr:rex to trigger the kick drum sample in the Redrum, which then triggered the SubTractor. You could also have drum samples in programmed patterns of the Redrum trigger the SubTractor or any other sound module device with a gate input.

A } ReWire

ReWire was originally created by Propellerhead Software several years ago to enable users of Steinberg's Cubase VST and Propellerhead's ReBirth to run the audio output of ReBirth directly into the mixer of Cubase VST by creating a virtual audio connection between the two applications. Since then, several audio applications have adopted ReWire support, including Reason. With ReWire you can run the audio output from Reason devices directly into another audio program such as Cubase SX, Sonar, or Digital Performer.

ReWire Master/Slave and Audio Connections

ReWire has two application modes: master and slave. Master mode is the application to which all audio is routed for mixing, and the master controls the synchronization of all connected ReWire applications. The slave application sends its audio to the master application and follows the master's synchronization. The mode is set by the application itself and usually cannot be changed; however, some programs run as either slave or master. Reason is a slave-only application.

Starting Reason in ReWire Slave Mode

Starting Reason in ReWire slave mode is straightforward. Simply start the ReWire master application first, and then start Reason. When Reason loads on your computer, it checks to see if a ReWire master application is already running. If a master application is running, Reason will automatically be set to run in ReWire slave mode. When Reason is running in ReWire slave mode, the hardware interface will indicate this.

✳ REWIRE APPLICATIONS

There are several ReWire master applications available. If you're running an application that supports ReWire, check that application's documentation for more information on what modes it supports.

A The hardware interface indicates when Reason is in ReWire slave mode.

ReWire Audio Input and Output Connections

In Chapter 2, "Fast Start," you looked at the hardware interface at the top of the rack, which is used to connect the devices to the output of your audio card. With ReWire you'll still need to use the hardware interface to connect the device to the ReWire channels. Reason supports 64 outputs; therefore, 64 channels to the master application are available with Reason in ReWire slave mode.

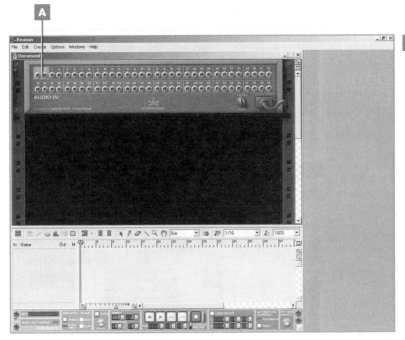

A When in ReWire slave mode the hardware interface's inputs are used to connect the devices to a ReWire channel.

Connecting to the Master Application

When Reason starts in slave mode, all 64 ReWire channels are available to send audio to the master application; however, the master application must be set up to receive audio from these channels. Since there are several applications that can be ReWire masters, it is hard to provide a generic description of how to set up a master. However, below is a brief description of the applications that can be ReWire masters, along with information about setting them up to receive audio through the ReWire channels.

❋ **FOR MORE INFORMATION**

This information is intended to provide a general explanation of setting up some common ReWire master applications. For more detailed information on setting up a ReWire master application, please consult your application's documentation.

Cubase SX/SL and Nuendo

For users of Cubase SX/SL and Nuendo:

A Use the Reason device panel to activate ReWire channels with SX.

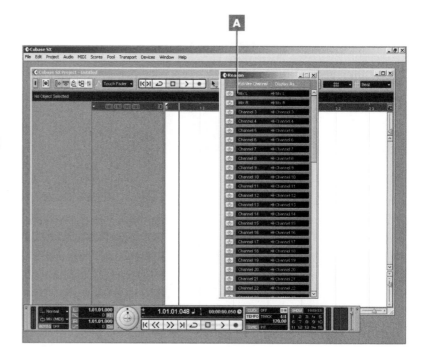

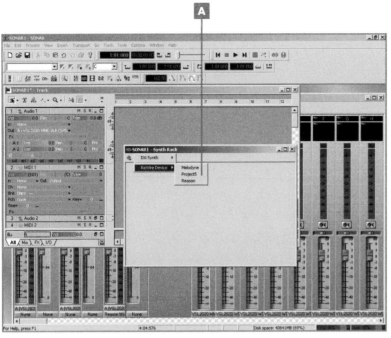

SONAR 2.0

If you use SONAR 2.0:

A Use the Synth rack in SONAR 2.0.

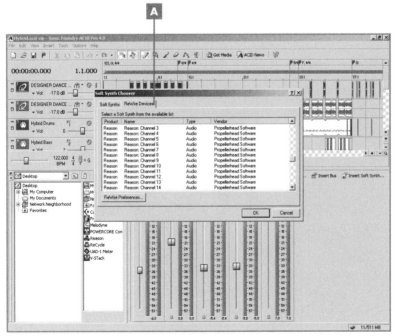

ACID 4.0

If you're an ACID 4.0 user:

A Use Soft Synth Chooser to add a Reason channel to ACID.

❈ ❈ ❈

B } Saving Your Work and Getting Your Song on CD

After you have created your own work of art in Reason and the song sounds just right, what's next? One obvious answer might be to save the song so you can load it and play it back at any time without having to load Reason every time. Reason offers you a few different ways to save your work. In this appendix, you'll get a look at the options for saving your work, and you'll also learn how to prepare your songs to be put on CD to be played in an CD audio player.

Saving the Song

You have spent hours tweaking and adjusting all the devices that make up your song, as well as capturing and editing the perfect performance. You would hate to see it lost. Before you shut down Reason for the night you'll need to save your work, so it will be there when you return to it the next day.

To save your song:

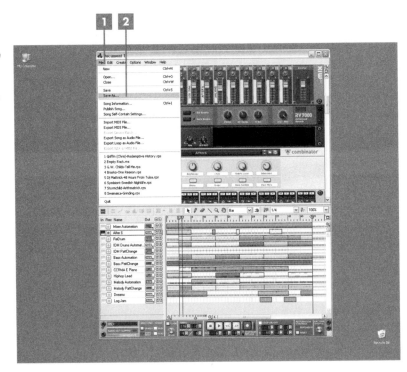

1 Click on the File menu. The File menu will appear.

2 Click on Save As. The Save As window will appear.

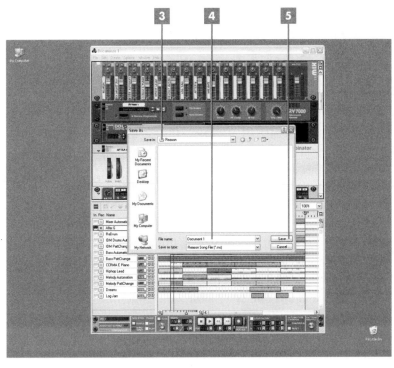

3 Navigate to the location where you wish to save your song.

4 Type in the desired song name.

5 Click Save. The song will now be saved to your hard disk.

❀ ABOUT SAVING

If you are continuing to work on a song that you saved previously, you need only click on Save from the File menu. The changes in the song will be written to the song's file.

❀ SAVE OFTEN

While working on a song that has already been saved, it is a good idea to save your work every 10 minutes or so, in case of a computer crash or a loss of power. This way, once you get Reason back up and running, you should have most of your work saved.

Saving Your Work as a Published Song

Imagine that you have worked many hours on a song for which you imported several of your own samples (samples that were not included with Reason). You save the song and take it to your buddy's house (he also has Reason). You load up Reason on your friend's machine and open your song, but your samples are not there! That's because when you save a song in Reason, the samples that you used are not saved with the song file. The song file will save only a reference pointing to where the samples are on your hard disk, and because they are not on your buddy's hard disk, Reason will load blank samples. There is a way to get around this—save your work as a published song. A published song will save all the samples and song information into one file so that when it's opened in Reason, on any machine, all the samples will be loaded along with the song.

❄ PUBLISHING ALLOWS YOU TO SHARE

A published song lets people share their songs, whether on CD-R or posted on the Internet. A published song also provides your song with a certain amount of protection. Published songs, when opened in Reason, cannot be saved; Copy and Paste are disabled, and the song cannot be exported to a stereo audio file. Published songs essentially can only be played back in Reason.

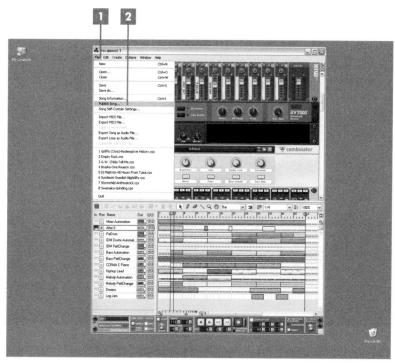

To save your work as a published song:

1 Click on the File menu. The File menu will appear.

2 Click on Publish Song. The Publish As window will appear.

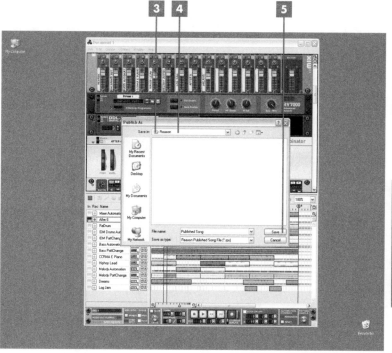

3 Navigate to the location where you wish to save the song.

4 Type in the desired song name.

5 Click on Save. The song will be saved along with all the samples used into a single file.

❋ SAMPLES AFFECT FILE SIZE

When saving your work as a published song, try to keep in mind how many samples you have imported. If you are using a large number of samples, the file size of the published song can be quite large.

Preparing Your Song for CD

To some people, the final goal of working on a song is to pop a CD into a CD player and listen to the masterpiece through a home stereo. To do this, you must first save your song to a stereo file that can be written later to CD. This process is referred to as a *mixdown* or *export*.

To perform a mixdown:

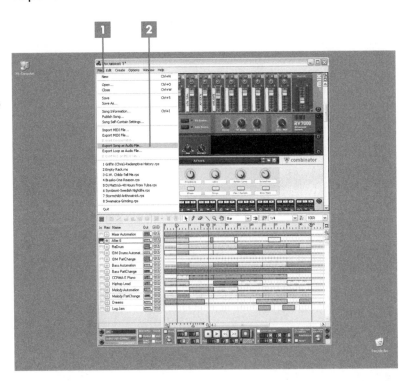

1 Click on the File menu. The File menu will appear.

2 Click on Export Song As Audio File. The Export Song window will appear.

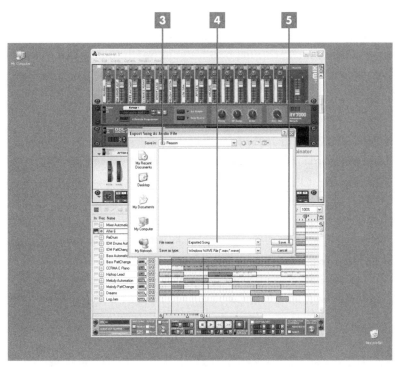

3 Navigate to the location where you wish to save the file.

4 Type in the desired file name.

5 Click Save. The Export Audio Settings window will appear.

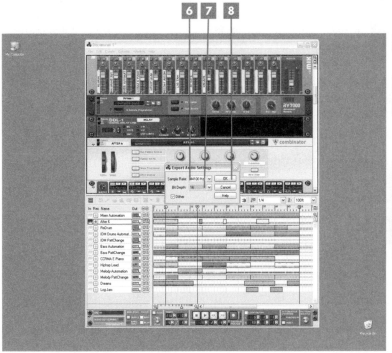

6 Set the Sample Rate to 44100 Hz.

7 Set the Bit Depth to 16.

8 Click OK. Reason will begin to export the song to a stereo file.

❄ **DEFAULT SETTINGS**

By default, the file settings are 44100 Hz and 16 bit; however, if these settings have been changed you will need to change them back to the default values because this is standard CD format.

To place the song onto CD you need to use a CD-writing program. There are plenty of options and loads of resources on the Internet to research which program best fits your needs. Below are some links to some popular titles:

❋ **Ahead Software's Nero Burning ROM** (www.nero.com). Nero is perhaps the most popular CD-burning software for Windows users.

❋ **Roxio's EZ CD Creator** (www.roxio.com). Roxio's EZ CD Creator has been around for a while and has a proven track record.

❋ **Stomp Inc. Click 'N Burn** (www.stompinc.com). A newer kid on the block, Click 'N Burn offers some nice features for audio users with the addition of Click 'N Edit Sound LE, which gives you a simple but effective audio editor to clean up your tracks before burning them to CD.

❋ **Roxio's Toast** (www.roxio.com/en/products/toast/index.jhtml). Yet another offering from Roxio, but this one is for Mac users. Toast is perhaps the standard for CD-burning on the Mac OS X platform.

❋ BURNING CDS ON WINDOWS XP OR MAC OS X

If you own Windows XP or a Mac OS X operating system, CD-burning software is already at your fingertips. Windows' Media Player, installed with XP, is capable of burning music to CD. For more information on using Media Player, consult your Windows documentation. Mac OS X users can burn their music using the iTunes application that is part of the OS X operating system. For more information on iTunes, consult your Mac OS X documentation.

C

The Combinator

Many classic bands are remembered as much for their signature "sound" as for their songs. Think of the one-of-a-kind guitar sound created by Jimi Hendrix, the heavy blues of Led Zeppelin, and the dense synth and instrument combinations of the progressive rock bands of the '70s. When you heard one of these songs for the first time, you knew who the band was, because you were so familiar with their unique sound. The same applies to the electronic composers of today. With the Combinator, you can save and recall the unique "build" of devices and effects that you have so painstakingly put together to create *your* individual sound. In this appendix, you'll learn how to

❋ Load a Combinator patch.

❋ Route devices in the Combinator.

❋ Create a Combinator patch.

❋ Use the Combinator Programmer.

❋ Add a backdrop.

Loading a Combinator Patch

As with so many Reason devices, there are pre-prepared patches just for the Combinator. Unlike the other devices, however, the Combinator is the "full-meal deal" and includes devices and effects with their pre-loaded patches and complete routing.

1 Click on the Create menu.

2 Select the Combinator.

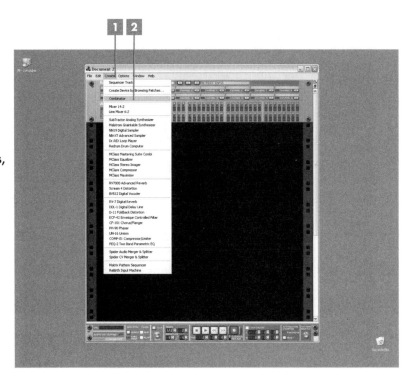

3 Click on the Combinator Browse Patch button.

4 Click on the Reason Factory Sound Bank in the Locations window.

5 Double-click on the Combinator Patches folder.

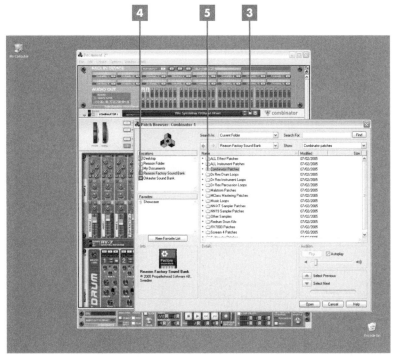

7 **6** **8**

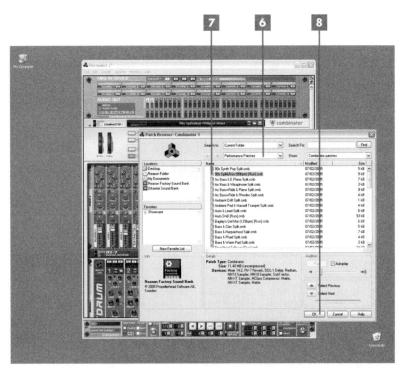

6 Browse **to the** Performance Patches **folder.**

7 Click **on the** 90s Split&Run (90bpm) [Run].cmb **Combinator patch.**

8 Click OK. **The patch with all of the devices and effects will be loaded into Reason.**

9

9 Click Play **to hear the unique sound of this patch.**

❋ ❋ ❋

Combinator Routing

The important thing to remember when using the Combinator is that even though it can be made up of a large variety of devices and effects, within Reason it is seen only as one device. Visually, Combinator's face extends around the devices within it.

When the Combinator is loaded, the Show Devices button is lit up by default, indicating that all the devices are visible within the Combinator Rack display window.

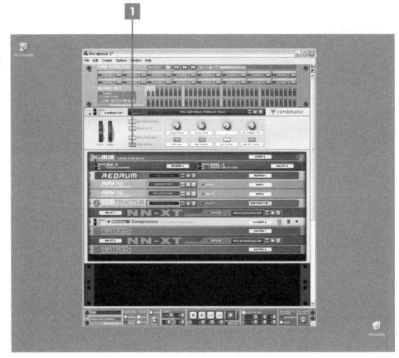

1 Click on the Show Devices button to deactivate it . The red light will go out, and all of the devices within the Combinator are hidden.

2 Press the Tab key to toggle to the rear view of the rack.

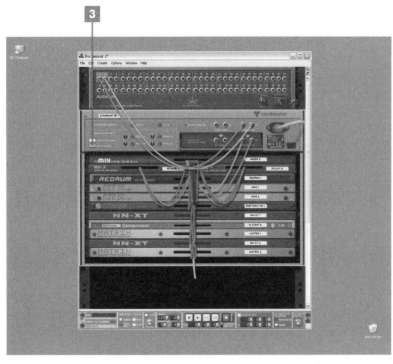

3 Click on the Show Devices button again to activate it. The button will light up red, and all of the devices within the Combinator are revealed.

Whether or not your devices are hidden, they all end up routed into the Combinator, which in turn is routed into your mixer or whatever setup you have created.

MULTIPLE COMBINATORS

Since the Combinator is treated like another device within Reason, you can load multiple Combinators within a song. You can also incorporate your Combinator with any other devices.

EXTERNAL ROUTING

If you have routed any of the devices in your Combinator to another software application (such as a sequencer), this external connection will not be saved with the patch.

Creating a Combinator Patch

Reason allows you multiple options for creating a Combinator patch. Use the methods you learned from previous chapters to add a mixer and a few devices and effects, and load any patches you desire. Route or re-route as necessary and listen to the results.

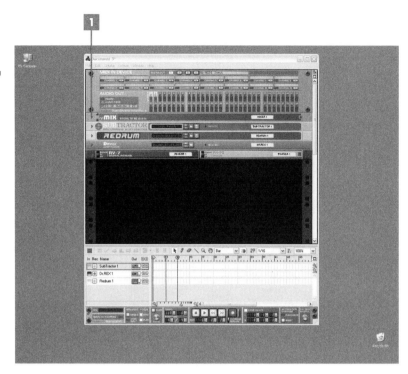

1 Click on the small arrow to minimize all of the devices you wish to combine.

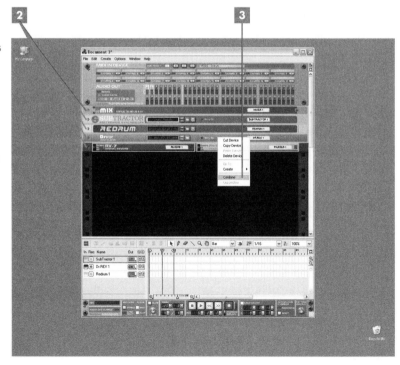

2 Shift-click on the all the devices you wish to combine.

3 Right-click (Command-click for Mac users) on any of the selected devices and choose Combine. The devices are combined and are now part of the Combinator.

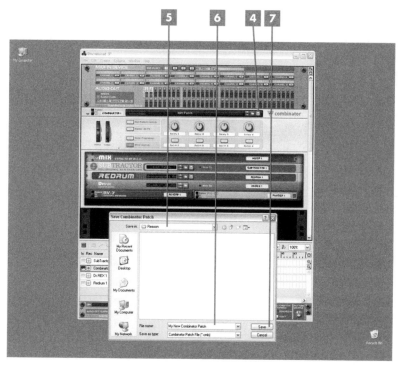

4 Click on the Save Patch button.

5 Browse to the location you wish to save the patch to.

6 Name the patch.

7 Click Save to save the file to that location.

ANOTHER COMBINING METHOD

Try creating a patch using the Combinator by creating a mixer first, then adding the Combinator. "Fill" the Combinator by dragging and dropping devices and effects that are already on the rack into the Combinator Rack display window. Once the devices are "in" the Combinator, route them together.

The Combinator Programmer

The Programmer portion of the Combinator allows you to map key-zone and velocity-zone regions and also allows for the routing of modulation features to the four buttons and dials on the Combinator's face.

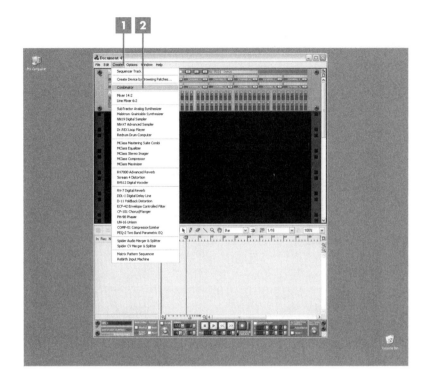

1 Click **on the** Create **menu.**

2 Select **the** Combinator.

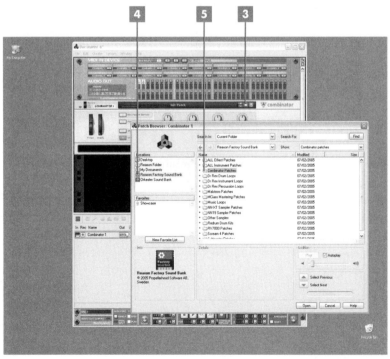

3 Click **on the Combinator Browse Patch button.**

4 Click **on the** Reason Factory Sound Bank **in the Locations window.**

5 Double-click **on the** Combinator Patches **folder.**

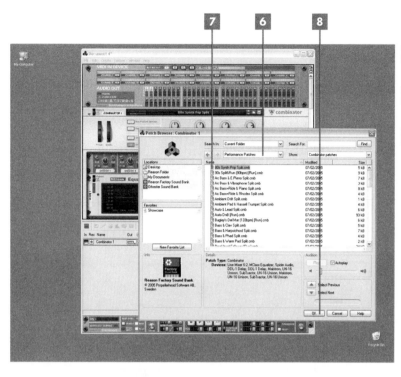

6 Browse **to the** Performance Patches **folder.**

7 Click **on the** 80s Synth Pop Split.cmb **Combinator patch.**

8 Click OK. **The patch with all of the devices and effects will be loaded into Reason.**

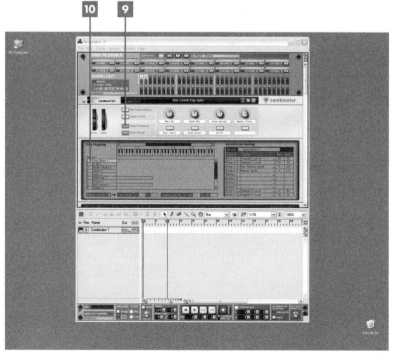

9 Click **the** Show Programmer **button. The Programmer will appear.**

10 Click **on** Line Mixer 2.

Under Modulation Routing you can see the parameters and values for the rotary dials and buttons.

Adding a Backdrop

Since the Combinator holds the devices and effects that represent your sound, it would be nice to customize it with a backdrop that's all your own.

❄ CUSTOM BACKDROP SPECS

You can create custom backdrops for your Combinator using image-manipulation software such as Adobe Photoshop. Reason 3.0 accepts both .jpg and .psd (Photoshop) files for use as backdrops with the dimensions 754 x 138 pixels at 72 dpi.

1 Right-click **(Command-click for Mac users) on the** Combinator **face.**

2 Choose Select Backdrop **from the menu.**

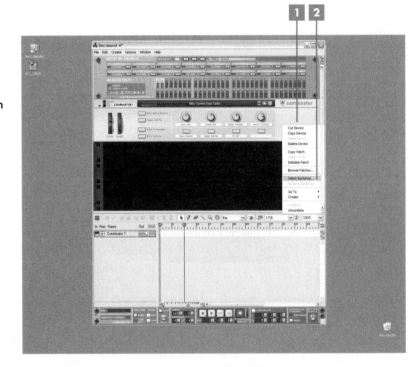

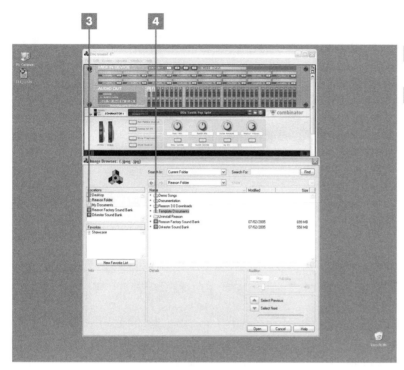

3 Click on the Reason folder in the Locations window.

4 Double-click on the Template Documents folder.

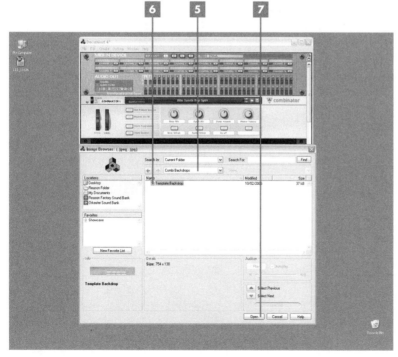

5 Browse to the Combi Backdrops folder.

6 Click on Template Backdrop.

7 Click Open.

Your template is now loaded as the new backdrop for the Combinator.

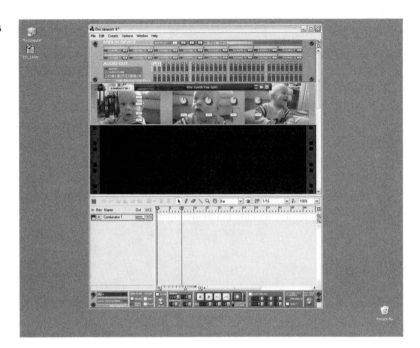

D } The MClass Effects

Your very long journey is almost over. You've sweated, cried, and poured your heart into your music. Well, maybe the experience wasn't that dramatic, but you can finally say that the composing of your song is complete. Now it's time to switch hats and use a different type of creativity. After composing, you assemble and mix your song in the sequencer. Whether your final composition is destined to be broadcast over the radio, satellite, or the Internet, or distributed on CD, DVD, mp3, or online, if your audience can't hear all the particular nuances you've built in to your song, all your hard work won't pay off. That's why mastering your final mix is so critical before distributing it. Reason has added a powerful suite of tools to help put a final, high-gloss polish on your song. In this chapter you'll learn about the following tools:

❋ MClass Equalizer

❋ MClass Stereo Imager

❋ MClass Compressor

❋ MClass Maximizer

❋ MClass Mastering Suite Combi

❋ Line Mixer 6:2

MClass Equalizer

The MClass Equalizer has three different kinds of EQ available: A high- and low- shelf equalizer, a two-band parametric equalizer, and a lo cut switch. You can turn on all or any combination of these different EQ effects. You'll now simulate doing EQ on a completed composition, so first load up a pre-made song.

Adding a Completed Song

1 Click on the File menu.

2 Select Open.

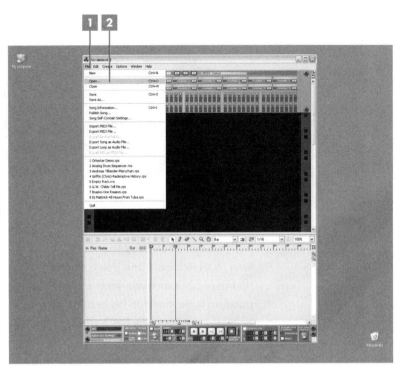

3 Select the Reason folder from Locations.

4 Double-click on Demo Songs.

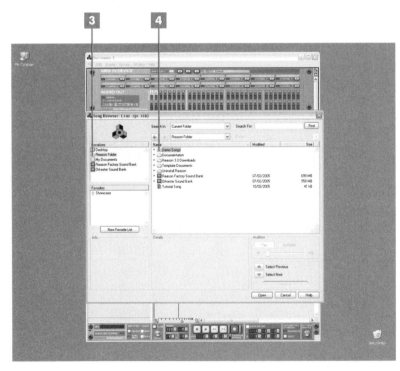

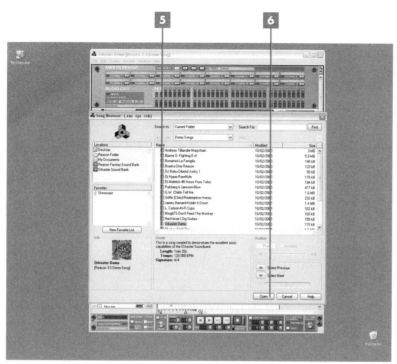

5 Click on the Orkester Demo.

6 Click Open. Now the Orkester Demo is loaded into Reason.

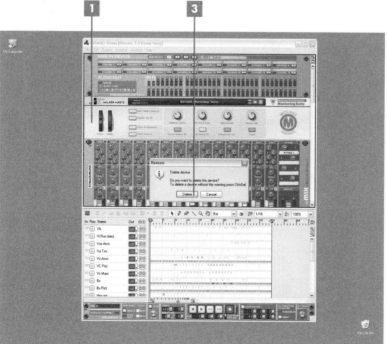

Removing the MClass Combi

There is already a pre-configured MClass Combi loaded as part of the song. You need to get rid of it so you can add your own EQ.

1 Click on the MClass Combi to select it.

2 Press the Delete key.

3 Click Delete in the dialog box. The MClass Combi will be deleted.

Adding the MClass Equalizer and Routing It to the Audio Out

1 Click on the Remix mixer so that it is selected.

2 Click on the Create menu.

3 Select the MClass Equalizer. It now appears in the rack.

You now have to route the MClass Equalizer so that it is the last device before output.

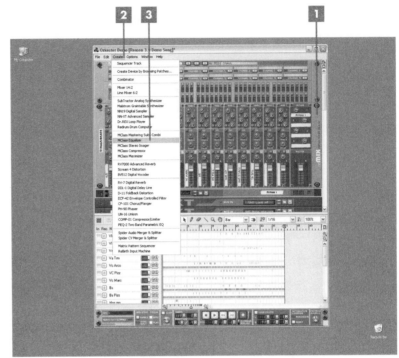

1 Press Tab to toggle to the back of the rack.

2 Right-click (Command-click for Mac users) on the Left Master Out of the ReMix mixer called Strings/Brass.

3 Choose M EQ 1 > Left from the drop-down menu.

4 Repeat steps 1 and 2 to route the Right Master Out to M EQ 1 > Right.

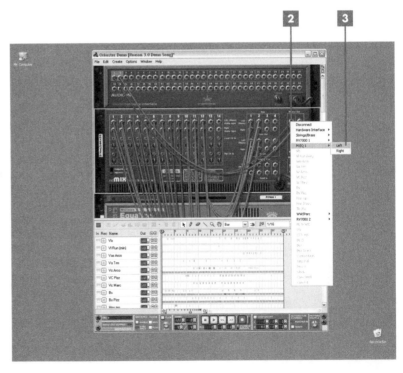

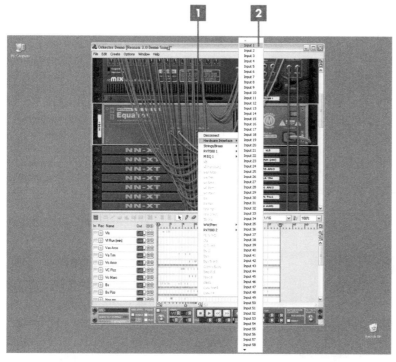

Now the Equalizer has to be routed to the audio output.

1 Right-click (Command-click for Mac users) on the Left Audio Output of the MClass Equalizer.

2 Choose Hardware Interface > Input 1 from the drop-down menu.

3 Repeat steps 1 and 2 to route the Right Audio Output to Hardware Interface > Input 2.

4 Press Tab to return to the front view of the rack.

Now the Equalizer is routed to Reason's Hardware Output.

EQ'ing the Completed Song

Since the Orkester Demo Song you loaded is full of high-pitched string songs, you'll EQ some of the high-end part of the signal.

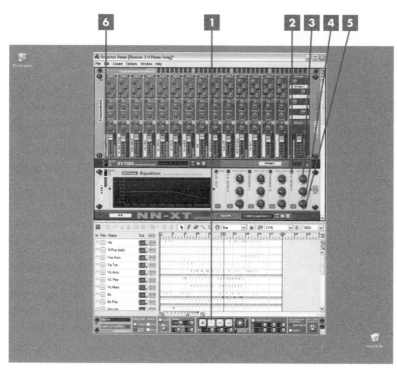

1 Click on the Play button.

2 Click on the High Shelf On/Off button to activate it.

3 Turn the Frequency knob to the 1/4 position.

4 Turn the Gain knob to the 1/4 position.

5 Turn the q knob to the 1/4 position.

6 Toggle the Enable button between On and Bypass to listen to the amount of signal you have EQ'ed.

MCLASS EQUALIZER GRAPHIC DISPLAY

Use the graphic display as a visual guide to see the amount of db cut over particular frequencies.

MClass Stereo Imager

The MClass Stereo Imager takes two different frequency bands (high and low) and allows you to control how wide or narrow the stereo image is of each. Let's pick up from the last example and add a Stereo Imager.

Adding the MClass Stereo Imager

1. Click on the MClass Equalizer to select it.

2. Click on the Create menu.

3. Select MClass Stereo Imager.

4. Press the Tab key to toggle to the rear view of the rack.

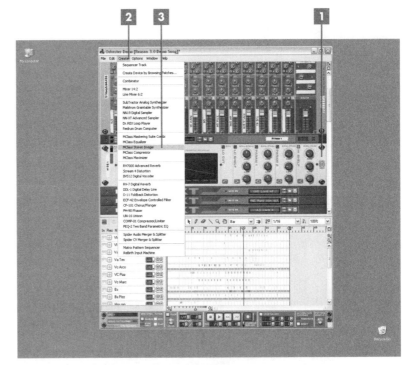

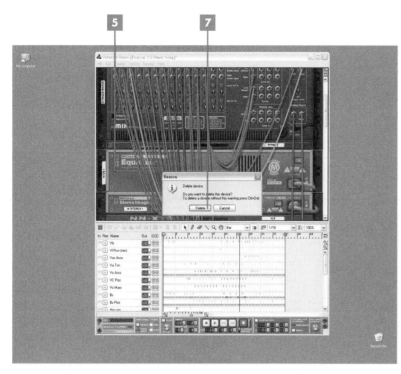

5 Click on the MClass Equalizer to select it.

6 Press the Delete key.

7 Click on the Delete button in the dialog box. The Equalizer is removed and the routing goes from the mixer to the Stereo Imager to the Audio Out.

8 Press the Tab key to toggle to the front view of the rack.

Adjusting the Stereo Image

1 Press Play.

2 Turn the Hi Band knob to the 3/4 position.

3 Turn the Lo Band knob to the 3/4 position.

4 Turn the X-Over Freq knob from the 10 o'clock to 2 o'clock position. Listen to the difference in stereo image when you alter the frequency crossover point between the hi and lo bands.

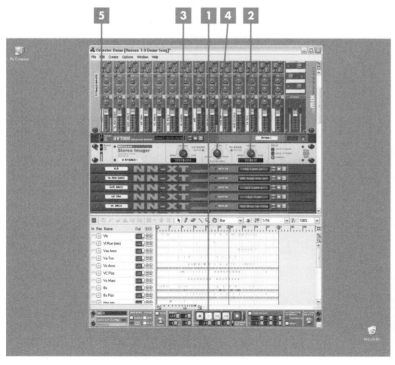

5 Toggle the Enable button between On and Bypass to listen to the difference between no stereo image change and the changes you've made. You'll hear a "widened" stereo sound.

❄ **STEREO AND MONO**

The Stereo Imager is not a magician! It cannot create a stereo "effect" from a mono source.

MClass Compressor

The MClass Compressor is a dynamic processor that allows you to compress the overall signal ranging from subtle to aggressive.

Adding the MClass Compressor

1. Click on the MClass Stereo Imager to select it.

2. Click on the Create menu.

3. Select MClass Compressor.

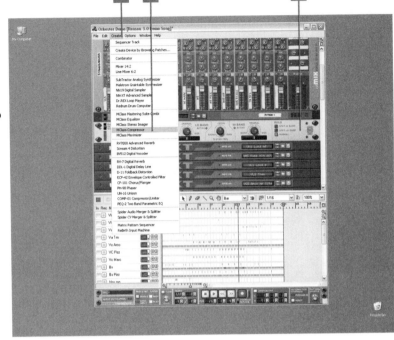

4. Click on the MClass Stereo Imager to select it.

5. Press the Delete key.

6. Click on the Delete button in the dialog box. The Stereo Imager is now gone and the Compressor is automatically routed.

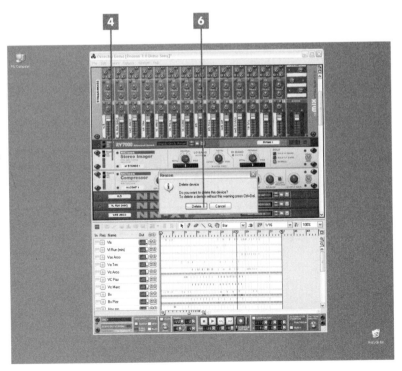

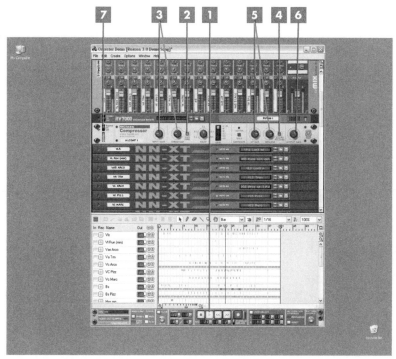

Adjusting the Compression

1 Press Play.

2 Turn on the Soft Knee button. The button will light up red when it's activated.

3 Turn the Soft Knee Input Gain and Threshold knobs to the 1/4 position.

4 Turn on the Adapt Release button.

5 Turn the Attack and Release knobs to the 3/4 position.

6 Turn the Output Gain knob to the 2 o'clock position.

7 Toggle the Enable button between On and Bypass to listen to the difference between the compressed and uncompressed signal. Also look at the VU meter to see how compression affects the volume level.

MClass Maximizer

The MClass Maximizer is a unique type of limiter that can maximize the amount of loudness of a mix without creating clipping or distortion.

Adding the MClass Maximizer

1 Click on the MClass Compressor to select it.

2 Click on the Create menu.

3 Select MClass Maximizer.

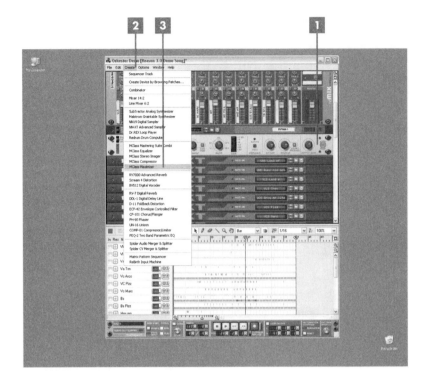

4 Click on the MClass Compressor to select it.

5 Press the Delete key.

6 Click on the Delete button in the dialog box. The Compressor is now gone and the Maximizer is automatically routed.

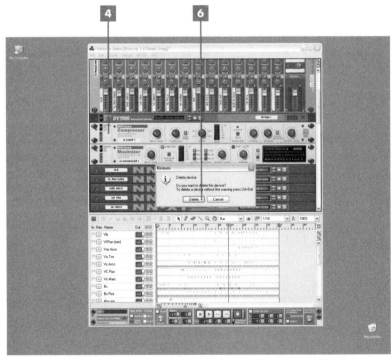

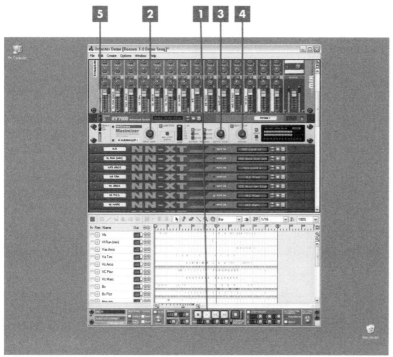

Boosting the Loudness

1 Press Play.

2 Turn the Input Gain to the 2 o'clock position.

3 Turn the Output Gain to the 2 o'clock position.

4 Turn the Amount to the 4 o'clock position.

5 Toggle the Enable button between On and Bypass to listen to the difference between the output with and without maximized loudness.

MClass Mastering Suite Combi

The MClass Mastering Suite Combi incorporates two of the new tools added to this version of Reason. Essentially it is the Combinator loaded with all of the new MClass effect devices: Equalizer, Stereo Imager, Compressor, and Maximizer. Because it is the Combinator, it is seen as one device and makes mastering your song even easier.

Adding the MClass Mastering Suite Combi

1 Click on the MClass Maximizer to select it.

2 Click on the Create menu.

3 Select MClass Mastering Suite Combi.

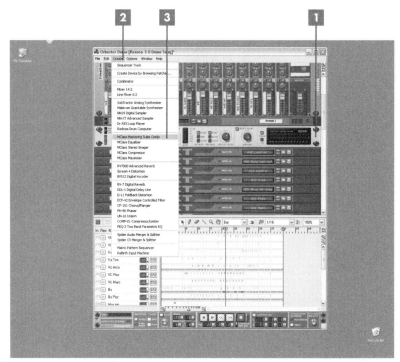

4 Click on the MClass Maximizer to select it.

5 Press the Delete key.

6 Click on the Delete button on the dialog box. The Maximizer is now gone and the Combi is automatically routed.

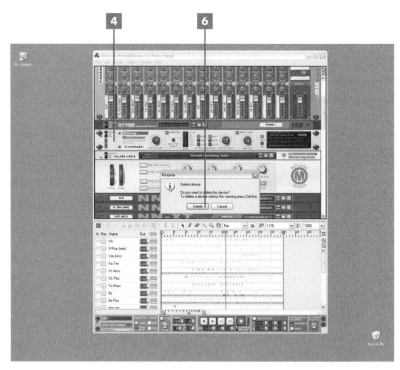

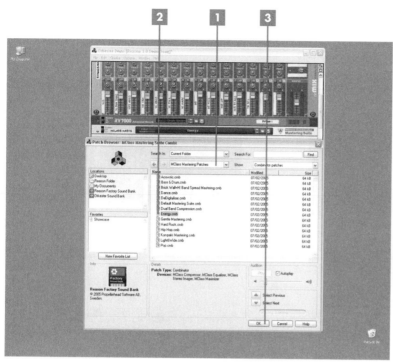

Loading an MClass Mastering Patch

1 Click on the Load Patch button. This will open the Patch Browser window with the MClass Mastering Patches folder contents visible. (If not, select Reason Factory Sound Bank and navigate to MClass Mastering Patches.)

2 Select Energy.

3 Click OK.

4 Toggle the Enable button between On and Bypass to listen to the difference between multiple-effects mastering the song and no mastering.

5 Try using the up/down arrows to select other loaded MClass Mastering Patches and hear their effect on the final mix.

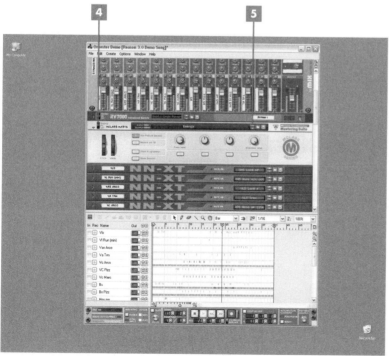

For those new to mastering and the MClass effects, using a pre-made patch is a great way to start when finalizing the sound of your song. This will allow you to hear the difference between an instantly mastered and pre-mastered version of your song. Also, by trying the different mastering patches you'll be able to hear how each one makes nuanced changes to your mix.

The Line Mixer

The Line Mixer (a.k.a. microMIX) is the baby brother to the ReMIX 14:2 mixer. With six stereo channels and one stereo effect/return, it offers basic pan and level controls. It is ideally suited for mixing outputs within the Combinator.

1 Click on the Create menu.

2 Select Line Mixer 6:2.

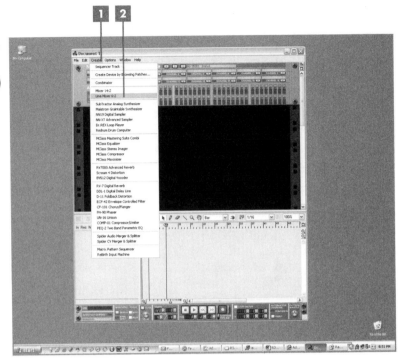

Using these tools will help you to create the final, presentation-quality version of your song, making it ready for distribution. You've gone through the whole process of composing, planning, building, and layering your song; you've mixed it and mastered it, and now you're finally done. Congratulations on creating your first Reason song!

Index

A

algorithms (RV7000 reverb), 131
alignment. *See* panning
Amp Envelope
  NN19, 84
  NN-XT global controls, 111-113
  SubTractor, 60
animation (cables), 15
attack (faders), 59
audio card preferences, 5-9
auditioning. *See* previewing
automapping samples (NN-XT key zones), 108-110
automation
  device indicator preferences, 15
  Redrum, 164
  sequencers, 188-189
  transport panel, 29

B

back view, racks, 24–25
background playing, 9
boxes (device parameters), 15
browser (Song Browser), 19–21
buffer size, 7–8
busses, 10
BV512. *See* vocoder effects
bypassing effects, 124

C

cables
  animation preferences, 15
  connecting, 222
  routing devices, 34, 37
  stereo, 222
CF-101 Chorus/Flanger, 123, 142–144
chaining. *See also* linking
  effects
    expanding, 227

inserts, 224-227
  loading, 227
  overview, 224
  sends, 228-231
filters, 59
mixers
  faders, 233
  sends, 231-234
  volume, 233
SubTractor, 59
channels
  devices, racks, 26
  hardware interface, 26
  mixers, routing effects, 222-224
  preferences, 8
  Redrum trigger pads, 171-173
chords (SubTractor), 51-52
choruses, 123, 142-144
click, transport panel, 28
clipping, transport panel, 28
clock source, 8-11
COMP-01, 123, 149-151
compatibility, Windows, 1
compressors, 123, 149-151
computers, external synchronizing, 255-257
configuring. *See* setting
connecting cables, 222
control panels, 9
controlled voltage. *See* CV control
controls. *See also* parameters
  CV control. *See* CV control
  devices, commonality, 45
  global controls. *See* global controls
  mapping remote MIDI controls, 247-254
  mouse preferences, 14
  NN-XT global controls
    Amp Envelope, 111-113
    filters, 110-111
    frequency, 111
    modulation, 113
    overview, 110
    pitch, 113
    resonance, 111
    volume, 111-113